Marilyn

writing clear paragraphs

Second Edition

ROBERT B. DONALD   JAMES D. MOORE
BETTY RICHMOND MORROW
LILLIAN GRIFFITH WARGETZ   KATHLEEN WERNER

Community College of Beaver County

Illustrations by RAYMOND E. DUNLEVY

PRENTICE–HALL, INC., Englewood Cliffs, New Jersey   07632

Library of Congress Cataloging in Publication Data
Main entry under title:

Writing clear paragraphs.

Includes index.
1. English language—Paragraphs. 2. English
language—Rhetoric. I. DONALD, ROBERT B.
PE1439.W7 1983   808'.042   82-18587
ISBN 0-13-970004-8

CREDITS
Page 58   Henry Bragdon, "George Washington: Monument or Man?" *American History Illustrated,* February 1967. Reprinted by permission of the National Historical Society.
Page 58   ANDERSONVILLE: A STORY OF REBEL MILITARY PRISONS by John McElroy. Fawcett Publications, Inc. Copyright ©1962 by Fawcett Publications, Inc.
Page 63   From CANNERY ROW by John Steinbeck. Copyright 1945 by John Steinbeck. Copyright renewed 1973 by Elaine Steinbeck, John Steinbeck IV, and Thom Steinbeck. Reprinted by permission of Viking Penguin Inc.
Pages 91, 92, 93   From YOU CAN'T EAT PEANUTS IN CHURCH AND OTHER LITTLE KNOWN FACTS by Barbara Seuling. Copyright ©1975 by Barbara Seuling. Reprinted by permission of Doubleday & Company, Inc.
Pages 92, 145–46   Specified brief excerpts from "Here Is New York," p. 123 and p. 121 in ESSAYS OF E. B. WHITE. Copyright 1949 by E. B. White. Reprinted by permission of Harper & Row, Publishers, Inc.
Pages 94–95, 198   Specified excerpts from ONLY YESTERDAY by Frederick Lewis Allen. Copyright, 1931, by Frederick Lewis Allen; renewed ©1959 by Agnes Rogers Allen. Reprinted by permission of Harper & Row, Publishers, Inc.
Page 149   Wallace Stegner, *The Sound of Mountain Water,* Doubleday, 1969. Reprinted by permission.
Page 152   From THE POPULATION BOMB, Revised Edition, by Dr. Paul R. Ehrlich. Copyright ©1968. Reprinted by permission of Ballantine Books, a division of Random House, Inc.
Pages 163–64   From page 37 in WHERE DO WE GO FROM HERE: CHAOS OR COMMUNITY?, by Martin Luther King. Copyright ©1963 by Martin Luther King. By permission of Harper and Row, Publishers, Inc.
Page 165   From WHO'S AFRAID: THE PHOBIC'S HANDBOOK by Barbara Fried. Copyright 1941 by Barbara Fried. Used with permission of McGraw-Hill Book Company.
Page 182   Entry for *cunning* from the *Random House College Dictionary, Revised Edition,* copyright ©1982, 1975, by Random House, Inc.
Page 191   Entry for *moving* © 1978 by Houghton Mifflin Company. Permission granted from the *American Heritage Dictionary of the American Language.*
Page 192   Synonyms for *give* used with permission. From *Webster's New World Dictionary,* Second College Edition. Copyright ©1982 by Simon & Schuster, Inc.
Page 198   From *With Every Breath You Take* by Howard R. Lewis, ©1965 by Howard R. Lewis. Used by permission of Crown Publishers, Inc.
Pages 201–202   *Eating May Be Hazardous to Your Health* by Jacqueline Verret and Jean Carper. Reprinted by permission of Simon & Schuster, Inc.
Pages 257–58   From pages 84–86 in "Letter From Birmingham Jail," April 16, 1963, in WHY WE CAN'T WAIT, by Martin Luther King. Copyright ©1963 by Martin Luther King. By permission of Harper and Row, Publishers, Inc.

Printed in the United States of America

10 9 8 7 6 5 4 3 2 1

ISBN 0-13-970004-8

PRENTICE-HALL INTERNATIONAL, INC., *London*
PRENTICE-HALL OF AUSTRALIA PTY. LIMITED, *Sydney*
EDITORA PRENTICE-HALL DO BRASIL, LTDA., *Rio de Janeiro*
PRENTICE-HALL CANADA INC., *Toronto*
PRENTICE-HALL OF INDIA PRIVATE LIMITED, *New Delhi*
PRENTICE-HALL OF JAPAN, INC., *Tokyo*
PRENTICE-HALL OF SOUTHEAST ASIA PTE. LTD., *Singapore*
WHITEHALL BOOKS LIMITED, *Wellington, New Zealand*

contents

iii

iv

v

preface

A NOTE ON THE SECOND EDITION

Since *Writing Clear Paragraphs* was first published in 1978, we have been delighted by its ongoing acceptance throughout the country on both the college and the high school level. We are grateful, specifically to you, our colleagues, for your enthusiastic acceptance of *WCP;* your continued use of our book, in combination with steadily increasing adoptions, clearly points out the need for a book of its type and its value as an instructional tool. As with any textbook, however, there is always room for improvement, and after four years of use, we have been able to evaluate objectively its major strengths and weaknesses. As a result, we now offer a fresh, expanded edition that still retains the best qualities of the original. In any revision, one always wonders just how far to go, and, for us, the process was initially a little like attempting to perform an autopsy on a being who had not expired. After combining notes, though, we determined that our basic model was sound but that some sections would be more effective if reorganized and/or expanded.

The following are some of the more significant additions and improvements:

A new arrangement of chapters, placing the factual detail paragraph near the end of the book

A new section on pronoun-antecedent agreement

Questions for discussion and suggested activities

Expanded sections on sentence combining, diction and usage, subordination, and dictionary use

Expanded and improved chapter on definition

More student examples

More exercises

We are confident that this new edition will challenge your students even more effectively and better enable you to deal aggressively with the special problems of the inexperienced writer.

ACKNOWLEDGMENTS AND THANKS

No book is simply the product of its authors but also represents the assistance and support of colleagues. We are grateful to Dr. Terry L. Dicianna, our president, and Dr. William K. Bauer, Vice-President for Academic Affairs, for their continuing support for this project. We also thank our fellow English teacher, David Anderson, and our endlessly helpful librarian, Linda Ciani. Three great secretaries, Carol Kunzmann, Mary Williams, and Alice Watson, were prompt, intelligent, and uncomplaining in their help to us.

We feel gratitude to a number of people beyond our campus. Particularly, we thank the painstaking and perceptive critics who read our manuscript, Patricia Grignon, *Saddleback College;* Eric Hibbison, *J. Sargeant Reynolds Community College;* William Luttrell, *DeKalb Community College;* and Joe Mosley, *Richland College.* In addition, we extend sincere appreciation to Joan Wilson, our Prentice-Hall Sales Representative, and to Joyce Perkins, our production editor, who must be magic.

We also thank our students, those who have permitted us to use their writing, and those who share the learning process with us in the classroom.

For permission to use the selections reprinted here, the authors are grateful to the publishers and copyright holders listed on the copyright page.

A NOTE TO STUDENTS

This book is concerned mainly with the paragraph and the ways to write a good paragraph. At first glance, the paragraph is only a visual thing: it is a unit of writing that begins with an indentation—a series of sentences put together for the convenience of the reader. A closer look, however, reveals that the paragraph is a sequence of related sentences that deal with one central idea. This central thought or controlling idea, as it is usually called, is the single most important thing to be considered in writing good paragraphs.

The controlling ideal, however, is just one requirement in three series of threes that the writer must consider to produce a clear paragraph. The first series of three in this book concerns the organization of the paragraph. The standard paragraph is made up of, first, the **topic sentence,** which is a statement of the controlling thought. The second part of the structure is the support for the controlling thought, which is called the **development** or **body** of the paragraph. The third part of the structure is the **conclusion.** Every paragraph you will be asked to write will have this three-part structure.

The second three requirements for clear writing are the three skills you will practice: first is **the organization of the paragraph;** second are **the forms of sentences,** and third is **the selection of words.** Each unit in the book will discuss organization, sentences, and words.

The third series of three that will be discussed repeatedly deals with the three qualities that make a good paragraph: **unity, coherence,** and **adequate development.**

Unity means "oneness." In trying for unity, always remember that the principal unifying device is the topic sentence itself, since it states the controlling idea to which everything else in the paragraph must relate. The topic sentence provides the guiding purpose; thus the wording of the topic sentence must be clear and specific, so that there is no doubt about what the paragraph concerns. Also, the controlling idea must be sufficiently limited, so that it can be adequately developed within the paragraph. The first consideration, then, is a carefully worded topic sentence. A paragraph has unity when its controlling idea is clearly stated and when every sentence it contains is clearly related to that controlling idea.

Coherence means that the sentences within a paragraph are linked smoothly to provide the reader with an evident progression from beginning to end; they are not isolated islands of thought. Abrupt shifts from one idea to another, even when each sentence is related to the controlling idea, create a disjointed paragraph. Coherence is achieved by relating each sentence to the sentences surrounding it in the paragraph.

Adequate development is more difficult to define. It cannot be measured in terms of a given number of words or sentences. Since a paragraph can best be thought of as the complete development of a single controlling idea, the writer must carefully consider what a given topic sentence needs in the way of explanation, illustration, or other support. You must train yourself to see what the body of the paragraph needs in order to clarify the controlling idea. A good paragraph provides the reader with a sense of wholeness and completeness, with no unanswered questions and no loose ends.

Since the paragraph is the basic building block for writing at any length or on any subject, the main purpose of this book is to help you to write good paragraphs. With a clear understanding of the paragraph, you can write almost anything.

the

paragraph

ORGANIZATION

What does a paragraph do, and what are the characteristics of a good paragraph? Both the writer and the reader need the paragraph. The writer uses the paragraph to help stay on the subject and to organize the material in a logical way, and the reader uses the paragraph to see what specific idea the writer wants to present. An effective paragraph (for writer or reader) has three major characteristics:

1. It should deal with one main thought—the controlling idea—and should contain *only* material that supports or proves that controlling idea.
2. It should contain sufficient material to support that controlling idea.
3. It should have a basic structure of Beginning—Middle—End (Topic Sentence—Body—Conclusion).

One simple principle will guide you in writing most of the paragraphs you will ever need to write. That simple principle is referred to as "The Ministerial Three."

The minister stands behind the pulpit and, in ringing tones, announces the text to the congregation:

THE MINISTERIAL THREE

1. **He tells 'em what he is going to tell 'em.** (Or, to put it more politely, he introduces the subject and indicates what he is going to say about it.)
2. **He tells 'em.** (He expands the subject, fills in details about it.)
3. **He tells 'em what he's told 'em.** (He sums up and reaches some conclusion about the subject.)

The sermon that comes from the minister's three is just like the paragraphs you will write. They will have the same basic structure: Beginning—Middle—End.

1. Beginning: "Tell 'em what you're going to tell 'em—**the topic sentence.**
2. Middle: "Tell 'em"—the discussion or explanation, that is, the **body** of the paragraph.
3. End: "Tell 'em what you've told 'em"—**the concluding sentence.**

Let's look at this basic three-part structure in greater detail.

Topic Sentence

The topic sentence is the key: a clear paragraph demands a carefully worded topic sentence that clearly expresses the controlling idea. Then every sentence in the paragraph should relate, either directly or indirectly, to the controlling idea as expressed in the topic sentence. Since the topic sentence is the most important unifying element in the paragraph, the whole structure of the paragraph will be weakened if the topic sentence is not clear and to the point. If the controlling idea in the topic sentence is clear, then it will be much easier to organize the ideas needed to illustrate, explain, and support the main point.

Therefore, you start your paragraph by telling the reader "what you're going to tell 'em": announce your controlling idea in a clear topic sentence. For the beginning writer, it is best to place the topic sentence at the very beginning of the paragraph.

**SUBJECT
PLUS
ATTITUDE**

The topic sentence must present both a **subject** and an **attitude** toward that subject. For example, "Dogs" is merely a subject, but "Dogs stink" is both a subject and an attitude: "dogs" (the subject you are going to write about) and "stink" (what you are going to say about dogs—your attitude).

Another thing to remember about the topic sentence is that it determines everything that follows. All sentences that follow your original statement must go back to your controlling idea. Thus, "Most dogs have halitosis" would support your topic sentence, but "Dogs are fun to play with" would not.

Notice that not all sentences are topic sentences, only those that have both a subject and an attitude. Simple statements of fact, such as "My watch is a minute slow" or "I know Edmond Smith," require no explanation or development. These are complete and self-sufficient statements, but they are *not* topic sentences. However, if you say, "Edmond Smith is the *stingiest* man I ever knew," you go beyond a mere statement of fact in that you express an attitude toward your subject. You think your subject is terribly *stingy*. If you say, "Old MacDonald had a farm," that is not a topic sentence, but merely a statement of fact. However, if you say, "Old MacDonald had the *noisiest* farm in Lawrence County," then you have an attitude expressed in *noisiest*.

Since everything in the paragraph must pertain to the topic sentence (the subject plus attitude), choosing the controlling idea is very important.

EXERCISE Ia
In the following topic sentences, circle the word or phrase that expresses attitude.

1. The muppets on "Sesame Street" act as though they were real people.
2. Larry's weird sense of humor annoys many people, especially my father.
3. Liberals deplore the welfare cuts in the new budget.

No attitude.

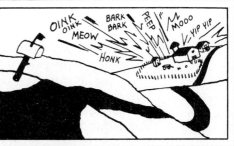

Here an attitude, there an attitude, everywhere an attitude.

4. Job hunting depresses even cheerful people.

5. Much modern history debunks traditional stories of great men.

6. Two advantages of assembly-line production are efficiency and uniformity.

7. Clothes often suggest the personality of the wearer.

8. The collie mastered all the tricks in the obedience course.

9. The richness of the English language creates two basic problems for the writer who wishes to be clear.

10. Some unanswerable questions stir up vigorous discussion.

BEING SPECIFIC

The controlling idea must be as *specific* (to the point) as you can make it. Try to limit or narrow your subject and attitude by choosing the most exact words possible. Use a specific word instead of a general one. For example, if you say "There is a *picture* on my desk," the reader might wonder whether you mean a painting, a drawing, a cartoon, or a photograph. If you say "I'm going to a *show* tonight," the reader might wonder whether you mean a play, a movie, an exhibition, a fashion show, or an opera.

Being specific is necessary for several reasons.

1. **If you are specific, the reader will know what you mean.** If you write "Painting is worthwhile," the reader will not know whether you mean painting a house or painting a portrait, or whether it is worthwhile for your ego or for your wallet.

2. **If you are specific, you have a better chance of proving your point.** If you write "No animal in the world does more for humans than a dog," you might try to support it with many examples of the dog's usefulness. However, dozens of examples would not prove the dog is more useful than the horse, the cow, the goat, the water buffalo, and many other work animals throughout the world. A specific sentence, however, such as "The dogs trained in the Seeing Eye Program enable their owners to lead active lives," gives you a chance to prove your point.

3. **If you are specific in your controlling idea, you can make the body of the paragraph more specific.** If you start with "Everything that lives on this earth needs nourishment," you will be forced to support your statement with vague generalities, not to mention having to talk about "everything that lives" because that is what your topic sentence promised you were going to do. If, however, you start with "A so-called good breakfast ruins my day," the body of your paragraph can be very specific. Consider these as specific details: "Just looking at two eggs quivering on a white plate makes my stomach churn" or "I can never concentrate in my eight o'clock math class because all my energies are being used to digest lumpy oatmeal."

First Try at a Topic Sentence

One way to make your attitude more specific is to keep asking yourself "Why?" Thus you move from a general idea to a more specific one, as in the following illustration.

"I like the book *Huckleberry Finn*."

"A so-called good breakfast ruins my day."

ASK YOURSELF: "Why do I like it?"
ANSWER: "*Huckleberry Finn* is interesting."
ASK YOURSELF: "Why is it interesting?"
ANSWER: "I don't know."
ASK YOURSELF: "Think! Try harder. Why is it interesting?"
ANSWER: "I like the way Huck is."
ASK YOURSELF: "Why do I like the way Huck is?"
ANSWER: "He seems real."
ASK YOURSELF: "Why does he seem real?"
ANSWER: "He is all mixed up. He thinks he's sinful, but he's really good."
FINALLY, ASK YOURSELF: "Now can I write a topic sentence that says that?"
ANSWER: "Sure."

Second Try at a Topic Sentence

A real joy of the book *Huckleberry Finn* is discovering the difference between what Huck thinks he is and what he really is.

Notice that once you begin to ask "Why," you change your subject from "I" to "*Huckleberry Finn,*" and that is exactly what you want to do. You want to discuss the book *Huckleberry Finn*—not "I."

As you can see from the topic sentence about Huck Finn, a topic sentence has to do more than just tell the reader what you are going to write about. What you are going to write about is only your topic, not your topic sentence. Don't confuse a topic with a topic sentence. For example, if you say that you are going to write about Ronald Reagan, you have only provided yourself with a topic—Ronald Reagan—but if you tell the reader what you want to say about the topic, then you're on your way to a good topic sentence. Now, you might be thinking, "What can I say about Ronald Reagan?" At this point you have to spend some time thinking about your topic and narrowing it down. Writing good topic sentences takes time. You can't just say anything about Ronald Reagan, such as "Ronald Reagan won the presidential election of 1980."

5

If this were your topic sentence, how would your reader know what to expect in the paragraph? The reader has to have an idea to hang on to. When you give your reader a topic sentence, you should be giving a guide that tells exactly which direction your paragraph is headed. Look at this topic sentence again, and see if it gives you any kind of a guide:

Ronald Reagan won the presidential election of 1980.

Do you know exactly what the writer is going to be talking about? Will it be something about Ronald Reagan or something about the presidential election of 1980? Will it be about Ronald Reagan's former occupation as an actor or will it contrast Ronald Reagan with Richard Nixon? Obviously, the paragraph could be developed in a hundred different directions. The topic sentence fails to provide a guide to either the reader or the writer because it contains no controlling idea. It is simply a statement of fact, and that shows why facts alone make such terrible topic sentences. They let the writer veer off in too many directions, thus making the paragraph incoherent and forcing the poor reader to try to make sense out of it.

NARROWING YOUR TOPIC SENTENCE

Once you understand that a topic sentence has to say something about your topic, you can concentrate on narrowing your topic. For example, suppose you were writing a paragraph about one of the following general topics.

Pollution	Antiques
Medicine	Television
Music	Sports

These are all extremely broad subjects. You would have to write a book to cover any one of them adequately. However, if you narrowed these topics, you could more easily find an idea for a paragraph. Consider the following, for example:

pollution
    water pollution
        water pollution in Star Lake
TOPIC SENTENCE: Water pollution has been *disastrous* for the fishermen of Star Lake.

medicine
    prescribed drugs
        the cost of prescribed drugs
TOPIC SENTENCE: The cost of prescribed drugs is *outrageously high.*

music
    music therapy
        the effects of music therapy
TOPIC SENTENCE: Music therapy has proved *quite successful* in the treatment of emotionally disturbed children.

antiques
    antique dealers
        sales strategy of antique dealers
TOPIC SENTENCE: Antique dealers sometimes use *deceptive* sales tactics.

television
    television commercials
        how women are portrayed in television commercials
TOPIC SENTENCE: Many commercials on television are *insulting* to a woman's dignity.

sports
    high school football
        high school football coaches
TOPIC SENTENCE: High school football coaches frequently *pressure players* to win at any cost.

Note that each of the topic sentences above contains a key word (or words) that makes a comment on the topic: "The cost of prescribed drugs is *outrageously high.*" "Many commercials on television *insult* a woman's dignity." The italicized words tell the writer's attitude—his or her impression, reaction, or point of view—about the topic and thus make the sentence a topic sentence. Words such as *outrageously high* and *insult* provide the reader with the controlling idea of the paragraph.

EXERCISE Ib
Using the three-step pattern illustrated above, narrow each of the following broad topics. Then use your specific topic to write a clear topic sentence.

1.	Movies	**6.**	Family reunions
2.	Alcoholism	**7.**	Divorce
3.	Country music	**8.**	Motorcycles
4.	Violence	**9.**	Sports
5.	Politicians	**10.**	Restaurants

EXERCISE Ic
Pick out the subject and the attitude in each of the following sentences. Underline the complete subject and circle the attitude.

1. Giving advice can be dangerous.
2. Doing homework during a warm spring day requires discipline.
3. One of the most difficult swimming skills to acquire is coordinated breathing.
4. Typing is a useful skill.
5. A parfait can be a tasty and artistic creation.
6. The modern American car is expensive to buy, to repair, and to operate.
7. Housework need not be boring.
8. The greatest rip-off in the country today is drugs.
9. The police officer's job is a demanding one.
10. A visit to the dentist is a harrowing experience.

EXERCISE ld
Rewrite the following sentences so that the subject and attitude are clear and specific.

EXAMPLE
GENERAL: Englebert Humperjelly is so popular.
SPECIFIC: Crooner Englebert Humperjelly draws hordes of fans by what he calls his "mood rock."

1. Working with food is rewarding.

   _____

2. Dogs are better than cats.

   _____

3. To write a paragraph, one must know how.

   _____

4. I like good books.

   _____

5. Working in a hospital is a worthwhile experience.

   _____

6. The English language is too difficult.

   _____

7. Women are bad drivers.

   _____

8. Married women shouldn't work.

   _____

9. Picasso did everything.

   _____

10. Austrians are music lovers.

    _____

EXERCISE le
Keeping in mind the need for a clear subject and attitude, put a check on the blank to the left if the sentence is acceptable as a topic sentence.

_____ 1. I have a dog named Jumper.
_____ 2. My math teacher is hard to please.
_____ 3. There are several things you should check before buying a used car.
_____ 4. Although she is over eighty, my mother still charms everyone.

_____	5.	I walked to the top of the hill and stopped there.
_____	6.	I run five miles every day.
_____	7.	Jogging really keeps the heart and lungs in good condition.
_____	8.	It all started at 8:15 P.M. on March 9, 1981.
_____	9.	Maintaining a home today requires a lot of time, money, and energy.
_____	10.	I bought a new car yesterday.

EXERCISE If

Read the following sentences and decide whether or not they would make good topic sentences. Tell what is wrong with each bad topic sentence and rewrite it to correct the fault.

1. Harry Truman was a good president.

_____

_____

2. Getting from here to the airport along the old highway or the new expressway.

_____

_____

3. I went to visit my Aunt Sue.

_____

_____

4. On a sunny day last October when the leaves had turned to scarlet and gold.

_____

_____

5. The gadget is unworkable.

_____

_____

6. I want to tell you about my father.

_____

_____

7. Sermons put me to sleep.

_____

_____

8. Every time Carlos gets up in the morning.

_____

_____

9

9.   President Kennedy was assassinated on November 22, 1963.

_____

_____

10. The art of playing a good game of pool.

_____

_____

Body

Now that you have announced your controlling idea, you must develop it; you must discuss, explain, support, or prove that controlling idea. You may use facts, reasons, illustrations, comparisons, contrasts, definitions, or other techniques, but you must remember the three essential qualities discussed in the Introduction: *unity, coherence,* and *adequate development.*

UNITY

A good topic sentence is the key to a unified paragraph. You won't have a good paragaraph unless **every** sentence supports one clear, controlling idea. If you begin with a vague controlling idea, you can easily stray from your topic and destroy the unity of your paragraph with irrelevant details.

Once you have stated your controlling idea, **stick to it.** Your reader doesn't want to be distracted and bored with extraneous points. If someone starts to tell you a story but gets sidetracked on a lot of unrelated details, you may not bother to listen. A reader who doesn't see any connection between the details in your paragraph and your controlling idea will become confused and quickly lose interest. In the following paragraph, for example, the italicized sentences add nothing to the controlling idea. **A potentially good paragraph has been ruined because it lacks unity.**

The city of Toronto, Canada, is a pleasant place to spend a summer vacation. Upon arriving in Toronto, one sees a remarkably clean city. The streets are not littered with dirt or debris, and Toronto's buildings are in such good condition that even the old ones look new. *In some cities, the buildings look like they are falling apart. Other cities are using specially treated steel to build their skyscrapers. Pittsburgh has one of these buildings.* Toronto is also a delight to shoppers. The streets in the shopping district are closed to traffic and lined with shady trees and outdoor cafes to provide the shopper with a pleasant, relaxed atmosphere away from the noise, the exhaust fumes, and the general chaos of congested city streets. The stores themselves are fun to shop in because, in addition to the usual big department stores one usually finds in such a city, Toronto also has many smaller stores which specialize in such goods as native Indian crafts and hand-carved wooden art objects. *Department stores are convenient, but I often find them boring. You see the same items in all of the department stores and, besides, they usually charge too much for their goods—especially clothes. Another reason I don't like them is because, even though most of them make millions in annual profits, they pay their employees as little as possible.* Toronto's restaurants also add to the city's appeal. Besides good food, they have nice atmosphere, and, best of all, reasonable prices. *Pittsburgh has some nice restaurants, too.* The people who live and work in Toronto also add immeasurably to the charm of the city. Because of their diverse cultural backgrounds, they are very interesting people, and their warm, friendly personalities make a visitor feel welcome. Toronto is one of the few large cities in the world where one can still feel safe walking along the streets at night. For many visitors, Toronto's low crime rate is its most appealing feature. *In some cities, the people are afraid to walk the streets at night. Of course, there aren't too many places left today where one can really feel safe. Cities have no monopoly on crime.*

COHERENCE

Make sure that your sentences follow an orderly sequence so that the reader can follow your development of the controlling idea. The reader must be able to see that the sentences link together in a logical pattern to make a connected whole. You might, for example, use time order (such as first to last) in telling a story, space order (such as left to right) in describing a place, comparison or contrast in illustrating a point, or the order of importance in arranging a series of facts to prove your point. You cannot expect your reader to understand you if your sentences are not in some kind of logical order. Notice how confusing the following paragraph is:

My day yesterday was a mess. I hope I don't have such a frustrating day soon again. My fan belt broke when I was on my way to work. The baby-sitter was sick so we couldn't go to the movie we were looking forward to. Because I was upset, I burned the steak I had splurged on. We got off to a bad start because I had forgotten to buy coffee. When I finally got to work, I found the interesting project I'd been working on was cancelled and I spent the whole day doing boring filing. My husband forgot I didn't have a car, so he failed to pick me up after work. Feeling there was nothing else to do, I flung myself on the bed—which immediately collapsed.

Notice that when sentences are in order, the reader can follow easily.

My day yesterday was a mess. We got off to a bad start because I had forgotten to buy coffee. My fan belt broke when I was on my way to work. When I finally got to work, I found the interesting project I'd been working on was cancelled, and I spent the whole day doing boring filing. My husband forgot I didn't have a car, so he failed to pick me up after work. Because I was upset, I burned the steak I had splurged on. The baby-sitter was sick so we couldn't go to the movie we were looking forward to. Feeling there was nothing else to do, I flung myself on the bed—which immediately collapsed. I hope I don't have such a frustrating day soon again.

**ADEQUATE
DEVELOPMENT**

Although adequate development cannot be measured by the number of words alone, you should work to construct an ample paragraph. Don't just add words, but build up the paragraph through unified and detailed development of your central idea. Look at the following paragraph, which states a central idea but fails to develop it adequately.

Taking the easy way out is often the way to missing out on some of life's most precious rewards. We often put off until tomorrow things that, for our own good, we ought to do today. It is often all too easy to avoid facing up to difficulties and responsibilities. Taking the easy way out seldom leads to well-being and happiness.

This paragraph is underdeveloped and suffers from malnutrition of thought. It lacks the detailed support necessary to develop the central idea.

Read the following paragraph as an example of adequate development of the same central idea.

Taking the easy way out is often the way to missing out on some of life's most precious rewards. By evading the problems and difficulties of life, one may appear, for the moment at least, to make things easier for oneself. In the long run, however, the easy way out may lead to dissatisfaction and regret. For example, if a shy girl takes the easy way out by avoiding the difficulty and embarrassment of meeting boys, she may later suffer greatly from the feeling of having missed out on life. Similarly, it is the easy way out for a shy boy to avoid making advances to a girl he likes when he fears he might be rejected. However, he may eventually suffer far greater pain in seeing someone else sharing her life and her charms. In other areas of life as well, it is often all too easy to avoid facing up to difficulties and responsibilities. It is often easy, for instance, to evade the concerted effort necessary to learn a particular skill, but if that skill is necessary for one's happiness and well-being, a person may suffer throughout life for having taken what was, for the moment, the easy way out.

PARAGRAPH LENGTH

Lincoln is reported to have said that a man's legs ought to be long enough to reach the ground. A paragraph ought to be long enough to reach the readers, to tell them all they need to know in order to understand what you want them to understand about your controlling idea. The body of your paragraph must do the whole job of developing your controlling idea for the reader. At the end, your reader should be able to say, "Yes, now I understand exactly what you mean."

Conclusion

If your discussion is to be complete, you need a concluding sentence to pull together the group of sentences that make up the body of your paragraph.

Usually a single sentence will provide an adequate conclusion. As "The Ministerial Three" suggests, one of the best ways to complete the paragraph is with a concluding sentence that refers to the controlling idea expressed in the topic sentence.

Look at this paragraph as an example:

Introduction

Although the New Testament writers used the popular language of their day, they often achieved great dignity and eloquence. Desiring to spread Christianity among all classes, they avoided high-flown style and, instead, chose language familiar to ordinary men and women. Since they were convinced of the greatness of their message, they often wrote naturally and directly, as earnest men might speak to their friends. Although St. Mark's writing

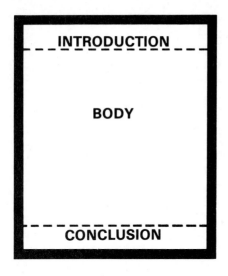

INTRODUCTION

BODY

CONCLUSION

Body

Conclusion

was not necessarily polished, he wrote with singular vigor and economy. St. John struggled with the language until he produced sparse and unadorned prose of great beauty. St. Paul, at his best, reached heights of eloquence which some consider unsurpassed in literature. St. Luke, the most brilliant of the New Testament writers, gave us Jesus' Parable of the Prodigal Son. **Taken as a whole, the work of these great Christian writers of the first century has a dignity and splendor all its own.**

Do you see how the concluding sentence refers to and echoes the controlling idea of the topic sentence?

NOTE: The conclusion doesn't simply repeat the topic sentence word for word: it restates the controlling idea.

A paragraph that just stops is incomplete, like a church without a steeple. That final sentence, by summarizing the discussion and reemphasizing the controlling idea, gives the paragraph unity and completeness.

There is one thing, however, that the conclusion must **not** do: **it must not add new material.**

The Four Kinds of Discourse

Discourse means "communication, the exchange of ideas, information, and feelings through language." When you communicate with someone, you satisfy one of four basic human needs: the need to tell how something looked or sounded or felt, the need to tell what happened, the need to convince someone, and the need to inform.

These needs are satisfied with four kinds of communication:

1. *Description* recreates, through words, an experience the writer had through his or her five senses.
2. *Narration tells a story*. It tells what happened, how it happened, and why it happened.

3. *Persuasion* uses words to make people think something or do something. The clergy, editorial writers, advertisers, teachers, and politicians rely heavily on persuasion; they want you to change your thoughts or behavior.

4. *Exposition* explains something. In one sense, exposition takes in all the others because a writer may describe something in order to explain it, may explain it by using narration in the form of illustration or examples, and may be using explanation in order to persuade.

In this broad sense, this textbook is concerned only with exposition, and all the paragraphs you write will be expository.

QUESTIONS FOR DISCUSSION

1. What is the best way to give someone directions to a specific destination?
2. When you receive instructions by telephone, what is the best way to make sure that you have understood them correctly? What if you are giving the instructions?
3. What is the best method of giving a person instructions on how to perform a routine task?

Suggested Activities

A vital part of your education since childhood has been learning to follow and to give instructions. Sometimes the instructions you received were clear and precise; at other times, no doubt, they were downright confusing. The truth is that giving clear instructions is far more difficult than it appears.

One common failing in giving instructions is the C.O.I.K. Fallacy: the instructions are Clear Only If Known. Most of you, at one time or another, have encountered this fallacy. For instance, you are looking for the home of an old friend who has moved out to the country. You stop to ask for directions, and you get something like this: "Now just go on down the road a piece until you pass old Hipplewaite's turkey farm. Then you'll come to a dip in the road where there's a big tree on the left. Now you take that road that bears to the right, and you go up there just a short ways and you'll see a green house set back in the trees."

The trouble with such instructions is what you don't know and the instructions don't tell you. How far down the road is "a piece"? How do you recognize old Hipplewaite's turkey farm? Is there a sign? Which side of the road is it on? How can you be sure which dip in the road is the right one? How big is that big tree, and what kind of tree is it? Does the road to the right just branch off or does it cut across? How far is "a short way"? Is there only one green house? Can you see it clearly from the road?

In giving instructions, you need to consider the knowledge, experience, and skill of those who are to perform the task. Who is going to follow your instructions? Curious schoolchildren? Adult amateurs? Skilled technicians? For example, if you are writing instructions for someone who knows little about cars, it is not enough to say "Clean your car's cooling system," "Adjust the spark plug gap," or "Check the timing." Unless your reader is a mechanic, you must give explicit directions on how to perform each of these operations.

It is also easy to forget some important detail. One way to prove this is to ask another student to tell you how to put your coat on. Have this student face the back of the room while the rest of the students face the front. As the student giving directions tells you what to do, follow the directions **exactly.** You will soon find yourself and the coat in a ridiculous position.

If you want to be sure that your instructions are clear and precise, the best thing to do is to test them. Have members of the group for whom the instructions are designed perform the task or operation following your instructions. You may find that your instructions are not so clear as you thought.

ASSIGNMENT
Put into practice what you have learned from this chapter. Select one of your topic sentences from Exercise Ib and write a well-developed paragraph that clearly supports your controlling idea.

SENTENCES

Just as a paragraph is a group of sentences that deals with one controlling thought, a sentence is a group of words that expresses a single idea. A complete sentence contains two essential elements: a **subject** (who or what the sentence is about) and a **verb** (what the subject is or does). A group of words that does not have both these parts is not a sentence at all, but a **fragment** of a sentence.

One-Word Sentences

One kind of sentence seems *not* to have a subject but really does. In such sentences (usually giving orders or making requests), the subject is **understood.** The reader or listener supplies the subject *you*. Look at the following sentences in which the subject *you* is understood.

[you] Help!	[you] Stop.
[you] Shut the door, please.	[you] Go.
[you] Call me.	[you] March.
[you] Take a running jump.	[you] Flee!

In all these examples, the sentence does not have a subject, but you know that the meaning is not "I help!" for instance, or "She shut the door, please."

All one-word sentences have some element understood. In "Help!" both the subject, *you*, and the object, *me*, are understood. In a sentence "Murder!" something like "A murder is going on here, and I need your help!" is meant. But under the circumstances, that would be a little wordy.

Two-Word Sentences

Here is the simplest form of sentence containing a subject and verb:

Fish swim.

That two-word sentence contains the **two** essential elements of a complete sentence:

1. It has a subject, *fish,* about which something is being said.
2. It has a complete verb, *swim,* that says something about the subject.

Fragments

A sentence fragment is less than a complete sentence. Some part of the basic subject-verb unit is incomplete or missing.

There is a difference between verbs and *verbals.* Verbals are incomplete verb forms that function as nouns, adjectives, or adverbs, but **not** as verbs. Note the following examples.

Fishing is his main hobby. [Verbal functions as a noun.]
The girl *dancing* is Ron's sister. [Verbal functions as an adjective.]
The boys came *to see* the pretty girls on the beach. [Verbal functions as an adverb.]

One of the main types of sentence fragment comes from using a verbal instead of a complete verb.

Fish *swimming.*
Fish *swimming* from the coast of Alaska to inland rivers every year.

Putting a period after these word groups does not make them sentences. Since their verb forms are incomplete, both are sentence fragments. The correct versions should be:

Fish swim.
Fish swim from the coast of Alaska to inland rivers every year.

Similarly:

1. Salmon *swimming* up the river to spawn.
2. Atomic power plants *operating* in the European countries.
3. The witness *being questioned* by the prosecutor.

These fragments can be made into complete sentences in several ways:

1. Salmon *are* [or *were*] *swimming* up the river to spawn.
    Salmon swim [or *swam*] up the river to spawn.

Salmon swimming up the river to spawn *overcome* seemingly impossible obstacles.

2. Atomic power plants *are operating* in the European countries.

    Atomic power plants *operate* in the European countries.

    Atomic power plants operating in the European countries *supply* a major portion of Europe's electric power.

3. The witness *is* [or *was*] *being questioned* by the prosecutor.

    The witness *is* [or *was*] *questioned* by the prosecutor.

    The witness being questioned by the prosecutor *told* one lie after another.

Note that the subject in each sentence has a *verb,* one or more words that show **action.** Remember that verbals such as *swimming, operating, being questioned* act only as modifiers; they do not show action.

EXERCISE Ig
Mark the complete sentences with a *C,* fragments with an *F.*

_____ 1. Having passed through Slippery Rock Grade School, Gates Junior High, and Ambridge High School.

_____ 2. He left.

_____ 3. I graduated from Harvard in 1982.

_____ 4. My cat, kind of a calico, orange and white striped one.

_____ 5. The past, the present, and the future passing before Scrooge this Christmas Eve.

_____ 6. The "castle" built by Randolph Hearst many years ago.

_____ 7. When I get nervous, I get sick.

_____ 8. The very exciting basketball game between Benedict Arnold High School and Calvin Coolidge Tech.

_____ 9. Running is a national craze.

_____ 10. Having stood alone for hours waiting for my late date.

EXERCISE Ih
Mark the complete sentences with a *C,* fragments with an *F.* Add whatever is necessary to make the fragments into complete sentences.

_____ 1. The fat man sitting in the stands, drinking beer, eating hot dogs, and swearing at the umpire.

_____

_____

_____ 2. The workers on the assembly line having decided to go on strike.

_____

_____

17

_____ 3. People coming to class late and fooling around and never answering questions.

_____

_____

_____ 4. Especially after having learned how to drive.

_____

_____

_____ 5. John looked out the window to check the traffic.

_____

_____

_____ 6. Alone and afraid, the girl with the red hair.

_____

_____

_____ 7. The traffic was heavy and the lack of police and directional signs.

_____

_____

_____ 8. John and Bill rode the bus to the city and hitchhiked back.

_____

_____

_____ 9. The snowfall was heavy and cars skidding all over the road and commuters stuck.

_____

_____

_____ 10. Passing the test was my greatest achievement.

_____

_____

EXERCISE Ii
The following exercise consists of groups of jumbled words that cannot be made into a sentence because they lack one of the essential parts of a sentence—a subject or a verb. Put the words into some sort of order; then add the missing subject or verb that will make the sentence complete.

EXAMPLES
interesting I the book   [verb is missing]
COMPLETIONS: I *found* the book interesting.
                 I *read* the interesting book.
                 I *returned* the interesting book.
lawn across the limped   [subject is missing]

18

the
paragraph

COMPLETIONS: The *man* limped across the lawn.
The *dog* limped across the lawn.

Try these:

me the dog brown

_____

long a slept time

_____

Did you answer "The brown dog bit me" or "The brown dog kissed me"? "Rip Van Winkle slept a long time" or "I slept long time"? (Your answer may tell you something about yourself.)

Now make sentences from the following word groups. Don't add s's or articles (*a, an, the*). Add only the necessary word, and change nothing but the order of the words.

1. drug pusher undercover an the officer

_____

2. ambitious workers the

_____

3. me to Helen Phillip at the party

_____

4. as the stocking cap the bank robbed six witnesses the man in

_____

5. the grill chicken on outdoor an Jeff

_____

6. of a speaker state emotional often facial expressions his

_____

7. the barroom into back staggered the of

_____

8. admitted jewels queen's the stealing

_____

9. Florence leather would to I visit a to buy jacket

_____

10. a brother player my classical guitar

_____

the
paragraph

EXERCISE Ij
Make the following fragments into complete sentences.

EXAMPLE
INCOMPLETE: The day I learned the true meaning of forgiveness.
COMPLETE: Last summer, my four-year-old daughter taught me the true meaning of forgiveness.

1. The accident I had on New Year's Eve and how it changed my life.

   _____

2. To enjoy your in-laws.

   _____

3. All the reasons why I hate cats.

   _____

4. The thrill of finding a sunken treasure.

   _____

5. Why jogging is helpful.

   _____

6. Five distinct categories of Monopoly players.

   _____

7. My definition of a good teacher.

   _____

8. Baking bread the easy way.

   _____

9. The frustrations of trying to go to college, work full time, and raise a family.

   _____

10. Watching the plane crash.

   _____

WORDS

As a paragraph is made up of sentences, a sentence is made up of words. The purpose of the word section in this book is to help you choose the best words you can, the words that make your meaning clear to the reader. Since subjects and verbs are the most important words in the sentence, work on those first.

A Clear and Specific Subject

General words are words of broad meaning and wide application. Words like *condition*, *situation*, and *eventuality* do have their place in our language, but if you want your reader to know exactly what you mean, you must select the most specific word possible for your subject.

Consider the following words:

Things	Actions
vehicle	aspect
device	malfunction
contraption	modification
matter	asset
entity	movement
article	misbehavior
feature	maladjustment
factor	circumstance

Each of these words represents a broad class of things or actions. *Feature*, for example, could refer to a movie, a story, a special attraction, or a nose, a chin, an Adam's apple, or even a belly button; it could refer to a cartoon that appears regularly, or a special characteristic of a house or a car or an author or an athlete.

Don't say *device* if you mean a can opener.
Don't say *vehicle* if you mean a Chevrolet Impala.
Don't say *article* if you mean a T-shirt.
Don't say *movement* if you mean a karate chop. *waltz step*

The following lists illustrate the relationship between broad, general terms and specific words that point directly to objects. As you move down the lists, you find words that become increasingly more specific with each step. *Cow* is much more specific than *living creature*, and *motorcycle* is much more specific than *vehicle*.

living creature	vehicle
animal	motor vehicle
quadruped	two-wheeled motor vehicle
cow	motorcycle
Jersey cow	Honda
old MacDonald's Jersey cow, Bossy	a red and black Honda 350

If you want your writing to be clear, be as specific as possible. If your subject is specific enough, all your readers will see the same picture; if your subject is too general, the meaning of your sentence will not be clear. For example, consider the following:

21

1. *Something* is floating in your soup.

   What do you see floating in your soup? A contact lens? A dandelion? A popsicle stick? Obviously, the word *something* is much too general.

2. A *creature* is floating in your soup.

   What do you see now? A monster? A mouse? A yellow-bellied sapsucker? You are probably thinking of something living, but that doesn't narrow the subject down very much.

3. An *invertebrate* is floating in your soup.

   If you know that *invertebrate* means "without a backbone," you can narrow the picture down to a spineless creature, but you still don't know exactly what is floating in your soup. A clam? A bug? A coward?

4. A *cockroach* is floating in your soup.

   Now your subject is specific. The picture is clear; the only thing you can see floating in your soup is a cockroach.

   ### EXERCISE Ik
   In each of the following, make the subject (the italicized word) more specific.

1. The *thing* in his hand could cut your arm off.

   _____

2. The *animal* next door broke its chain.

   _____

A cockroach is floating in your soup.

3. The *item* she bought is not returnable.

    _____

4. The *weather* made the roads treacherous.

    _____

5. Her *heart condition* prevented her from attending school.

    _____

6. *Facilities* are provided.

    _____

7. The *drink* she served was potent.

    _____

8. A *publication* lay on the coffee table.

    _____

9. The *place* where they live is badly in need of repair.

    _____

10. *Something* kept the car from starting.

    _____

A Clear and Specific Verb

If you want your paragraphs to make sense, you have to learn to say exactly what you mean. Using the wrong word in a sentence can be just as serious an error as using the wrong number in a math problem. For example, suppose you had to describe an extremely intoxicated neighbor trying to reach his back porch after a night of bar-hopping. If you wrote,

My neighbor *walked* across the back yard,

when you really meant

My neighbor *staggered* across the back yard,

then you would have made a serious error in communication and conveyed an inaccurate picture to your reader. Changing the verb from *walked* to *staggered* creates a different image in the reader's mind. That's why it is so important to choose the right verb. Look at the following sentences and see how the image in your mind is altered by the change of only one word in each sentence—the verb.

My neighbor *stomped* across the back yard. [Do you see an angry man?]

My neighbor *paced* across the backyard. [Do you see a nervous man?]

My neighbor *glided* across the back yard. [Do you see a happy man?]

23

My neighbor *jogged* across the back yard. [Do you see an exercise buff in a gray sweatsuit?]

How does verb choice change the meaning of the sentences below?

May *looked* at John.
May *glared* at John.
May *gazed* at John.
May *stared* at John.
May *gawked* at John.
May *glanced* at John.

Suggested Activity

There are more than a hundred verbs in English that specify some particular kind of walking. Have each student suggest a specific verb for the general verb *walk*. For example, "He *strutted* down the street." The words should be written on the blackboard. (Try to get sixty.)

Notice that by making the verb more specific, you create a picture not only of the way a person walks but also of the person walking. What or who might be likely to be *strutting?* or *tiptoeing?*

Try this same exercise with *talk* and *laugh*. (Try to get twenty each.)

EXERCISE II
Replace the italicized verb with one that is more specific.

1. He *came* into the room.

   _____

2. She *put* the package on the table.

   _____

3. The boy *went* home.

   _____

4. The doctor *spoke* to the patient.

   _____

5. He *took* a gun from the wall rack.

   _____

6. The child *worked* on his project.

   _____

7. The woman *talked* a long time.

   _____

8. My grandfather *told* the man to come in.

   _____

9. He *laughed* at the joke.

_____

10. She *disliked* her boss.

_____

EXERCISE 1m
For each italicized word or phrase in the following paragraph choose a more specific term. Note how the paragraph changes when you make the *person* a cowboy or a *ballerina*.

A *person came out* of an *enclosed area* and went down the *thorough-*

_____

fare. He *got into* a *vehicle* in another *enclosed area* and *went on his way.* He

_____

turned a corner in a hurry and almost hit *another person* who was *walking* along

_____

the street *looking* at the sky. The driver *said* to the *person* walking, "Why don't

_____

you *pay attention* to *what you are doing?*" As he *went on,* he *said* to himself,

_____

"How does a *person* expect to be seen *late in the evening* when he is wearing

_____

dark apparel?" The *person* walking stopped *looking* at the sky and *looked* at

_____

the retreating *vehicle.* "That driver almost *did me an injury,*" he said.

_____

25

CHAPTER II

narrating

ORGANIZATION

"Mummy, tell me a story."
"Daddy, read me a story before I go to sleep."
"Hey, Sam, have I got a story for you!"
"My grandfather is full of stories of 'the Good Old Days'."

Everybody from baby to Gramps likes a story. Your assignment in narrative writing will be to write a paragraph about a personal experience—something that has happened to you.

What Is a Narrative?

Did you ever tell a friend about an experience that embarrassed you or amused you or terrified you or in some way changed you? If you did, then you already have some practice in composing a narrative, because when you related your experience to a friend, you were actually narrating a story. The word *narrate* means "to tell, to give an account of"; when you write a narrative paragraph, you are

telling your readers a story, giving them an account of something that happened to you, such as an unforgettable personal experience.

Organization of a Narrative Paragraph

Narrative in the sense used in this chapter is a story told to support a point. The narrative paragraph has the same organization discussed before:

1. The topic sentence tells what you are going to talk about (your subject) and what you think or feel about it (your attitude).
2. The body supports or develops your topic sentence. One of the easiest and most effective ways to do this is through narration—by telling a story to prove your topic sentence.
3. The concluding sentence restates the topic sentence and points out the significance of the narrative in the body of the paragraph.

Thus, in the narrative paragraph you again have the "ministerial three."

The Narrative of Personal Experience

One of the most common kinds of narrative is that of personal experience. In this kind of narrative, you tell the reader what happened and why it was important to you. Remember, you are not going to tell the reader your whole life story, certainly not in one paragraph; so you need to focus sharply on a single event that affected you in some way.

Perhaps the most effective way to pursue your search and get down to the essence of what you want to say is through a series of questions such as these:

What stands out in my memory?
Why was that so important to me?
What difference did it make to me?
Why did I act that way?

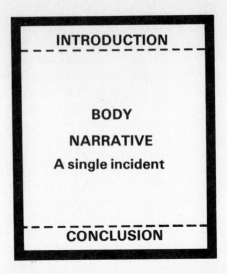

```
┌─────────────────────────────┐
│      INTRODUCTION           │
│  - - - - - -    - - - - -    │
│                             │
│                             │
│          BODY               │
│        NARRATIVE            │
│      A single incident      │
│                             │
│                             │
│  - - - - - -    - - - - -    │
│       CONCLUSION            │
└─────────────────────────────┘
```

What did it do to me?
How have I changed?

Asking such questions will help you understand your own experience better, and answering them will usually provide you with the controlling idea of your paragraph. The incident or event you select provides the *subject,* and your response to the event provides the *attitude.* As soon as you have your controlling idea clearly in mind, write down one clear sentence that tells at least your general subject and clearly expresses an attitude toward that subject. For example:

Perhaps the funniest thing I ever saw was two policemen trying to catch a cow in a shopping center.

One hot summer night last August, I saw an accident that left me horrified.

My first encounter with a harmless garden snake had disastrous consequences.

You must have a point to your story, and the place to make that point is in your topic sentence. Once you have that topic sentence down on paper, then make sure that everything you write contributes to developing its controlling idea.

Remember, the narrative paragraph portrays action. It is like a moving picture in which objects are in motion from one moment to the next. The writer must capture that action for the reader. Your sentences must have a sense of direction and carry your main idea forward. If your controlling idea does not progress as you develop your paragraph, the reader will lose interest. Keep the story moving at all times, and your reader will stay with you.

Write honestly and directly in natural language. Don't use stilted and phony wording in a mistaken attempt to impress somebody. Be honest with yourself, too, and don't attempt to hide your own failings and doubts. After all, where is there a human being who has never done anything selfish or stupid or frivolous?

What kind of words will be most appropriate for your topic and your reader? Words that express feelings, that appeal to the senses, or that portray a mood are good for narrative paragraphs. You don't want merely to **relate** something to your reader—you want to **recreate** it. Your reader should share in your experience, and your choice of words can cause him or her to have vibrations similar to your own. This response is called *empathy*.

If, for example, you are writing about a terrifying experience, you should choose the words that best describe your exact perceptions and emotions at that time. In this way, the reader can see the experience through your eyes and feel its emotional impact; in effect, you and the reader become one person. It is important, therefore, to remember exactly what you saw and how you felt—then carefully choose the appropriate words. After reading the next sample student paragraph, analyze your immediate reaction to see whether you share a feeling of empathy with the writer. If so, how did she create this feeling for you?

At the age of nineteen, I had a horrifying, gruesome experience. The nightmare occurred in the barracks at Ft. Gordon, Georgia, where we were preparing for an inspection. Four girls were assigned to various duties in the latrine. Shivbby, our barrack's sergeant, and Debbie Howell volunteered to strip the latrine floor using turpentine and a buffer. Meanwhile MacDonald and I waited outside until they were finished so that we could go in and complete our details. Suddenly there was a blast followed by a flash fire, and both MacDonald and I were thrown backward from its impact. Debbie Howell came tearing out of the latrine screaming like a banshee, and I saw that both of her feet were burning. Immediately, MacDonald and I threw her to the floor and quickly extinguished the flames which engulfed her feet. Then, as we turned and looked at each other, horror filled our eyes. MacDonald screamed—her eyes filled with disbelief: "Oh my God, Bessie, Shivbby is still in there; she is still in the latrine!" We both ran to the latrine and were horrified as Shivbby, who was burned black from head to toe, came staggering out of the latrine and collapsed into Mac-Donald's arms. After witnessing this gruesome sight, I went into shock, unable to believe that the figure before me, burned beyond recognition, was once my barrack's sergeant. The sight and smell of burning flesh and hair almost made me vomit, but I held it back. However, when the ambulance attendants arrived and lifted Shivbby, some of her burned flesh remained on MacDonald's arms. That was my breaking point. I dashed out of the building and did not care where I went, for I was running away from the scene of a nightmare. Still, to this day, seven years after her death, I can see Shivbby's burned body and smell the rancid flesh and hair. This nightmare will linger in my memory forever. *Bessie Young*

Notice how the first sentence tells the writer's *attitude* toward the experience. Notice, too, that the story moves straight forward until the last two sentences. Then note how the last two sentences bring the story to a conclusion. The last sentence, especially, echoes the controlling idea expressed in the words of the topic sentence, ". . . horrifying, gruesome experience."

At this point you may be saying to yourself, "But nothing like that ever happened to me. I have nothing exciting to write about." It may be true that none of your experiences seem to have been earth-shaking or heroic, tragic or hilarious; but that is not the important thing. The important thing is not what happened but **what effect it had upon you,** your response to the experience. Even a seemingly trivial incident, if it had an effect upon you, has the power to involve your reader in a genuine sharing of experience.

What Can I Write About?

At this point, you may still be saying to yourself, "I can't think of anything! Life has been a drag. What could I possibly write about that anyone else would be interested in reading?"

Don't panic.

Think about your past and remember that **your life is unique.** No one else has lived a life exactly like yours; therefore, it must be full of experiences that no one else has had. Even if another individual has shared a similar experience, such as a disappointing blind date or a terrifying plane ride, that person could not have reacted in exactly the same way as you did. So look inside yourself and examine honestly what you think and feel.

When you explore the events of your own life as honestly and accurately as possible, you will find that you do have something worth writing about. Perhaps you have had experiences that few of your fellow students have shared: making a life-or-death decision, witnessing the birth of a child, visiting a foreign country, meeting a famous person, having a serious operation, or being involved in a divorce. The key to the beginning of a good narrative lies in choosing the right experience to write about. Think about your childhood. Where did you grow up? In a small town? On a farm? In a ghetto? Think about your grade school and your high school years. Did you have any memorable experiences—any traumatic, humorous, embarrassing, or glorious moments?

Or think about some possible firsts:

Your first date
Your first love
Your first child
Your first plane ride
Your first taste of defeat
Your first glorious success
Your first encounter with death
Your first day on a new job
Your first Christmas away from home

THE CENTRAL PURPOSE

Telling a story is **not** just listing a series of events; the account of events, when placed in a logical order, **must make a point.** Otherwise, your composition will not be a paragraph because it will not develop an idea; it will remain simply a series of events. Your reader must be able to see *why* you are writing about a particular experience.

Why was it terrifying?
Why was it funny?
Why was it humiliating?
Why was it valuable?

narrating

I ate a good breakfast Wednesday morning and then I went to school. My last class wasn't over until about four o'clock. I was hungry so I stopped at McDonald's and ate a Big Mac and two orders of French fries. After I got home, I studied math for a while and then looked over my psychology notes, but I soon got tired of studying. I decided to go over to my girlfriend's house. We went out for a pizza and then I drove back home. I fell asleep on the couch while I was watching the Johnny Carson Show.

Do you think you would look forward to this student's next "interesting" story, or would you find yourself developing a strong urge to walk the other way the next time you saw him coming? Do you think you might have asked yourself: "Why is he telling me this? What point is he trying to make?" If your reader asks these same questions after reading your narrative, then you have failed to meet the most important requirement of a good narrative paragraph—**a central purpose.** When you tell your reader why you are writing about a particular experience, you automatically provide your narrative with a controlling idea. The writer of the following narrative, for example, has a clear purpose—to tell the readers about an embarrassing experience.

Although I can laugh about it now, the experience that took place last Saturday afternoon was actually quite embarrassing. As part of my duties as a state policeman, I was assigned to give driver examinations. It was a very hot and humid day that progressed much too slowly, but, finally, I gave my last test—to a woman. I failed the lady because she had driven her car up over a curb. I took time to explain to her that I could not possibly pass anyone who drove a vehicle up over a curb during a driver's test. She accepted the explanation calmly, and then we went inside the exam center where I stamped "Did Not Pass" on her permit. The disappointed woman then stepped outside to wait for her husband. By this time, I was falling behind schedule, so I hurried from the building to my marked patrol car and started the engine. I backed up a few feet, cut the wheels to the right, and then started to drive away, but, suddenly, I heard a loud bang. As my car rocked and swayed, my face grew redder and redder. Much to my embarrassment, I had driven the patrol car over a high curb and damaged the front end. As fate would have it, the woman I had failed was standing about twenty feet away—shaking her finger at me and laughing hysterically. I wanted to crawl into a hole; I quickly departed and prayed that I would never have to meet my lady friend in the exam center again.   *John Hudson*

This narrative makes sense because it has a controlling idea. The writer is not simply listing a series of facts; he is telling you about an **embarrassing** experience. In the first sentence, he tells you **why** he is going to relate his experience to you (" . . . what took place last Saturday afternoon was actually quite embarrassing"), and then he presents a step-by-step account of what happened.

Here is another student paragraph, one in which the writer emphasizes the time order of a narrative by discussing how time passes in his accounting class. Notice also the vigorous expression of his attitude in his topic sentence.

If I had but one hour to live, I would spend it in my accounting class. There the seconds seem like hours, the minutes like days, and the hour like the longest

month during a cold and bitter winter. Placid-faced clock-watchers surround me as we all think the same thought. When will it end? The lecture drags on like a sermon: no beginning and certainly no end. Drowsiness seems to overtake all, as our heads nod sleepily, giving one the impression of children bobbing for apples. Not even blinking my eyes seems to help; in fact, Charles Atlas couldn't hold them open. Suddenly the instructor's voice changes, removing the spell-like trance he has cast upon me. Alert now, I shift my weight in search of a more comfortable position. A slight yawn escapes me. Now I've done it! The instructor shifts his eyes toward mine. He's going to ask me a question. Make it an easy one, I think to myself. The class, turning in my direction, awaits my answer. They look like vultures anticipating their next meal. To their dismay and my surprise, I answer the question correctly. With no apparent change in the tone of his voice, the instructor immediately resumes his lecture where he had stopped. Unlike E. F. Hutton, when the instructor talks, people fall asleep. Inconspicuously, I glance at my watch and find, much to my surprise, that ten minutes have already passed.
David McKay

Topic Sentence

CHOOSING THE RIGHT KIND OF TOPIC SENTENCE

As the little group of sentences at the beginning of this chapter indicates, everyone likes a story. Because we all like stories, narratives provide a good method for developing topic sentences that can be supported by a single example.

Here are some topic sentences that can be proved by a single incident.

Having an overly friendly dog can cost you a job.

Driving when angry can be disastrous.

Falling in love is very time-consuming.

At age seven, I learned that honesty is not always the best policy.

My baby brother can ruin any date.

An article I read last year changed my life.

An incident that happened to a friend of mine made me appreciate my parents.

Be careful. Not all topic sentences can be developed or proved by a single incident. Some topic sentences need many examples. Other topic sentences need facts to support them. The following topic sentences, for example, could **not** be proved by a single incident or story. Why not?

A waitress encounters several kinds of irritating customers.

Students at CCBC can be divided into three groups: the brain, the worker, and the goof-off.

Attending a large university has many advantages over attending a branch campus.

EXERCISE IIa.
Tell which of the following sentences could be successfully developed by the narrative method.

_____ 1. The need for technicians has increased rapidly in the last ten years.

_____ 2. The Arabic alphabet is quite different from ours.

_____ 3. My sister's wedding reception was a disaster.

_____ **4.** There are two kinds of degrees given at our college—the Associate in Arts and the Associate in Science.

_____ **5.** An automobile wreck I had last year changed my life.

_____ **6.** Being arrested and booked frightened me into conformity.

_____ **7.** Today there's a market for cars of all sizes.

_____ **8.** The custom paint job on Jimmy's van was spectacular.

_____ **9.** The flying saucer landing in our back yard made me a believer.

_____ **10.** The day we moved from Elm Street is the day our honeymoon ended.

Body

The body of the paragraph developed by narrative consists of the relating of a single incident or story. The sentences are put in order by time; that is, events are recorded in the order in which they happened. In this kind of paragraph, just write the topic sentence, and then tell the story that proves the topic sentence.

Note how the narrative body of the following paragraph supports the controlling idea:

As a trainer and breeder of horses, I've worked with many smart horses, but the smartest I've ever known was a big, black gelding called Baron. I was teaching Baron, my own horse, some of the tricks of "high dressage," a special training in which the horse learns to dance, walk on his hind legs, kneel down, and do a lot of showy things like that. Baron was doing very well, but he was still my saddle horse, too. One December 24 I rode over to take a friend his Christmas present. Once I was there, my friend and I decided to have a little Christmas cheer. Time sped past, but suddenly I realized that dark had fallen and so had about three inches of snow. Hurriedly jingling out a few last Christmas wishes to my friend and his family, I mounted Baron and trotted down the drive. My wife would be seething that I was late for dinner on Christmas Eve. If I cut through the woods on a little trail only Baron and I knew, I could save about four miles. So, I curved left to the trail. At first, it was beautiful in the woods, white and silent. That horse and I could have been alone in the world. Then, crash! Baron stumbled over a deadfall branch and we both thudded to the ground. Baron struggled to his feet and bolted fifty yards away. But I knew I wasn't going to get up without help; something important was broken. There I was, helpless, in the middle of the woods with the snow filling up the hoof marks, the one clue that led to me. It would be hours, maybe days, before anyone found me—too long, anyway. It was up to Baron and me. I called him, softly. He came and nuzzled me. Then I commanded, "Kneel, Kneel." He'd done it in the ring, but would he do it now in the snow and underbrush? I couldn't reach him to give him the hand signals, just the words over and over and over. But he did it! He kneeled. Then, somehow, half-fainting, I draped myself across the saddle. On command, he rose. On command, he followed that path home, walking. Baron probably saved my life that night.

The topic sentence for this narrative paragraph could be worded in various ways:

My experience as a small-time trainer and breeder of saddle horses has convinced me that horses are not as dumb as many people think.

Although most people think that horses are beautiful but dumb, I, as an expert, know better.

The main thing is that the story is told with a clear purpose in mind—**to make a point.**

By clearly stating your opinion in the first sentence, you avoid having your reader ask, "So what? Why are you telling me this?" Even though others may disagree with you, just state your opinion and tell the story to support it. Indeed, having a number of people disagree with you can lend your paragraph strength. You often want to have an argumentative edge that provokes people into listening to you, even if they listen only to contradict. Suppose the reader finishes the horse story and shouts, "Well, let me tell you a story about two dumb horses I know." That's far better than having the reader yawn and ask, "Who cares?"

Conclusion

You also need a concluding sentence for your narrative, one that restates your topic sentence so that what you leave your reader with is your controlling idea. The following is an acceptable conclusion for the horse story:

I'll agree that horses are beautiful, but I'll never be convinced that they are stupid; Baron and I know better.

If your paragraph has a clear topic sentence, a narrative body to support it, and a sound conclusion to end it, no one will ever ask you, "So what?"

EXERCISE IIb

Narrative paragraphs follow a chronological order: first this happens, then this, and so on. Rearrange the following sentences to form a coherent narrative paragraph. On the line at the bottom, use sentence numbers to show the correct sequence.

(1) My roommate, Linda, taught me that. (2) They were one of the big college romances. (3) As Linda left school, she said, smugly, that Johnny would shape up. (4) She was smart, beautiful, rich, but, most of all, she knew what she wanted—and got it. (5) That was his character. (6) When she returned, ready to forgive and forget, she found Johnny had made up his mind. (7) I have always liked the saying that "Character is fate," especially since I learned that it means people get what they deserve. (8) Linda didn't seem to know what had hit her. (9) In the little college we went to, Linda was the girl who had everything. (10) She got him, too. (11) If she'd grown up with Johnny, as I had, she would have known that she couldn't push him too far. (12) After vacation, they would either announce their engagement or break up. (13) One of the things she wanted was darling Johnny Spencer. (14) When spring vacation came that senior year, Linda told Johnny that she'd give him two weeks to make up his mind. (15) Linda planned on marriage right after graduation, but, for once, Johnny didn't seem to go along. (16) But I knew: her own demanding character had been her fate. (17) He'd married a girl from his home town.

Some Do's . . .

1. **Do** arrange the details of the narrative in chronological order, the order of the time in which things happened.

2. **Do** limit your subject and narrow its scope to a single significant event or possibly a single thread of closely related events. (All of the details are then arranged in time order from beginning to end.)

3. **Do** use the past tense. There are exceptions, of course, but usually the **simple past tense** will serve you best in telling your story: "We **strolled** toward the lake. . . . We **saw** the speedboat. . . . Then we **heard** the boy in the water scream. . . . etc.

    If you need to include some detail which occurred before the action of your story takes place, all you need to do, in most instances, is to add *had* or *had been* to the simple past form: for example, "I **had been** told. . . . . I **had** heard. . . . . I **had** looked. . . .

4. **Do** make sure your narrative is unified. To achieve that unity, your paragraph as a whole needs to make a unified statement about your personal experience. You need (1) a clear and specific topic sentence which states the controlling idea, (2) detailed development clearly related to the controlling idea, and (3) a conclusion that reemphasizes, clarifies, or restates the controlling idea.

. . . and Don'ts About the Narrative

1. **Don't** try to cover too much. Remember that you are not writing your autobiography.

2. **Don't** include details that are not required to support your main point. You need to be highly selective. If your narrative is about something that happened to you late at night, don't start by talking about what you had for breakfast, unless it has some direct reference to your nighttime adventure.

3. **Don't** write a pointless account of events. No matter how dramatic the details may be, they need to be interpreted in terms of your reaction to them. It is not enough, for example, to tell your reader about a fiery auto crash; you must show the reader how the accident influenced your life. Although your experience need not be dramatic or spectacular, you do need to have a point to make, and everything in your narrative needs to be related to that central point or controlling idea.

Suggested Activities

The telling of tall tales is an American tradition carried on today by such organizations as the Liars' Club and by countless hunters, fishermen, and yarn spinners.

1. Taking no more than two minutes for the telling of each story, see who can come up with the biggest whopper.

2. Give one student at the front of the class a brief item from the news—preferably no more than three or four sentences. Have the student read the item silently and turn it face down. Then have him or her whisper the message to the next student. Have the second student pass the message

35

to a third, and repeat the process until the message has been relayed to the last person in class. Have the last person repeat the message aloud. Now compare the last person's version of the message with the original news item.

QUESTIONS FOR DISCUSSION

1. What happens when a story is passed by word of mouth through a chain of people who hear the story and then tell it to someone else?
2. Suppose you hear a report of a strange incident which happened in some remote area—the Amazon jungle, Outer Mongolia, or an Eskimo settlement. Should you rate the report as probably true, doubtful, or highly doubtful? Why? What difference would it make if the incident being reported took place in New York's Times Square?

ASSIGNMENT

Write a paragraph using the narrative method of development. Be sure that the subject is important enough to warrant retelling and that the topic sentence can be supported by the telling of a single incident.

SENTENCES

Comma Splices and Fused Sentences

Your mind always works faster than your pen or your typewriter; as a result, you may make the mistake of running separate ideas and sentences together. When you do that, you make your writing difficult for your reader to follow. If you are to eliminate comma splices and run-on sentences, you must show your reader clearly where one complete thought ends and another begins.

If you have completed a thought, show the reader with a period (.).
If you're asking a question, show the reader with a question mark (?).
If you are making an extremely emotional statement, show the reader with an exclamation mark (!).

These marks tell your reader that a sentence has been completed. If you place a comma at the end of a sentence, your reader won't know that you have completed a thought and will be confused. For example:

Jerry won the dance contest, when his girlfriend saw him dancing, she developed an uncontrollable urge to laugh.

Similarly, if you fuse two complete thoughts together without any punctuation at all, the reader will become even more confused:

Jerry won the dance contest when his girlfriend saw him dancing, she developed an uncontrollable urge to laugh.

When two complete thoughts are coupled together with a comma, as in the first example, the error is called a **comma splice.** The comma splice is considered a serious error because it reflects an error in logic (failure to recognize a complete thought) as well as an error in punctuation.

The basic rule concerning the comma splice is that independent clauses (complete subject-verb units that could be separate sentences) cannot simply be spliced together with a comma. For example:

A meeting of the PTA is scheduled tonight, several important items are on the agenda.
We are permitted to use a dictionary, that is the only book we are supposed to bring.

When two complete thoughts, often not very closely related, are run together without any punctuation, as in the second sentence about the dance contest, the error is called a **fused sentence.** Here are some more examples.

The river was more than a mile wide he could not swim across.
I often do my studying in the attic it is the quietest room in the house.
After law school he hopes to become a trial lawyer that is what he has always wanted to be.

Comma splices and fused sentences such as these can usually be corrected in several ways:

1. Make two separate sentences.

We are permitted to use a dictionary. That is the only book we are supposed to bring.
A meeting of the PTA is scheduled tonight. Several important items are on the agenda.

2. Use connecting words, such as *and, but, or, nor, yet, so,* plus a comma. (These words, called **coordinating conjunctions,** are discussed in Chapter III.)

We are permitted to use a dictionary, but that is the only book we are supposed to bring.

A meeting of the PTA is scheduled tonight, and several important items are on the agenda.

3. Use a stronger mark of punctuation, the semicolon (;). You might think of the relative strength of these marks of punctuation as a formula: comma (,) + coordinating conjunction = semicolon (;)

A meeting of the PTA is scheduled tonight; several important items are on the agenda.

We are permitted to use a dictionary; that is the only book we are supposed to bring.

4. Use a **conjunctive adverb,** a linking word or phrase such as *therefore, moreover, consequently, as a result.*

The river was more than a mile wide; therefore, he could not swim across.

The presidential train made only brief halts at the prairie towns; consequently, the President did little more than exchange greetings at these whistle stops.

5. Make one of the independent clauses subordinate by using subordinate conjunctions such as *because, before, after, since, while, until, if, so that, as, as if, as though, once, as long as,* and so on.

Although we are permitted to use a dictionary, that is the only book we are permitted to bring.

Since bowling has become very popular, there is a bowling alley in almost every neighborhood.

6. Separate two independent clauses into two sentences with a conjunctive adverb at the beginning of the second sentence.

The river was more than a mile wide. Therefore, he could not swim across.

NOTE: Coordination and subordination are dealt with more fully in Chapter III.

Run-on Sentences

The **run-on sentence** consists of several main clauses loosely joined together by a series of coordinating conjunctions such as *and, but, so, for,* and *yet.* A reader who is forced to read a long string of thoughts without pausing can easily become confused. Some students have actually written one-page paragraphs which consisted entirely of one or two run-on sentences.

Jack decided to take Karen dancing and he needed some money so he stopped at the bank on his way home but it was closed and he started getting desperate because this was her birthday and he had promised to take her out so, as a last resort, he borrowed ten dollars from his dad but to get the money he had to agree to clean out the garage the next day.

narrating

       Venice is a city of bridges because it is built on a series of islands which are laced with canals, and the only way one can get from one place to another is by bridge or by boat, so every block or so, there is a small bridge for pedestrians, but there is no need for large bridges for buses and taxis because the buses and taxis are boats and gondolas.

       A run-on sentence can be corrected by dividing it into two or more shorter sentences. Notice how much clearer the meaning becomes when you can pause at the end of major thought groupings:

       Jack decided to take Karen dancing, and he needed some money. He stopped at the bank on his way home, but it was closed. He started getting desperate because this was her birthday, and he had promised to take her out. As a last resort, he borrowed ten dollars from his dad. To get the money, he had to agree to clean out the garage the next day.

       Venice is a city of bridges. Because it is built on a series of islands which are laced with canals, the only way one can get from one place to another is by bridge or boat. Every block or so, there is a small bridge for pedestrians. There is no need for large bridges for buses and taxis because the buses and taxis are boats and gondolas.

Punctuation Between Clauses

       1. If you use a coordinating conjunction—*and, but, or, for, nor, yet, so*—between two independent clauses, always put a comma **before** the conjunction. (Remember, a clause contains both a subject and a predicate. An independent clause states a complete thought, but a dependent clause cannot stand alone.)

[independent clause], and [independent clause].
[independent clause], but [independent clause].
[independent clause], yet [independent clause].

CAUTION: These conjunctions are used at other times without commas. Look at the following examples:

Jack spends his morning playing golf and his afternoons swimming.

       In the above sentence, *and* does not join two independent clauses. There is no comma in front of the *and* because "and his afternoons swimming" is simply an additional phrase, not an independent clause.

The boss and the secretary were driven to the airport.

In this sentence, *and* simply joins the two parts of a compound subject. Use no comma.

Jack bought a new car and promptly wrecked it.

In this sentence, the *and* does **not** join two independent clauses; it simply joins the two parts of a compound predicate, *bought* and *wrecked*.

NOTE: A comma **is** needed before the *and* in a series of three or more terms.

The colors of the flag are red, white, *and* blue. [a series of three or more words]
Smiling faces, clean fingernails, *and* polished shoes were what he looked for in his morning inspection. [a series of three or more phrases]
When Jack will arrive, what he will have to say, *and* when he will have to leave are the only questions on her mind. [a series of three or more clauses]

2. If the two ideas are closely related, you can write both independent clauses as one sentence and separate them with a semicolon(;). The semicolon indicates that both ideas are related, but it provides enough of a pause to keep them from running together.

[independent clause]; [independent clause].

3. If you use a **conjunctive adverb**—*therefore, moreover, besides, nevertheless,* etc.—between two independent clauses, use a semicolon before the conjunctive adverb and a comma after it.

[independent clause]; therefore, [independent clause].
[independent clause]; moreover, [independent clause].
[independent clause]; besides, [independent clause].

CAUTION: A common error is the comma splice that involves the use of conjunctive adverbs such as *consequently, however, besides, nevertheless, then, thus, still,* and so on.

COMMA SPLICE: We had lunch at the Woodman, then we all went out to Lake Pomeran.
CORRECT: We had lunch at the Woodman; then we all went out to Lake Pomeran.
COMMA SPLICE: We were sure we would be late, nevertheless we got there before the curtain went up.
CORRECT: We were sure we would be late; nevertheless, we got there before the curtain went up.

NOTE: The short conjunctive adverbs *then, thus,* and *still* don't always need a comma **after** them, but they always need a semicolon **before** them.

John studied hard; *still* he failed the test.

It is important to know the distinction between two kinds of conjunctions or connecting words.

First are the coordinate conjunctions—*and, but, or, nor, for, yet, so.* (This is the complete list; there are no other coordinate conjunctions.)

Second are the conjunctive adverbs—*also, besides, consequently, however, therefore, likewise, nevertheless, then, thus, still.*

What is the difference?

The words in the first group are always used as conjunctions, but the words in the second group are **not** always used as conjunctions. When they are used as adverbs, their location in the sentence can shift.

Look at this example:

However, his boss told Jerry to finish the job by noon.
His boss, *however,* told Jerry to finish the job by noon.
His boss told Jerry, *however,* to finish the job by noon.
His boss told Jerry to finish the job, *however,* by noon.
His boss told Jerry to finish the job by noon, *however.*

Do you see how adverbs can be moved around in the sentence? Now notice that the coordinate conjunctions—*and, but, or, nor, for, yet, so*—do not have this mobility. Try moving an *and* around in a sentence. You quickly see that it cannot be moved around.

A conjunctive adverb, then, is just an adverb used to provide a connecting link between independent clauses. For example:

The boss told Jerry to finish the job; *however,* he couldn't get it done that day.
He thought she was being wasteful; *besides,* he was saving up for a new car.

NOTE: A number of phrases, such as *in fact, as a result, to be sure, after all, for instance, for example,* can be used to perform the same function as the single-word conjunctive adverbs.

Nature has a way of taking care of her mistakes; *as a result,* no living species should be considered useless or dispensable.

A FINAL NOTE ON CONJUNCTIVE ADVERBS

When words such as *however, consequently,* and *nevertheless* do not join independent clauses, do not use a semicolon. Simply put a comma before and a comma after the word.

WRONG: The senator's wife; *however,* did not want him to run again.
CORRECT: The senator's wife, *however,* did not want him to run again.
WRONG: All the avid fishermen; *to be sure,* would be out on the lake before dawn.
CORRECT: All the avid fishermen, *to be sure,* would be out on the lake before dawn.

Read the following examples, and observe why each is punctuated differently:

Sally has the flu; therefore, she cannot attend class today. [*Therefore* separates two independent clauses.]

John is, therefore, the best player we have on the team. [*Therefore* does not join independent clauses.]

It seems to me, however, that your plan does not consider every alternative. [*However* does not join independent clauses. The "that" clause is dependent.]

I would like to go; however, there is no available transportation at that time of day. [*However* separates two independent clauses.]

REMEMBER: You must know the difference between coordinate conjunctions and conjunctive adverbs before you can punctuate correctly. You also need to recognize the difference between dependent and independent clauses. A review of the sections on fragments will help.

EXERCISE IIc
Selecting the method you consider best, correct the following. Explain why you think that the method you chose is the best.

1. Marcella had a lot of money she spent it freely.

   _____

   _____

2. The cafeteria is large it can seat 750 people.

   _____

   _____

3. I threw the football forty yards in the air Stanley caught it.

   _____

   _____

4. Carla had pneumonia she was in the hospital for a week.

   _____

   _____

5. Sometimes I think my teachers hate me I never get good grades.

   _____

   _____

6. Two shoplifters were arrested one was a thirteen-year-old boy.

   _____

   _____

7. Struthers had been blacklisted by the union he could never get another job as an engineer.

   _____

   _____

8. She always wanted to be a nurse that was her childhood ambition.

_____

_____

9. I'll pick you up at nine o'clock don't be late.

_____

_____

10. He started to get angry his sense of humor stopped him.

_____

_____

11. The owner was furious he found a dent in the fender.

_____

_____

12. The weather had been glorious it was in the eighties every day.

_____

_____

13. We took the wrong turn at Saginaw we were headed east instead of north.

_____

_____

14. Boys of that age are adventurous they will try anything once.

_____

_____

15. Look for the complete subject-and-predicate units they will help you separate the clauses.

_____

_____

EXERCISE IId
Supply only the needed punctuation to correct comma splices and fused sentences:

1. Many people have tried to quit smoking some have even tried hypnosis.
2. Have you seen any of the new electric cars they are surprisingly small.
3. Your intelligence is insulted by television commercials the automobile ads are especially bad.
4. Carol's mother is an excellent cook even though her budget is limited, she still prepares delicious meals.
5. Patty bleached her hair it became very dry and brittle.

6. Senator Slick said that he never accepted any illegal campaign contributions, he doesn't know where that extra $50,000 came from.

7. Bob took a course in transactional analysis last semester then he got a divorce.

8. I went to bed late last night I forgot to lock the front door.

9. If you see some guy in an orange shirt and a purple tie then you've found my husband he's color blind.

10. Proofread your paragraph before you turn it in put your name on the outside.

EXERCISE IIe
Punctuate or rewrite the following run-ons to make clear to the reader where one idea stops and another begins:

1. My dog has a tendency to run away so I went to the hardware store to buy a chain to tie him up but when I got there I didn't have enough money to get a heavy chain but I did have enough to buy some clothesline so I did but he chewed through that the first day and ran away as usual but he came back that night because he was hungry I guess.

2. Since my sister went to college she has become a big pain in the neck because she acts so conceited and she thinks she is so smart that she doesn't have to listen to Mom or Dad anymore and she will hardly even notice me and she looks down on everybody, even her boyfriend but she still goes out with him, I notice.

3. My friends think I'm crazy because I really like to study, especially English because I think it's just wonderful how the authors use just the right words to get their messages across and I would like to be able to do that too, and I think I will be able to some day because I like to study English.

4. I think car salesmen are immoral because they would do anything to sell a car even lie to you and I'm sure of this because I've been shopping for a used car and I've gone to see a lot of salesmen and they all say that they have a car that was owned by an old woman who only drove it to church but I notice the seats are all worn out and the engine seems about shot so she either must have gone to church a lot or the salesmen are liars.

5. I want to go on a vacation because I have never been more than thirty miles out of this town and I would like to see some new scenery and some new people and some new things but I guess vacations will have to wait until I finish my education and earn some money and then I will go and explore the world.

EXERCISE IIf
Make whatever changes in punctuation are necessary to correct the following sentences. Do **not** add periods or capital letters.

1. Most of the houses have street numbers, however; it is hard to see the numbers at night.

2. We drove around town for a while, then we went to the beach.

3. I never once said that his story sounded fishy, I only said that I would need to see some solid evidence.

4. Unemployment was high in the cities of the Northeast however the Sunbelt cities were booming.

5. He must be rich he has everything he wants.

6. Come to my house tonight we will play air hockey after dinner.

7. What he does what he thinks and what he says should not concern you at all.

8. Everyone claims that the Mercedes is a superior automobile I feel however that it is overrated.

9. The weatherman predicts frost therefore we should not plant the tomatoes until next week.

10. My dog has been treated like a human being for seven years and I don't have the heart to tell her the truth.

11. After the race Sam crumpled to the ground and was unable to move.

12. You were right to stand up for what you believed to be sure you had no other choice.

13. The surf was becoming treacherous besides I was already tired and chilled to the bone.

EXERCISE IIg
The punctuation in the following passage from the Bible has been altered. On the lines below the exercise, use sentence numbers to indicate any fragments, comma splices, or fused sentences you find in the paragraph.

The Adulteress

(1) Then each went off to his own house. (2) While Jesus went out to the Mount of Olives. (3) At daybreak he reappeared in the temple area, and when the people started coming to him, he sat down and began to teach them (4) The scribes and the Pharisees led a woman forward who had been caught in adultery. they made her stand there in front of everyone. (5) "Teacher," they said to him, "this woman has been caught in the act of adultery. (6) In the law, Moses ordered such women to be stoned what do you have to say about the case?" (7) (They were posing this question to trap him, so that they could have something to accuse him of.) (8) Jesus bent down and started tracing on the ground with his finger. (9) When they persisted in their questioning, (10) He straightened up and said to them, "Let the man among you who has no sin be the first to cast a stone at her." (11) A second time he bent down and wrote on the ground, then the audience drifted away one by one, beginning with the elders. (12) This left him alone with the woman, who continued to stand there before him. (13) Jesus finally straightened up and said to her, "Woman, where did they all disappear to? (14) Has no one condemned you?" (15) "No one, sir," she answered. (16) Jesus said, "Nor do I condemn you, you may go, but from now on, avoid this sin."   *John 7:53*

Fragments _____

Comma Splices _____

Fused Sentences _____

WORDS

The Actor-Action Sequence: The Active Voice

English is a complex language, and there are few absolute rules regarding sentence structure. However, two essential elements of good writing are **precision** and **economy** (saying exactly what you mean in the fewest possible words). Applying a few simple rules of sentence structure can help you to achieve economy and precision in your writing.

The basic sentence structure in English is the simple, active sentence.

Fish swim.
Joe hit John.
The power plant polluted the atmosphere.

The important thing to note here is the **actor-action sequence:** Somebody or something **does** something—swims, hits, pollutes, sings, plays, fights, runs, or **performs some act.**

Although it is not the solution to all problems in sentence structure, one rule that will help you to write with precision and economy is this: whenever the context permits, have somebody or something do something; make the subject of your sentence the **actor,** and use an **active** verb.

Suppose, for example, that you wanted to tell someone what Tom did this morning. The most logical and direct word sequence would be to begin with Tom (the actor) and then immediately tell what he did (the action):

Tom milked the cow this morning. (active voice)

Sometimes, however, the focus shifts, and the cow is emphasized instead of Tom:

The cow was milked by Tom this morning. (passive voice)

Notice what happened. The actor (Tom) is no longer so important, and Old Bessie steps into the spotlight. In effect, the actor-action sequence has been reversed so that the reader now pays more attention to the cow than to Tom. This type of sentence is called **passive voice.**

Look again at both examples:

Tom milked the cow this morning. (active voice)
The cow was milked by Tom this morning. (passive voice)

Which of the two do you think is the more direct and less wordy? **Active voice** is best, of course, because it puts Tom (the actor) first and immediately tells your reader, in fewer words, what Tom is doing.

NOTE: Does this mean, then, that you should never use passive voice?

No, but try to use active voice whenever possible because it places the emphasis on the actor and does not bury him or her somewhere else in the sentence.

In some cases it is correct to use passive voice. For example, sometimes the actor is unknown or unimportant. In a sentence such as "The road was built in 1867," the actor—who built the road—is unknown. In a sentence such as, "The Populist Party was defeated," the actors—who did the defeating—are unimportant. In both situations, therefore, it is appropriate to use passive voice.

CHOOSING A CONCRETE SUBJECT

To be able to choose an active verb, you must first select the right subject. If you choose the wrong subject, you may find it difficult to use an active verb. For example, use the best action verb you can with each of the following:

Their plans *interferred*
His intentions
Her conclusions *clashed w mine*
My excuse *puzzled the teacher*

Not too easy, was it? The reason for the difficulty is that these subjects cannot **act** with many verbs—they cannot smile or jump or swim or frown or bite. The following words, however, are subjects more easily put into an active sentence.

> dogs
> my Uncle Bill
> the duck
> Jack's Corvette
> the county sheriff

Once you have selected a concrete subject, then choose an active verb so that the reader can see who is doing what.

EXERCISE IIh
Revise the following sentences using the active voice to make them more direct and forceful.

EXAMPLE
The ball was hit by him. (weak)
He hit the ball. (stronger)

1. I was bitten by the big black dog.

_____

2. The pendant was worn by Stella around her neck.

_____

3. That football is a dangerous sport is known by everyone.

_____

4. My excuse for failing the test was because I did not study.

   _____

5. The car was driven over the cliff by the drunken driver.

   _____

6. Your letter of July 15 has been received by me today.

   _____

7. The rock group got applause and praise from the excited students.

   _____

8. The policeman was thrown to the floor and mauled by the rioters.

   _____

9. The term papers were carefully marked and graded by the instructor and returned by him on the last day of class.

   _____

10. The decision was handed down by the jury and was printed subsequently in the newspapers.

    _____

11. The conclusion that spanking was more effective than words was reached by his mother.

    _____

12. Marjorie's graduation picture was placed on the television set by her mother.

    _____

13. A log was thrown across the stream by the rangers.

    _____

14. The troops were not told by anyone about the attack plan.

    _____

15. A decision was made by the committee to change the rules.

    _____

Economy of words makes meaning stand out

One measure of the efficiency of your writing is the meaning per word. Putting your sentences in *actor-action sequence* cuts down the number of words so that your meaning stands out more clearly.

The car was wrecked by Oscar. [6 words]
Oscar wrecked the car. [4 words]
A decision was made by the two families to travel together. [11 words]
The two families decided to travel together. [7 words]

48

An old railroad watch was given to me by my grandfather. [11 words]
My grandfather gave me an old railroad watch. [8 words]

narrating

Often good results are achieved when you replace wordy and round-about *it* and *there* sentences with a clear **actor-action sequence.** Note how much shorter and clearer the following sentences become when put in actor-action form:

ORIGINAL: It is the belief of the investigators that the fire had been started by an arsonist. (16 words)

REVISED: Investigators believe an arsonist started the fire. (7 words)

ORIGINAL: There is the feeling on the part of some atomic experts that the results of years of exposure to low-level radiation will be an increase in birth defects. (28 words)

REVISED: Some atomic experts feel that years of exposure to low-level radiation will increase birth defects (15 words).

ORIGINAL: It has been observed that there has been an increase of ten degrees in the water temperature as a result of the discharge from the power plant. (27 words)

REVISED: Discharge from the power plant increased the water temperature ten degrees (11 words)

NOTE: Sometimes sentences beginning with *it* and *there* are necessary, but they often lead to wordiness.

EXERCISE IIi
Rewrite the following sentences to make them shorter and clearer by taking the following three steps:

1. Pick out the actor and the action (ask yourself who or what does what).
2. Put your new sentence in actor–action sequence (make the actor your subject and use an action verb).
3. Eliminate all excess words.

1. The broken line has been repaired by the steamfitter.

_____

2. Permission was granted by the investigating committee for the hiring of a new chief counsel.

_____

3. It is predicted in the report that there will be an increase in the water pollution in 1990.

_____

4. It was clear to Polanski the reason his resignation had been requested.

_____

5. There were not many stars shining in the East.

_____

6. There is a lecture on physics that is given by Professor Zebrowski that is very interesting.

_____

7. It is a fact that the vegetables had been raised by the women, and the men had been the ones who brought the buffalo meat.

_____

8. It was Juanita's opinion that a trick had been played on her by one of the lab assistants.

_____

9. There is a belief on the part of some tribe members that there is bad luck in stepping in the footprints of another person.

_____

10. There are many truckers who will be attending the meeting on Tuesday.

_____

CHANGING WEAK VERBS TO ACTIVE VERBS

The most common weak and imprecise verbs are the *be* verbs: *is, was, were, have been,* and so forth. Take this sentence, for example:

exceed

The impurities *are in excess of* EPA standards.

Note the italicized words, *are in excess of.* Which word in that group could serve as the basis of a new verb to replace *are*?

If we replace *are in excess of* with one word, *exceed,* we have improved the sentence in both clarity and economy.

These impurities *exceed* EPA standards.

Here is another example.

The fifth chapter *is an explanation of* Henry George's economic theory.

Here again, it is not difficult to find a new verb to replace *is.* Just look at the phrase *an explanation of.*

The fifth chapter *explains* Henry George's economic theory.

To replace the generally weak and wordy *be* form, you look for another word in the sentence to serve as the basis of an active verb.

The claim of the investigator *is* that the cargo door flew open.
The investigator *claims* that the cargo door flew open.

EXERCISE IIj

In each of the following sentences, replace the italicized weak verb form with an active verb. Try forming the new verb from some other word in the sentence, as shown in the preceding examples.

1. The increase in the yield *will be* about 60 percent.

   _____

   Concluded

2. The conclusion of the investigators *was* that the witnesses had lied.

   _____

   operate by

3. All the pumps *are* of the electrically operated type.

   _____

4. The Olympic Committee *will be making* the selection of the finalists.

   _____

5. Figure 9 *is* an illustration of the graduated tax scale.

   _____

6. The contention of the critics *is* that the play is too long.

   _____

7. A faculty committee *will make* a determination as to which students are to receive awards.

   _____

8. A belief of many people in the underdeveloped countries *is* that Americans are all wealthy.

   _____

9. Whether or not to send a representative *is* a decision that must *be made* by the student government.

   _____

10. Electricity *is* what makes the motors operate.

    _____

REPLACING OTHER WEAK VERBS

Using other weak verbs, such as *provide*, *make*, *use*, *serve*, and *give*, usually weakens your writing. Wherever possible, replace these weak verbs with verbs that show action.

EXAMPLE: Paddle fans *provide* gentle circulation of air.
IMPROVED: Paddle fans gently *circulate* the air.

EXAMPLE: This type of heating and cooling system *makes* fewer demands on energy.

IMPROVED: This type of heating and cooling system *demands* less energy.

EXAMPLE: A heat pump *is used* for heating and cooling the house.

IMPROVED: A heat pump both *heats* and *cools* the house.

Note that these revisions cut down the number of words; as a result, every word works harder and the meaning of the sentence stands out more clearly.

EXERCISE IIk
Revise the following sentences by using active verbs to replace the italicized weak verbs.

1. The success of their experiment *will give* encouragement to others.

   _____

2. An electronic thermostat *serves* to regulate the temperature.

   _____

3. The funds raised by the banquets *will provide* the finances needed for Burke's campaign.

   _____

4. We must *make* a decision about next fall's schedule.

   _____

5. Building the houses on stilts *provides* protection for them during the spring floods.

   _____

CHAPTER III

describing

ORGANIZATION

Few people can make it through the day without describing something—a new teacher, an old boyfriend, the weather. You are probably no exception. Did you ever join a group of friends who were in the middle of a conversation about someone and find that you didn't know whom they were talking about?

FRIEND 1: ...and then Joe turned around and said—
YOU: Joe who?
FRIEND 1: Joe Reynolds.
YOU: Who's that?
FRIEND 1: You know Joe—the big guy with the mustache and the black curly hair.
YOU: No, I can't picture him.
FRIEND 2: The one who's always smoking a corncob pipe. He wears the old green army jacket.

**Use your senses of sight, sound, and smell
to form a picture in your reader's mind.**

YOU: No, I still can't picture him.

FRIEND 3:   You know—the one who's so hard to understand because he always mumbles when he talks.

YOU: Oh—You mean the guy who walks like John Wayne—the one that always smells like a bottle of Brut. Now I know the one you're talking about.

Think about how the image of Joe was actually formed. You pictured the way he looked, the way he talked, the way he walked, and even the way he smelled. In other words, you used your senses of sight, sound, and smell to create a picture in your mind. Anything you can see, you can describe, but it is not just what you see that can be described. If that were true, then you would never be able to tell a person how anything sounded or tasted or smelled or felt: you couldn't tell anyone that bells "clang" or that unsalted potatoes taste "bland" or that old milk smells "sour" or that sandpaper feels "rough." In order to create a clear, vivid picture, you must use your senses fully to observe what you are describing. Description attempts to give a feeling to the readers so that they may experience the same sensory and emotional effects that the writer is trying to communicate.

Using your senses is only the first step. You must **convey** the impression you learn through your senses. People constantly describe things as they talk to their friends and families, but as you can see from the following sentences, they often don't make themselves very clear.

Your room is cool, man.
That restaurant really has atmosphere.
This view is something else.
My favorite hangout is really neat.
My first sight of Sweet Thing Pettibon blew my mind.

54

Make your reader see what you see, feel what you feel.

These sentences make no clear impression. Of course, a speaker can muddle through by using hundreds of words, or by gesture, or by facial expression, or by tone of voice; but, as a writer, you can't do this. What do you do, then? Well, there is a way.

What you must do in writing a description is to **show** the reader, not **tell** the reader. You must try to make the reader see what you see, feel what you feel, hear what you hear, smell or taste what you smell or taste.

To provide a good description of a person or place, you must first of all be a good observer. You must make use of the five senses—**touch, smell, taste, sight,** and **sound.**

Then you must get your subject sharply into focus and limit your description in terms of time, place, and point of view. For example, consider the work of a fine photographer: in order to photograph birds in flight, children at play, an old man sleeping in the park, or a glamorous fashion model, he or she first gets the subject into focus. If you want to describe Uncle Henry or Aunt Susan, limit your focus to that one person. Better yet, get a sharper focus on such specific features as Uncle Henry's work-gnarled hands or Aunt Susan's crinkled smile.

To make your descriptive paragraph clear, you must go back to the 1-2-3 form, the beginning, middle, and end.

Topic Sentence: Central Impression

Your description may be confusing until all the details from your senses can be summed up in one clear central impression. Not until you have that central impression clearly in mind are you ready to write your description.

Get your subject into focus and limit your description.

1. Write one clearly worded topic sentence which identifies your subject and states your attitude, thus stating your central impression.
2. Put the topic sentence first in the paragraph.
3. Make sure that every detail in the body of the paragraph contributes to the topic sentence.

EXAMPLES: CENTRAL IMPRESSION ITALICIZED
Marty Singleton wore *a look of permanent disappointment.*
Even when sitting quietly, little Angelina makes you think of *a bird about to take flight.*
The tiny clearing in the depths of the bearded pine forest *seemed to whisper some secret that humans were not supposed to know.*

If you will look again at the group of sentences beginning with "Your room is cool, man," you will notice that they tell you very little. They have vague attitudes, and the reader has a wide variety of meanings to attach to each. Look at the possible interpretations of this sentence:

WRITER: Your room is cool.
READER 1:   There's a lack of heat; it's 60 degrees in here; there is a draft.
READER 2:   The room is painted and decorated in cool colors: soft green, avocado, turquoise.
READER 3:   There is lack of warmth here. It is a formal room, inhospitable, not cozy.
READER 4:   It's a perfect young person's room; it has lots of pillows, a good stereo, and great pictures.
READER 5:   The room is a perfect pad; it has strobe lights, a water bed, piped-in rock music, a heavy marijuana smell, and a good lock on the door.

The same is true of all the other sentences in that group. The attitude is not clear because it is subject to many interpretations. The first thing you must do is make sure that your central impression is clear, that the reader knows exactly

56

what you see and feel. Narrow your subject and attitude, and choose the precise word—the one that tells your feeling exactly. Go through the same process described in the "Huckleberry Finn" discussion in Chapter 1.

"Your room is cool" might then become a more specific sentence like one of these:

Your room is perfect for studying.
Your room is made for quiet meditation.
Your room is a perfect hideout for a runaway.

See how one student describes a special kind of room.

One of the most distinctive, and perhaps most easily recognizable, atmospheres is that of an athlete's locker room. As you enter, the unmistakable odor of perspiring bodies, damp leather, and dirty clothes hits you; it is a familiar one for the athlete, but sometimes unbearable for others. The room is usually large, dim, and long enough to be lined with rows of army-green lockers. The dryers hum in the background while the steam from the showers settles and penetrates every nook and cranny, making the floor and walls seem dripping wet. We bring our emotions into this sanctuary, away from prying eyes and ears, to release our joys and jubilation, disappointments and discouragements, and sometimes our tears. The language would make an English professor cringe, yet nothing could ever change it. It may sound offensive in many respects, but to an athlete it is part of his life that he cherishes and never forgets when those days are set aside for a different kind of life.   *John Navage*

EXERCISE IIIa
Tell which of the following would be acceptable topic sentences for a descriptive paragraph.

1. Carmelita's dress really suited her personality.
2. My date was six foot two with gorgeous blond hair and adorable baby blue eyes.
3. Mary's living room was uninviting.
4. Everything about Gerhardt's appearance seemed friendly and relaxed.
5. Walter Cronkite is smart.
6. Even today a Mexican village reflects the old culture.
7. There are three kinds of teachers who really bug me.
8. The word "prejudice" is often misused.
9. Sitting in the waiting room gave me a bad feeling.
10. The library is a forbidding place.

The Body

In developing your topic sentence, you must follow the same rules as always. All sentences should support or prove the topic sentence.

When you are writing a descriptive paragraph about a person, you put descriptive details together to arrive at a **central impression** of that person. **(Central impression = controlling idea.)** The most important thing to convey to your reader is this central impression. After using your senses to gather different kinds of information about a person, you've got to ask yourself: "What does all of this information add up to? What can I say about this person after observing all of these details? Does the person appear to be a rigid, conservative soul or an independent, free spirit? Does his or her appearance project a feeling of warmth and compassion or a feeling of coldness and insensitivity?" **Certain details will create certain impressions.** For example, the following description of George Washington as a young man creates a definite impression. After observing Washington, a fellow Virginia officeholder recorded these details:

Straight as an Indian, measuring 6 feet 2 inches in his stockings, and weighing 175 pounds
Well-developed muscles, indicating great strength
A well-shaped head, gracefully poised on a superb neck
Blue-gray, penetrating eyes overhung by a heavy brow
A face that terminates in a good, firm chin
A pleasing and benevolent though a commanding countenance, regular and placid features with all the muscles of his face under perfect control, though flexible and expressive of deep feeling when moved by emotion
Deliberate and engaging in conversation, looks you full in the face
Graceful movements, a majestic walk

These descriptive details about Washington lead up to a central impression, that of a strong, calm, dignified man. The observer concluded that Washington's demeanor (outward behavior) was "at all times composed and dignified." If this observer had been writing a descriptive paragraph about Washington, this central impression would have formed the basis of his topic sentence: "George Washington was a dignified-looking young man." Or, "George Washington's appearance as a young man projected an aura of composure and dignity." **Note,** however, that topic sentences such as "George Washington was a **good** man" or "I have a **positive impression** of George Washington" would **not** be good topic sentences because they would be vague. Your topic sentence must present a clear, specific, central impression.

Now contrast the descriptive details about Washington with those about Captain Henri Wirz, commander of Andersonville, the South's most notorious military prison during the Civil War.

An undersized, fidgety man with an insignificant face and a mouth that protruded like a rabbit's
Bright little eyes, like those of a squirrel or rat, which assisted in giving his countenance a look of kinship to the family of rodents
A little gray cap perched upon his head
Stepped nervously about
Gnat-brained and cowardly
A snarling little temper
Sputtered in very broken English

Is there any way that you can possibly add up these details to get a picture of composure and dignity? What is your impression of Captain Wirz? How would you describe him in a topic sentence?

SUPPORTING THE CENTRAL IMPRESSION

Suppose that you took as your topic sentence, "My physics teacher, Mr. Carson, **looked like a rumpled grizzly bear**." What sort of details would develop that central impression into a total picture?

Here are some that you might choose to include:

Hairy, barrel-chested man
Heavy arms that swing slowly with his lumbering, toed-in walk
Rumpled slacks and shirt, usually brown or gray
Scuffed brown loafers or carpet slippers
Big nose and beady brown eyes
Mottled gray hair, bristling on top, shaggy at the collar
Curly mass of gray hairs poking up out of his open collar.

Details such as these would support your central impression—"like a rumpled grizzly bear." In fact, if these details are all wrong, that is a good indication that your central impression is faulty and is simply not supportable.

Good choice of details building up to the central impression persuades your reader to "feel what you feel." In the paragraph below, underline the details that develop sympathy for the caged gorilla.

Seeing the gorilla at the zoo was an awesome experience. Relying on the protection of the heavy iron bars, I stood amid the group of kindergarteners, over whom I had been affectionately appointed homeroom mother, and stared open-mouthed at the ferocious beast. Inside his private cage, the wheezing ape ruled regally over one huge gray rock and one worn-out old tire, the latter which he intermittently lugged from spot to spot to rest upon. Perched atop his treadless throne, his humanlike hands clutched at each shiny, black cheek as he peered cautiously at the amazed faces of his cringing visitors. As my own bulging eyes wandered from the metal sign on the cage, which ordered, "Dangerous Animal—Do Not Feed," to the small darting eyes of this miniature King Kong, I wondered if he was as much in awe of

LOOKED LIKE A RUMPLED GRIZZLY BEAR!

me as I was of him. Several smart-alecky, long-haired hoodlums from another group of visitors shouted at this zoo's Mighty Joe Young, "You're ugly!" and "You stink!" I could not help but feel a bit of motherly sympathy for this innocent alien in his hot fur jumpsuit. His gargantuan appearance was frightening, but his guileless expression was as lovable as those on the faces of my hypnotized six-year-olds.   *Connie Susich*

When you write a descriptive paragraph about a person, you add up the details derived from your senses and form one central impression of that person. When you write a descriptive paragraph about a place, you also gather details to form a central impression—an **atmosphere,** a **mood.** What do you see? What do you hear? What do you smell? What do you feel? What time of the year are you observing this place? What time of day are you observing this place? Where is the place? In a rural area? In a desolate area? In a crowded city? In a building: a school, a home, a hospital, a steel mill? Again, certain details create a certain atmosphere. For example, look at the different atmospheres created by the descriptive details of the following rooms.

One Room
PLACE: A living room
WHERE: An old farmhouse in the country
WHEN: A cool evening in late autumn
SIGHTS: Soft, upholstered sofa and chairs in warm colors of rust, yellow, orange, and brown
A thick, rust-colored tweed carpet
An old brick fireplace with a carved wooden mantel
An oak coffee table covered with a newspaper, a pipestand, and a child's coloring book
An old wicker basket filled with freshly picked flowers
A handmade quilt lying over the back of a rocking chair
Antique paintings in wooden frames on the walls
SOUNDS: The laughter of children
The crackling of burning logs
SMELLS: Aroma of homemade bread baking in a nearby kitchen
The scent of cherry logs burning in a fireplace

Another Room
PLACE: A living room
WHERE: A high-rise apartment building in a city
WHEN: A rainy day in March
SIGHTS: Black and white shiny leather sofa and chairs
White globe lamps with black plastic bases
A gray tile floor with white shag rug in center
A glass coffee table with narrow steel legs
A glass end table covered with an arrangement of plastic flowers
Abstract prints on the walls in slim black metal frames
A china closet filled with crystal and sterling silver
Nothing out of place
SOUNDS: Rinse cycle of the automatic dishwasher in the kitchen
Outside traffic—beeping horns, screeching brakes

The living room in the farmhouse makes you feel cozy, but the living room in the apartment building gives you a colder, more formal feeling. Each room has its own atmosphere which forms the controlling idea of a descriptive paragraph—hence the topic sentence. Think about the place you are describing. How does it make you feel? Tense? Important? Scared? Relaxed? What kind of atmosphere does it project? Eerie? Tense? Peaceful? Determine the atmosphere of a place, and then present it to your reader in a topic sentence. Make sure that you have given your reader a **specific** controlling idea—"The living room of the old farmhouse had a warm, cozy atmosphere," **not:** "The living room had a **nice** atmosphere," or "Larry's apartment made me feel **cold** and **uncomfortable**," **not:** "Larry's apartment gave me a **bad** feeling."

Each of the following paragraphs presents and develops a clear central impression.

An air of death haunts my grandfather's old, red brick house. As I walk through the creaky oak door, the light barely creeps through the dirty old windowpanes. Slowly, I move into the once lively living room. While I reach for the light switch, the soft wisp of a spider's web brushes against my hand. The smell and taste of dust are thick in the air. The new gray, crushed velvet furniture is covered with thick, clear, plastic sheets. The white walls and ceiling are now a dull dingy gray, and there are little wisps of dust about the floor. Hearing nothing except my own heartbeat, I feel the loneliness and emptiness crash out even louder and harder. Standing there waiting for the kind, loving old gentleman to speak is the only thought in my mind. Then, with sadness, I realize—he's gone.   *John Hudson*

There was something melancholy about this place where people had lived and loved and died. From an old pine snag in what was once the front yard, a crow launched into hobbled flight across fields overgrown with brambles and scrub oak. Its forlorn "caw-caw" accentuated the emptiness. Only a shallow pit filled with briars and raspberry bushes now marked the spot where the old farmhouse had once stood. Something, a field mouse, perhaps, scurried away among the weeds. The rank odor of decay pervaded the back wall of the cellar where a crumbling fragment jutted above the tangle of underbrush. From the top of an old cherry tree, a hidden bird sang its short song and stopped. Around in all directions, the sunny afternoon stretched into silence and desolation.

An intensive-care unit is like a sterile waiting station between life and death. The gloom of a winter day seemed to add to the room's ominous atmosphere. Directly above my head was a long, slender, tubular-like tree with bottles of pale liquid hanging from its boughs. Next to the bed, on my left, stood an awesome technical genius with a screen busy with dots moving up, down, and across. Snuggled next to this was a vast, portable screen separating me from the next occupant. Along the far side of the room was an immense array of stainless steel instruments and machinery assigned to specific areas for expected crises. Immediately in front of me, I saw women in crisp, white uniforms whisking past a spherical clock hanging on a pallid wall. A huge, stationary desk surrounded by racks of metal clipboards sat along the right wall. Perched on the desk was a solitary cactus in an artless vase, leaving me with the distinct feeling of total solitude. The silence of the room was interrupted by the squeaking of rubber soles on the high-glossed floors. Intermittently, I could hear the muffled murmurs of pain and the whispers of the personnel trying to relieve the mental anguish of the patients. An antiseptic smell hung in the air like the smog over a densely populated city. It was, indeed, a purgatory to await the decision of my body and spirit—to succumb or to go on living.   *Carol Steele*

The caption below the newspaper photograph read: ''This site is an eyesore. Why doesn't someone remove this blemish from an otherwise peaceful, unmarred view of nature?'' The accompanying article went on to describe the abandoned, ramshackle shanty in rather degrading terms. How little they know. This structure and its land is not an eyesore, but rather a sight for sore eyes. This shanty was my grandparents' home, where my father was born and reared, where my brothers and I spent many enjoyable days during our childhood. As I gazed at the photo, I saw no blemish; I saw Grandpop sitting by the fire warming his bones and Grandma preparing supper on the wood-burning kitchen stove. That supper invariably became a feast. I saw Uncle, as always, trying to light the head of a match at fifty paces with his pump-action Winchester .22 rifle. With acres of land, wooded and pastured, we had much room within which to investigate the wonders of childhood. The property included White Day Creek, the local swimming hole which was banked by gigantic boulders and thick rhododendron bushes. Swimming always included taking a bar of soap along. Dusk was spent sitting on the porch joking and laughing while bullfrogs croaked and crickets chirped. Darkness would creep in and be filled with innumerable tiny beacons from the flashing fireflies. I can still picture the red glow of burning coals as we bedded down for the night. Dear irate journalist, I would that you saw this homeplace through the eyes of my heart.

Bob Hilpert

EXERCISE IIIb

Which of the following sentences do **not** contribute to the central impression—the controlling idea? Underline the irrelevant sentences, and then list them, by number, on the line below the paragraph.

(1) When I was a child, a desolate, gray mansion dominated our neighborhood. (2) Fragments had been broken off the outside edges of its overgrown gardens to make little yards for little modern houses, but the old house was still the queen of the street. (3) It was getting dingy and dilapidated, but it was still serene and gracious. (4) We used to go sled riding down its curving garden paths. (5) There were slates missing from the roof, but the roof line was ample and pleasing. (6) Once my father wanted to buy the house and fix it up. (7) It had four huge chimneys, with an occasional missing brick, that rose at least two stories above the little houses huddled below. (8) In nice weather, we played pirates and outlaws in the vast old clumps of lilac bushes. (9) The little houses bustled with life, noisy with kids and dogs. (10) The old house, silent and empty, loomed above them, seemingly content with time passing it by. (11) It was the favorite place to play in our neighborhood.

Irrelevant sentences _____

DESCRIPTIVE DETAILS

Once you have a dominant impression firmly in mind, select the descriptive details that will best convey this impression to your reader. All details must support your central impression as expressed in the topic sentence.

Details should also be concrete and visual; your reader should get clear, vivid impressions from your details as well as the feeling of being right there with you on the spot.

I tumbled end-over-end on the river bottom like a towel in a drier. "What a stupid way to die," I thought, as the icy water numbed my consciousness.

Read the following passage from *Cannery Row* carefully. Notice how well John Steinbeck uses image-making language to create clear, vivid pictures. Underline the words and phrases that make you feel you can almost reach out and touch the various creatures.

Doc was collecting marine animals in the Great Tide Pool on the tip of the Peninsula. It is a fabulous place: when the tide is in, a wave-churned basin, creamy with foam . . . . But when the tide goes out, the little water world becomes quiet and lovely. The sea is very clear and the bottom becomes fantastic with hurrying, fighting, feeding, breeding animals . . . . Starfish squat over mussels, and limpets attach their million little suckers and then slowly lift with incredible power until the prey is broken from the rock. And then the starfish stomach comes out and envelops its food. Orange and speckled and fluted nudibranchs slide gracefully over the rocks, their skirts waving like the dresses of Spanish dancers. And black eels poke their heads out of crevices and wait for prey . . . . Hermit crabs like frantic children scamper on the bottom sand . . . . Here a crab tears a leg from his brother. The anemones expand like soft and brilliant flowers . . . .
Then the creeping murderer, the octopus, steals out, slowly, softly, moving like a gray mist, pretending now to be a bit of weed, now a rock, now a lump of decaying meat while its evil goat eyes watch coldly. It oozes and flows toward a feeding crab, and as it comes close its yellow eyes burn and its body turns rosy with the pulsing color of anticipation and rage. Then suddenly it runs lightly on the tips of its arms, as ferociously as a charging cat. It leaps savagely on the crab, there is a puff of black fluid, and the struggling mass is obscured in the sepia cloud while the octopus murders the crab . . . . And down to the rocks come the black flies to eat anything they can find . . . the smells of life and richness, of death and digestion, of decay and birth burden the air. And salt spray blows in from the barrier where the ocean waits for its rising-tide strength to permit it back into the Great Tide Pool again. And on the reef the whistling buoy bellows like a sad and patient bull.

SPECIFIC DETAILS

One way that you help the reader see what you see and feel what you feel is to be specific in your detail. If, in your paragraph, you say "tree," your reader can "see" anything from a small flowering dogwood to a large stately oak. However, if you say "towering pine," your reader is likely to "see" what you "see." If you say, "He is handsome," your reader may picture anything from a tall, slim, blond dancer to a huge, dark, brawny wrestler. However, if you say, "He was six feet tall and weighed 250 pounds, but all anyone noticed were his springy black curls and flashing black eyes," your reader is with you.

If you say, "She was a rather attractive girl," does that give your reader a picture?

If you say, "It was sort of a lovely scene," does that give your reader a picture?

The answer is **no**!

There are millions of "rather attractive" girls; furthermore, who is attractive depends on the eye of the beholder. "Sort of a lovely scene" could be found almost anywhere and at any time from starry winter night to sunny August afternoon. Your description suffers whenever you use vague expressions such as "a bunch of trees." What kind of trees do you mean? Majestic oak? Towering pine? Leafy maple? Graceful poplar? Blighted elm? Swaying palm? Flowering dogwood?

EXERCISE IIIc USING SPECIFIC DETAILS

Rewrite each of the following in specific terms, making up specific details so that the reader will experience what you as the writer experienced.

1. Many smells came out of the kitchen.
2. The snack bar was noisy.
3. Crowds trying to go somewhere are interesting.
4. We saw a strange thing.
5. The institution does good work.
6. Your home is super.
7. Mr. Yacabowski has a nice appearance.
8. My English teacher's office isn't very neat.
9. We had a great view from the top of the mountain.
10. Mom's new hairstyle makes her look different.

ORDERING DETAILS

Once you have chosen the best details to fit your purpose, you must arrange them in a logical order. No matter what your paragraph describes—an object, person, location, or event—you cannot list details at random. There must be a pattern. When you observe something, you get a picture of the whole thing, and the order in which you think about its different parts or effects does not really matter. The reader, however, cannot visualize the whole as you did. You must therefore provide a pattern into which the reader can fit the details and recreate the whole in his or her own imagination.

The main pattern of organization in descriptive writing is **space order,** or spatial arrangement. You arrange details in an order that the eye might easily follow: top to bottom, left to right, far to near, and so on. Your location in relation to what you are describing can help you to arrange details effectively. From a fixed position, your eyes can sweep around a room, scan an object from top to bottom, examine a person from head to toe, or contemplate a landscape from the horizon to where you are standing. You may even choose a particular or unique characteristic and extend your pattern of details outward from it. If you are in motion, you can relate your impressions as objects come into view, as you pass something, or even as you walk around it. Details must be arranged to give your reader the view that you had as an actual observer.

Notice the spatial order used in the following paragraph.

Hank Belaire's whole appearance radiated an easygoing humor. As soon as you saw him swinging across the campus in his loose-jointed way, you could feel yourself start to smile at the broad lock of hair that bounced on his head and the way his jeans flapped against his cowboy boots. His own quick, loose grin lighted his angular face the moment he saw you. And no matter how far away, he'd boom out his ''Howdy pardner!'' As he sloshed his way toward you, his loose limbs flailed the air until you'd think he was about to disintegrate or start to fly. Yet, as he bore down on you with arms gesticulating in wide arcs, you always knew you were sure to hear "a good one," usually something about his crazy professors (all of his were) or about his rolling junk-heap of a car. Coming from anyone else, his stories could never have seemed half as funny because, most of all, he immensely enjoyed them himself. Even while he was flapping away across the campus to tell his story to someone else, you could still hear his muffled guffaw and see him slap his leg in glee. Hank had the kind of easy rolling humor that could brighten anyone's day.

EXERCISE IIId
Rearrange the following details in a logical order to describe a yard which, through the presence of children, has been changed from a lonely, vacant plot of grass to a center of constant activity. On the line at the bottom, use sentence numbers to show the correct sequence.

1. In the left-hand corner of the back part of the yard sits a huge, circular swimming pool with a Batman beach towel hanging on one side and a sliding board surrounded by floating balls and inner tubes on the other.
2. The left front part of the yard contains a swing set that has been used so often that the grass around it simply refuses to grow anymore.
3. The once deserted lot on Ivy Street has come back to life since the Maguire family bought it.
4. Now that the yard is a center of constant activity, one would never guess that it was once just a lonely, vacant lot.
5. The right side of the yard, which used to be lined with scraggly weeds and bushes, is now bordered by a cyclone fence to keep in the cat and the dog.
6. Next to the garage on the right side of the front part of the yard, stand a small red tricycle, a sleek new five-speed bike, and a scuffed, wooden skateboard.
7. Farther down the left side of the yard, one immediately notices the trampled hedges where kids have repeatedly taken a shortcut into the neighbor's yard to retrieve their baseball.
8. The old maple tree in the other corner of the back yard is now graced with a humble but sturdy homemade tree house complete with a "KEEP OUT" sign painted on the front.

Conclusion

We have learned that description, in order to be suggestive, must provide details that form a dominant impression—a feeling or effect that you want your reader to share with you. The conclusion of a descriptive paragraph should therefore be a detail of observation which permanently fixes that central impression in the imagination of the reader. (Note the concluding sentence in the paragraph describing Hank Belaire.) The conclusion is not just a way to bring your paragraph to a close; it is a final opportunity to create the desired effect on your reader. Here the details may be drawn together to provide a final unifying impression.

Your conclusion should restate or reinforce your general impression, the attitude in your topic sentence.

How would you describe the sensation you get from the following experiences?

1. Having a dentist drill a tooth.
2. Diving (or jumping) into a swimming pool on a hot day.
3. Stepping on a wad of bubble gum.
4. Taking the first bite of a big, juicy apple.
5. Looking at the stars on a clear night.
6. Driving down a dark road at night in pouring rain.
7. Accidentally stepping into a mud puddle.
8. Banging your shin against a hard object.
9. Walking through deep, soft sand in bare feet.
10. Suddenly encountering a snake.
11. Having a small child hold your hand.
12. Stubbing your toe on a rock or a cement curb.

Suggested Activity

Divide the class into two groups of equal number (if the groups are unequal, the teacher may take part or may pull a student out to help as a judge). Have each group turn its desks to face an opposite wall. Each group will be given a simple drawing. Being careful not to let the other group see its drawing, each group will write directions on how to draw the figure. Then the groups will exchange their directions and attempt to draw the figure as directed. This is a sure test of the worth of the directions.

ASSIGNMENT

1. Write one detailed descriptive paragraph of a place that leaves you with a feeling of sadness, joy, loneliness, contentment, or some other distinct impression. Make sure that all the details contribute to the mood or central impression. **Underline your topic sentence.**
2. Write a paragraph describing a person who made a distinct impression on you. Use concrete details to develop your central impression. **Underline your topic sentence.**

SENTENCES

Independent and Dependent Clauses

A sentence consists of words which, when arranged properly, express a complete thought; the clause is the basic sentence unit, containing a subject and verb.

THE INDEPENDENT CLAUSE The independent clause contains the main idea of the sentence; it can stand alone. That is, an independent clause is a simple sentence. For example:

John studied his English last night.

describing

This sentence makes sense because it gives you a clear and complete statement of John's doing something. Any independent clause can be a sentence.

Sally lost her comb.
The pitcher dropped the ball.
I like beer.

THE DEPENDENT CLAUSE

The dependent clause contains an idea of secondary importance and does not express a complete thought. Frequently, the dependent clause begins with a word that warns you the clause cannot stand alone. For example, if someone says to you. "Because he had a test today," you would wait to hear the rest of the sentence. A dependent clause *depends* upon an independent clause to make sense.

John studied his English last night because he had a test today.

Now, because you joined your dependent clause to an independent clause, the relationship of the two ideas is clear. This type of joining is called **subordination.** You can even join them in reverse order.

Because he had a test today, John studied his English last night.

When you put the dependent clause **before** the independent clause, you usually separate them with a comma.
Remember—a dependent clause cannot stand alone. It can only be used to help an independent clause.

The independent clause contains the main idea.
The dependent clause helps to explain the main idea or adds information to it.

Sometimes a sentence is made up of two or more independent clauses, and a dependent clause is not used.

I jogged down the road, and Sue followed on her bike.

Coordination

The process of joining independent clauses is called **coordination.** Words used to link independent clauses are called **coordinating conjunctions.** You should know these:

and
but
or
for
nor
yet
so

If you use one of these words to join two independent clauses, a comma should go in front of it:

[independent clause], **and** [independent clause].

Keep in mind that coordination gives the same rank or level of importance to each of the independent clauses. Joining independent clauses with *and, but, or, for, nor, yet,* or *so* implies equality in value and emphasis. Coordination is the right structure or grammatical form only when the two ideas expressed in the clauses are relatively equal in importance.

Bill joined the army, but Sam joined the navy.
Thunder filled the air, and black clouds rolled across the sky.

You also need to select the right coordinator.

TO INDICATE AN ADDITIONAL FACT OF EQUAL IMPORTANCE: *and*

Mary washed the dishes, and Susan made the salad.

TO INDICATE AN EXCEPTION, QUALIFICATION, OR REVERSAL: *but*

I love the music, but I can't dance.

TO INDICATE AN EXPLANATION OF THE FIRST CLAUSE: *for*

She refused to testify, for she was terrified of the defendant.

TO INDICATE AN ALTERNATIVE TO THE FIRST CLAUSE: *or*

Jack can return to school, or he can go to work.

TO INDICATE AN EXCEPTION, QUALIFICATION, OR CHANGE: *yet*

He said he had no money, yet he went to Florida last week.

TO CARRY OVER A NEGATIVE IDEA FROM THE FIRST CLAUSE: *nor*

The money was never received, nor was the monument ever built.

TO INDICATE A RESULT OF THE STATEMENT MADE IN THE FIRST CLAUSE: *so*

I studied all night, so I was ready for the test.

FAULTY COORDINATION

Most faulty coordination results from the overuse of *and. And* is often used when another coordinating conjunction shows the relationship better.

FAULTY: She had little formal art training, *and* she managed to become successful as an artist.

IMPROVED: She had little formal art training, *yet* she managed to become successful as an artist.

Another misuse of *and* is in connecting two ideas that are **not** of equal
value or importance. If the ideas are unequal, you must use **subordination.**

Conjunctive Adverbs

Independent clauses can also be connected with conjunctive adverbs, but they
establish a looser link between the ideas in the clauses. They are used primarily to
show special relationships other than those expressed by a simple *and* or *but*.
You must be sure to choose the right conjunctive adverb to show the relationship
that you intend. Here are commonly used conjunctive adverbs to suit various
purposes.

TO SHOW TIME: *afterward, later, finally, meanwhile, then, at the time,
soon, now, next, thereafter, last.*

Jimmy smashed in the grill of his dad's car; afterward, he did a lot of
hitchhiking.

TO SHOW ADDITION: *in addition, furthermore, moreover, besides, again,
too.*

The cost of building an atomic power plant is enormous; furthermore,
we still haven't solved the problem of disposing of atomic waste.

TO SHOW REASON, RESULT, OR CONCLUSION: *thus, consequently, therefore,
surely, in fact, as a result.*

All indications pointed toward his defeat; consequently, he withdrew
from the race.

TO SHOW CONDITION, QUALIFICATION, OR ALTERNATION: *otherwise, still,
anyhow, however, nevertheless, instead.*

She appeared to have little chance of getting the job; nevertheless, she
was determined to apply.

TO SHOW COMPARISON OR CONTRAST: *similarly, likewise, conversely, still,
however, on the other hand.*

Your investment could prove profitable; on the other hand, you could
lose every cent.

TO INDICATE AN ILLUSTRATION OR EXAMPLE: *for example, for instance.*

Many of the inventions that have altered our daily lives have come from
the laboratories of giant corporations; for example, Bell Laboratory scientists
have received more than 19,000 patents.

Subordination

Subordination enables you to arrange your ideas in terms of value and emphasis. While coordination leaves the two clauses on the same level of importance and emphasis, subordination enables you to make clear other relationships between the clauses, such as **when, where, why, how,** or **under what conditions.**

The words introducing the dependent clauses and indicating the relationship between clauses are called the **subordinating conjunctions.**

Whenever the cowboys came into town, there was sure to be a brawl. (when)
Wherever Mary goes, you can be sure to find Jack with her. (where)
Because he was almost broke, he decided to stay home. (why)
As if he hadn't a care in the world, Jack kept right on spending his money foolishly. (how)
Although he was dead tired, he got up and dressed quickly. (under what conditions)

The part of the sentence beginning with the subordinate conjunction is a dependent clause. "Although he was dead tired" is not a complete thought; by itself it would be only a sentence fragment. The part of the sentence that gets the most emphasis is the complete thought, "he got up and dressed quickly."

In the following two sentences, the main clause, italicized, expresses the main idea; the subordinate (dependent) clause expresses an idea of lesser importance. Which of the two versions is correct? The answer depends on what the writer intends to emphasize. The first version puts the emphasis on the bombing of Pearl Harbor, a fact of historical importance; the second version, however, puts the emphasis on a bit of biographical information. Obviously, the bombing of Pearl Harbor is the more important fact, yet it may be proper to put it in a subordinate clause if the writer intends to emphasize a personal detail—where he was at the time of Pearl Harbor.

When I was going to kindergarten in Rapid City, South Dakota, *the Japanese bombed Pearl Harbor.*
When the Japanese bombed Pearl Harbor, *I was going to kindergarten in Rapid City, South Dakota.*

FAULTY SUBORDINA-TION

In upside-down subordination, the emphasis is misplaced because the main idea appears in a subordinate clause.

UPSIDE-DOWN: As I witnessed the bank being robbed, I waited for Joe Fritz to make a phone call to an old girlfriend.
CORRECT EMPHASIS: As I waited for Joe Fritz to make a phone call to an old girlfriend, I witnessed the bank robbery.

Do not overload a sentence with too many subordinate clauses.

describing

OVERLOADED: Big cars like the Buick Electra and Mercury Marquis, *which* were high in popularity in the early 1970's, were near the bottom of the sales charts by the early 1980's *as* buyer preference, *which* had altered drastically in the face of increased gasoline prices, turned toward smaller, more fuel-efficient cars *which* were very often foreign made.

REVISED: Although highly popular in the early 1970's, big cars like the Buick Electra and Mercury Marquis had fallen to the bottom of the sales charts by the early 1980's. Buyer preference had altered drastically with increased gasoline prices, and buyers turned to smaller, more fuel-efficient cars—mostly foreign made.

THE SUBORDINATE CONJUNCTION

Here are some commonly used subordinate conjunctions.

after	even though	since	whatever	which
although	how	so that	when	whichever
as	if	that	whenever	while
as far as	in order that	though	where	who
as if	just as	till	whereas	whoever
as long as	now that	unless	whereby	whom
as soon as	once	until	wherever	whomever
because	once that	what	whether	why
before	provided that			

All the above words can be subordinate conjunctions, but they can also be used as other parts of speech. They are subordinate conjunctions only when they introduce a subordinate clause and show its relationship to the independent clause.

To show the precise relationship between the subordinate clause and the independent clause, you must choose the right subordinate conjunction.

TO INDICATE TIME: *before, after, since, when, while, as, just as, as soon as, as long as, whenever.*

Since Bobby went away, Freda has been unhappy.
While the teacher lectured, Frank took copious notes.

TO INDICATE CAUSE: *because, since, so that, in order that.*

He practiced constantly so that he could make the team.
Since the pool was contaminated, the swim party was cancelled.

TO INDICATE CONDITION OR CONCESSION: *if, though, even though, how, although, provided that, whether, even if, unless, as far as, as long as.*

Unless I get a raise in March, I'll quit.
As long as Ron is in charge, his brother-in-law will get all the overtime.

TO INDICATE MANNER: *as if, as though.*

describing

He acted as though he were the coach rather than the trainer.
As if I didn't know better, I accepted the chairmanship.

TO INDICATE PLACE: *where, wherever.*

I don't know where I left my textbook.
Wherever Julie went, Charles was sure to follow.

TO INDICATE CONTRAST: *whereas.*

Whereas the other nations have agreed, France remains adamant.
He is a prosperous attorney, whereas his brother is a criminal.

This list indicates only the general purpose of common subordinate conjunctions. The right subordinate conjunction is the one that shows the logical relationship of your ideas as accurately as possible. You must choose your subordinate conjunctions carefully to convey the exact meaning and emphasis that you intend.

RELATIVE PRONOUNS AS SUBORDINATE CONJUNCTIONS

Relative pronouns serve double duty. They act as both a subordinate conjunction and the subject of the subordinate clause. This is often true of the following relative pronouns:

that	whichever
what	who
whatever	whoever

The car **that** *hit me* crashed into the culvert.

Notice how *that* serves as both a subordinating conjunction and the subject of hit.

Whatever *happened to Judge Gater,* I don't know.

EXERCISE IIIe
The following sentences are examples of faulty coordination. Rewrite each sentence to place one of the ideas in a subordinate clause. (Try to select the right subordinate conjunction—*before, after, because, since, although, if, unless, until*, etc.)

1. I know him quite well, and I don't understand his strange ideas.

_____

2. Thunder rolls and lightning strikes, and the potato pickers retreat to the barn.

_____

3. I will never speak to her again, and she was very rude to me.

_____

4. You can be sure you'll be robbed, and you go into the Keg-O-Nails.

_____

5. Few travelers came that way, and the ancient ferry had sunk to the bottom of the river.

_____

6. I looked across the valley, and I saw the enemy advancing.

_____

7. The high priest begins to chant, and two assistants jiggle the sticks to make the puppets dance.

_____

8. I heard a horn honk, and I looked behind me.

_____

9. I studied hard, and I passed the test.

_____

10. I often feel lonely and left out, and I don't cry.

_____

EXERCISE IIIf
Use subordination to combine each of the following groups of sentences into one clear and concise sentence.

1. The garden was full of melons and corn. We crept in after dark and stole two melons.

_____

2. Jimmy was new to the neighborhood. He had few friends. He had no one to confide in.

_____

3. The famous author had left school in the eleventh grade. He was recently awarded an honorary Doctor of Letters.

_____

4. He was immediately sent back into combat. He had just been discharged from the hospital.

_____

5. He was born in Oil City. Oil City was only a small village then. His family moved to Pittsburgh. He was only three at the time.

_____

By coordinating equal elements and subordinating elements of lesser importance, combine the following groups to form one or two sentences.

1. a. It's too easy to knock television.
    b. People say there is too much violence.
    c. They also think there is too much sex.
    d. They will admit there are good shows.

    _____

    _____

2. a. Why don't they turn it off when it's bad.
    b. Television sets all have a special little button or knob.
    c. They're marked "off" and "on."
    d. That's a very good way to avoid a bad show.

    _____

    _____

3. a. I didn't like classical music until recently.
    b. I thought it was boring.
    c. I only liked rock and country music.
    d. I took a course in music appreciation and know more now.
    e. I find rock and country boring.

    _____

    _____

4. a. The chemistry teacher did not like his supervisor.
    b. He felt she did not know enough to supervise him.
    c. He said, "She doesn't know a molecule from a rose."
    d. He resented her.

    _____

    _____

5. a. People who love dogs don't think of them as animals.
    b. They treat them as if the dogs were people.
    c. In their houses, a guest doesn't dare sit in the dog's chair.
    d. Sometimes the dog seems to run the house.

    _____

    _____

6. a. The instructor stood at the blackboard.
    b. She was explaining chemical compounds.
    c. She was pointing out that compounds depended upon energy relationships.
    d. She was pointing out that no stable compound can be formed without a loss of energy.

    _____

    _____

7. a. Fast food restaurants are becoming increasingly popular.
    b. I don't see why.
    c. They don't offer anything but speed.
    d. The food is monotonous.
    e. It's too heavily salted and has too much fat.
    f. It's high in calories.

    _____

    _____

8. a. Fiction is considered to be made up of novels and short stories.
    b. Novels are usually longer than short stories.
    c. They also have more characters.
    d. They have more than one plot.

    _____

    _____

9. a. Coordinate conjunctions link ideas of equal importance.
    b. Subordinate conjunctions link ideas that have relationships other than equality.
    c. Relationships like *where, why, how,* or *under what conditions.*
    d. Using subordinate conjunctions results in complex sentences.
    e. Complex sentences are the ones most often used by mature writers.

    _____

    _____

10. a. John had dropped out of high school.
    b. He thought the money he could earn made going to school silly.
    c. After eleven years he wasn't earning a lot more than he had when he first started to work.
    d. Even worse, he was bored.
    e. So, he went back to school.

    _____

    _____

Review of Fragments

In Chapter I the sentence error known as a fragment was discussed. When you understand clauses, you do not write fragments.

A sentence is supposed to express a complete thought. You capitalize it at the beginning and punctuate it at the end. What happens, however, if you do not have a complete thought but decide to capitalize and punctuate anyway? You then have only a piece of a sentence—a sentence fragment.

Most students do not write sentence fragments deliberately. Sometimes they think they are writing a complete thought. Often the dependent clause is mistaken for a sentence and is capitalized and punctuated as such.

Because he had a test today.

The result is a fragment, because it takes more than a capital letter and a period to make a group of words into a sentence. There must be completeness of meaning. As you have already learned, one way of eliminating a fragment is to add an independent clause.

John studied his English last night because he had a test today.

Some fragments **almost** express a complete thought, and perhaps the elimination of one word will do the job.

~~Because~~ he had a test today

Now our fragment actually expresses a complete thought, and we can correctly capitalize and punctuate.

He had a test today.

Remember, the biggest problem you will have with fragments is being able to recognize them. The changes that you make to eliminate them will depend on what you want to say and how you want to say it.

Look at a few more fragments:

Going to college without having chosen a major.

What is missing?

You don't know **who** is going to college. You need more information to make a complete thought.

Most high school students go to college without having chosen a major.

By supplying the **who** (most high school students), you change your fragment into a sentence.

Joe finally realizing that she loved him.

What is missing?

You expect Joe to act—to do something. By supplying the action, you change your fragment into a sentence.

Joe, finally realizing that she loved him, *proposed the next evening.*

That she was the most competent person on the committee.

What is missing?

You need an actor and an action to complete the thought.

We knew that she was the most competent person on the committee.

Remember that sometimes you can eliminate a fragment by just changing one or two words. In other situations, you may want to link the fragment to a larger, more complete thought.

FRAGMENT: Thinking I was right. I continued up the hill toward the house.
CORRECTION: Thinking I was right, I continued up the hill toward the house.

EXERCISE IIIh
Find all the fragments in the following paragraph. Revise each fragment by attaching it logically to a preceding or following sentence, or rewrite the fragment so that it stands by itself as a sentence.

As a spectator, I am often amused by watching the workers at a construction site. Or, rather, I'm amused by the way their labors are shared. A frequent source of amusement to me is the flag waver. Invariably he seems burly enough to smash down stone walls. Frequently, however, it's some scrawny little fellow who does the backbreaking job. Just the other day, as I watched the construction work going on at a highway overpass. A huge gorilla stood with a tiny flag in his paw. He sluggishly moved the dainty red flag with what seemed to be enormous effort. While down in the ditch a shriveled little rabbit of a man swung a heavy sledge with resolution. Since the little man must have been at least sixty years old. I wondered why he couldn't change places with the Goliath who waved the flag. Union rules, I suppose. But it seems to me that this sort of thing happens so often that there must be some mysterious higher law. To amuse the gods, no doubt.

WORDS

The ultimate success of your paragraph will depend upon how carefully you select and arrange your words. To give the reader a clear picture, you need specific and concrete words. For example, suppose someone said to you, "There is a difficult traffic situation at the intersection." Do you get any picture at all? Now suppose someone said, "A Buick station wagon and a Thunderbird crashed head-on at King and Jefferson Streets, blocking the intersection." Now do you get the picture?

GENERAL: The fruit tree in my back yard flowers each spring.
SPECIFIC: In late May, that ancient, gnarled Northern Spy tree near the back porch was covered with white blossoms as big as snowballs. The sweet smell of apple blossoms permeated the air around it.

Civilization as we know it would not be possible without general words and the ideas or concepts for which they stand. The difficulty with these general words, however, is that unless they are used with great care, their meaning remains cloudy and indefinite.

Often we try to clear up these general words by referring to something concrete, something our reader can grasp through his senses. For example,

"Meaner than a junkyard dog."

"toughness" is a general quality; you might try to make it concrete by using such expressions as "tough as rawhide," "hard as old iron," or, in the words of the song, "meaner than a junkyard dog." (Such expressions are figurative language, but you don't need to worry about that now.)

What you need to remember is that general words such as *medication* or *transportation* stand for a whole group or class of things. If you are to write clearly so that the reader gets the picture, you need to use the most specific word possible: don't say *medication* when you mean *an aspirin tablet.* And you usually do need to show what you mean by a term such as *courage* or *horror* or *hate.* Show courage as a fireman charging into a flaming doorway, show horror in round eyes and bristling neck hairs, show hate in narrowed eyes and snarling lips.

What good description requires is *concrete detail*, details that your reader can see and hear and taste and smell and feel. You need words that will make him see the sparks fly, that will make him smile or frown or cringe.

Select words that match or nearly match your sense impressions. It is hard to describe the exact smell of apple blossoms, but the suggestion of air smelling "sweet" will stimulate your readers to use their own imagination.

Words that form comparisons are also useful. "Big white blossoms" does evoke a mental image, but "white blossoms as big as snowballs" creates a vivid portrait which not only is more precise but also suggests a sense of wonder or awe. Words that create pictures as well as feelings are essential. General and abstract words do not create pictures. Specific and concrete words do.

General words indicate classifications or broad categories of things like *tree.*

Specific words indicate individuals within that classification like *elm, maple, pine, oak.* Of course, it is possible to become increasingly specific. There are Dutch elms and Chinese elms, sugar maples and Norway maples and red maples.

Abstract words indicate ideas that are understood intellectually, like *color* or *noise.* Abstract words name qualities (*intelligence, patriotism*), concepts (*evolution, progress*), and conditions (*illness, poverty*).

Concrete words are understood through the five senses of sight, sound, smell, taste, and touch, because concrete words refer to things in the physical world like *orange* and *sandwich.*

Her dress was *red and navy blue.* [sight]
My skin felt *clammy.* [touch]
The drum went *boomlay, boomlay, boom.* [sound]
The pickle was *bitter.* [taste]
The *stench* of uncollected garbage was overpowering. [smell]

A Clear and Specific Modifier

For the precise and concise choice of words, three techniques have already been discussed: the choice of active verbs rather than passive verbs, the choice of a clear and specific subject, and the choice of a clear and specific verb.

A fourth technique is choosing clear and specific modifiers. A modifier is any word or group of words that change the meaning of another word. It changes meaning by making more complete the picture given of the modified word.

The boy ran down the street.

There's no modifier for boy—is he two or sixteen?

The *young* boy [or *The four-year-old-boy*] ran down the street.

We now know more, but what does he look like?

The *red-headed four-year old* boy ran....
The *freckled, red-headed, four-year-old* boy ran....
The *crying, freckled, red-headed, four-year-old* boy ran....

All these italicized words are modifiers acting on the word *boy*, so that the reader gets a more complete picture of him.

Like the subject and verb, the modifiers must be as **specific** as you can make them.

Adjectives and Adverbs

Modifiers fall into two main groups: those that modify nouns and those that modify other parts of the sentence. Modifiers of nouns function as **adjectives.** Modifiers of other parts of the sentence function as **adverbs.**

The following examples illustrate the confusion that arises when **adjectives** are not specific:

Mary is a *strange* child.

Does that mean that Mary is neurotic, unpredictable, old-fashioned, suspicious, quiet, isolated, frightened, or insecure?

Mr. Anderson is a *nice* man.

Does that mean that he is kind, warm, sincere, thoughtful, patient, or generous?

Senator Thompson is a *bad* politician.

Is the senator dishonest, incompetent, or unsuccessful?

The next examples illustrate the confusion that arises when **adverbs** are not specific:

It was a *poorly* developed paragraph.

Was it inadequately developed or illogically developed?

The money was *improperly* distributed.

Was the money distributed illegally, immorally, or haphazardly?

That magazine is published *periodically*.

Is it published weekly, monthly, or annually?

As a beginning writer, you might be tempted to heap one adjective upon another in order to clarify your nouns. But be careful: modification can easily be overdone.

The tired, feeble, gray, stooped old man wearily walked up the jagged, rocky, winding mountain path.

Often suggestion, instead of drawn-out description, can create a better picture for your reader:

The aged peasant, wasted by an eternity of suffering, leaned heavily on his stick and shuffled up the boulder-choked path.

Nouns, verbs, and adverbs can combine with adjectives to add variety in descriptive detail:

Moonlight creeping softly between the shadows revealed a mossy staircase leading down to the water.

It takes a lot of practice to write a good paragraph, but your choice of words—words that tell, that create pictures, that suggest, that convey emotions—will ultimately determine whether or not you communicate successfully with your reader.

EXERCISE IIIi
Make the following sentences more specific. Find the general words and change them to words referring to what can be pointed to, visualized, or remembered.

EXAMPLE
Once I *went* to a *big city.* [The italicized words can be made more specific.]
Last Tuesday, I *drove* to *Chicago.*

1. School was cold yesterday.

_____

2. I like some aspects of school.

_____

3. One day last week I found some money.

_____

4. Some police officers are crooked.

_____

5. My family is big.

_____

6. There are lots of sports events on TV.

_____

7. Doctors in some parts of the United States make a lot of money.

_____

8. For some reason, I like my chair.

_____

9. My dog is mean.

_____

10. I work at the shopping center.

_____

EXERCISE IIIj

Make the following sentences more concrete. Use words that allow the reader to see, hear, taste, smell, or feel.

EXAMPLE

VAGUE: The worker was *tired*. [The writer *tells* the reader.]

CONCRETE: His green work shirt soaked with sweat, the worker, eyes red-rimmed with fatigue, slumped into the chair and wiped his forehead with a trembling hand. [The writer *shows* the reader.]

1. Jim is accident-prone.

   _____

2. The lunch was good.

   _____

3. The snow-covered landscape was beautiful.

   _____

4. The concert was spectacular.

   _____

5. I was scared when I had to make a speech.

   _____

6. The barn smelled funny.

   _____

7. The cafeteria is noisy.

   _____

8. He was a good basketball player.

**Use words to create pictures
in your reader's mind.**

9. The meat was tough.

_____

10. The band was loud.

_____

EXERCISE IIIk
In the following paragraph, modifiers are left out of the 25 blank spaces. For each blank, the word list below the paragraph makes four suggestions. Choose the one you think works best in that sentence, and tell why you chose it. If you don't know the meaning of some of these words, look them up in the dictionary.

The colors and sounds of early spring are fresh and bright. Today (1) _____ the sky lightened to (2) _____ blue. An (3) _____ (4) _____ cloud (5) _____ drifted by, its underside (6) _____ from the rising sun. (7) _____ birds made (8) _____ sounds in the (9) _____ branches of the trees (10) _____ against the eastern sky. The (11) _____ chorus of the "peepers" in the (12) _____ meadows dwindled to a (13) _____ soloist. As the sun rose, the sky grew (14) _____ and the clouds lost their (15) _____ bottoms. The tree branches changed from (16) _____ gray and brown to a (17) _____ green. The birds, (18) _____ now, chirped and trilled and sang. Trees in (19) _____ greens formed a (20) _____ background for an oak tree whose (21) _____ leaves were (22) _____ balls of (23) _____ . Above the chorus of singing birds, a cardinal made his (24) _____ comment, "bir die, bir die, bir die." The colors and sounds of spring bring in the new season, driving out (25) _____ winter.

Choose carefully. As Mark Twain said, "The difference between the almost right word and the right word is really a large matter—'tis the difference between the lightning bug and the lightning."

1. early
   once
   at dawn
   in the morning
2. dim
   pale
   pallid
   faint
3. occasional
   random
   uncertain
   casual
4. tiny
   petite

   minuscule
   small
5. moderately
   languidly
   gently
   slowly
6. colorful
   bright
   rosy
   light
7. unseen
   hidden
   undercover
   invisible

8. soft
   whispering
   murmuring
   subdued
9. leafy
   shady
   shadowy
   flowering
10. drawn
   outlined
   silhouetted
   showing
11. unending
   heavenly

describing

demonic
nightlong

12. marshy
    wet
    damp
    swampy

13. lonesome
    solitary
    lonely
    single

14. brighter
    lighter
    more colorful
    bluer

15. loud
    shining
    garish
    rosy

16. dark
    colorless

dull
blackish

17. pale
    light
    yellowish
    golden

18. awake
    lively
    conscious
    sprightly

19. lots of
    many
    varying
    contrasting

20. mixed up
    messy
    spotted
    mottled

21. new
    young

infant
day-old

22. round
    irregular
    hazy
    misshapen

23. color
    red
    dark red
    maroon

24. long
    double
    loud
    two-note

25. cold
    bleak
    dreary
    dismal

CHAPTER IV

explaining with examples

ORGANIZATION

Exposition means explanation. An explanatory paper tells what a thing is, how it works, how it is made, how it is like or unlike something else, or how something is caused.

The primary purpose of an expository paragraph is to share your knowledge of something. In narrative, you shared an experience; in description you shared an emotion or a sensory impression; however, in exposition, you share or prove (in the case of an essay exam) your knowledge.

As a writer, you are often required to explain something to someone else. You may want to justify your opinion, or perhaps you want to clarify an idea or concept so that someone else can understand it. Whatever your purpose, good examples can help you to get the message across. They not only make things clearer, but they also help to persuade and convince. Examples often provide the supporting details in a paragraph that **explains.**

```
┌─────────────────────────────┐
│                             │
│       INTRODUCTION          │
│  ─ ─ ─ ─ ─ ─ ─ ─ ─ ─ ─      │
│                             │
│  EXAMPLExxxxxxxxx           │
│  xxxxxxxxxxxxxxxxxx          │
│  xxxxxxEXAMPLExxx            │
│  xxxxxxxxxxxxxxxxxx          │
│  xxxxxxxxxxxxxxxxxx          │
│  xxEXAMPLExxxxxxx            │
│  xxxxxxxxxxxxxxxxx           │
│  xxxxxxxxxxxxxxxxxx          │
│       CONCLUSION            │
│  ─ ─ ─ ─ ─ ─ ─ ─ ─ ─ ─      │
│                             │
└─────────────────────────────┘
```

There are two basic methods for developing a paragraph by examples:

1. Use a **series of examples** that make clear the controlling idea.
2. Carefully select **several extended illustrations** or brief anecdotes that directly support the controlling idea.

In either method, the purpose is to support the topic sentence. In this kind of development, as in the others you have studied, the basic organization of the paragraph remains the same.

1. Topic sentence
2. Body
3. Conclusion

Topic Sentence

Here, again, you must be very careful in choosing your controlling idea. If your subject is too large or your attitude is too general, you will have trouble providing the necessary support. As always, you must narrow your subject and attitude carefully before you start. Thus, before you consider how to develop your paragraph you should (1) decide exactly what subject you are going to discuss, (2) decide on some clear stand or attitude toward your subject, and (3) write down your topic sentence (subject + attitude) in the clearest and simplest words possible.

Look at the following topic sentences:

1. Moving was a real experience for him.
2. Moving to a new place altered his way of life.

3. When the family moved to a larger farm, John had to start doing a man's work.

> Which of these is the most specific?
> Why are the other two faulty as topic sentences?
> What are the key words in sentence 3?
> With number 3 as a topic sentence, what would you expect the paragraph to explain?
> What kind of examples might be used to support this topic sentence?

Now suppose that the writer had chosen different wording:

When his parents decided to move to another farm, John's childhood abruptly came to an end.

> What are the key words in this topic sentence?
> How would this topic sentence alter the emphasis of the paragraph?
> What kind of examples might be used to support this topic sentence?

Again, suppose that the writer had changed the wording of the topic sentence to read:

His family's move to a larger farm meant that John could no longer enjoy the carefree childhood he had shared with his brothers and sisters.

Even though each topic sentence deals with the same basic event, each new wording of the topic sentence would call for somewhat different development. This brings you to one of the qualities of the topic sentence that has not yet been discussed: the topic sentence tends to establish the kind of development the writer will use.

Look at the following topic sentence from Mark Twain's *Autobiography*.

It was a heavenly place for a boy, that farm of my Uncle John's.

Obviously, this sentence can be developed by examples, as Mark Twain does from his impressions and memories.

EXERCISE IVa
Tell which of the following sentences could be developed by examples.

_____ **1.** Three types of customers at the restaurant where I work really irritate me.

_____ **2.** Although many people use them interchangeably, *compare with* and *compare to* have different meanings.

_____ **3.** My English teacher is really funny at times.

_____ **4.** My mother is a generous person.

5. The books in my library can be divided into four types.
6. Disneyland has several unique attractions.
7. The word *discrimination* has several distinct meanings depending on how it's used.
8. Manuel's van is beautiful.
9. An odd thing happened to me on the way to school today.
10. Heart disease and cancer are the two leading causes of death in the United States.

Body

Right from the first word, you need to consider the information that is available to you in developing your paragraph. To be adequately developed, the body of the paragraph must offer the reader everything that is promised or implied by the topic sentence, leaving no loose ends or unanswered questions.

Consider the following situation, in which Betty tells Jan that she's thinking about going out with George.

JAN: I've met some cheap people in my lifetime, but I've never met anyone quite as tight as George.

BETTY: What do you mean?

JAN: Well, for example, I have never once seen George leave a tip in a res-restaurant, and he hates to go to expensive places. Whenever George dines with friends, he always manages to perform a neat little disappearing act right before the waiter brings the check.

Use examples to prove your point.

88

[Betty now has a better idea of what George is like, and she is probably having second thoughts about going out with him. Jan continues with her examples.]

JAN: You had better be prepared to do a lot of walking. George doesn't like to spend money on gas. If any destination is within walking distance (to George this means anything within a five-mile radius) plan on hiking. Even if he does take his car, you'll still be walking. George just refuses to waste money on parking. Instead of leaving his car in the parking garage next to the theater, he'll drive around until he finds a free parking lot or a space on a deserted side street somewhere.

With every example, Betty gets a clearer understanding of Jan's first remark about George.

Notice how a student develops his controlling idea by the use of specific examples in the following paragraph.

Although having more than one girlfriend can sometimes be an advantage, it does have its disadvantages. For example, when a birthday or holiday arrives, you have to buy a present for each of the girls, and that could cost a lot of money. Also, you always have to worry about one of the girls finding out about each of the others, and that could prove to be a hairy experience. Another occurs when two of your girlfriends ask you for your class ring and you have already given it to a third one. Scheduling dates usually turns out to be more of a carefully planned strategic move than a spur-of-the-moment decision. One of the biggest disadvantages is bringing one of the girls home for dinner and Mom slips and calls her by the wrong name. And what could be more of a disadvantage than when your birthday arrives and they all want to help you celebrate it. Last but not least, a final disadvantage is trying to remember what you said to each of the girls without acting like you can't remember. All of these examples prove that more than one girlfriend can be a *big* disadvantage.

Jim Presto

In the same way, examples help your reader understand because they narrow down general knowledge into specific knowledge. After reading a student's answer to an essay question, an instructor can usually tell whether the student had only a general idea of what he was talking about or whether he knew exactly what he was talking about. Writing a memorized definition of deviant behavior on a test does not prove that you understand the concept of deviant behavior, but if you can provide specific, detailed examples of deviant behavior, then you can prove to your instructor that you do indeed understand the concept. That's why essay questions are sometimes accompanied by the suggestion, "Provide as many specific examples as possible." What if this book had not provided specific examples of different kinds of paragraphs? Don't you think it would have been harder to write a narrative paragraph if you had never seen an example of one? How many times have you heard a confused student ask a teacher to give an example? **Examples are useful because they aid understanding.**

There are several things to remember as you write the body of your example paragraph.

1. **Be sure your examples are relevant:** that is, make sure they support your idea precisely. If you are discussing easy and tough professors, an

Food served in school cafeterias makes me choke.

example of a middle-of-the-road grader is out of place. If you are discussing the difficulty of reading highly complicated problems in technical books, an example of a clearly stated problem in the book is not relevant. If you are discussing the poor food served at college cafeterias, all the examples given should be from college cafeterias, not cafeterias in hospitals, high schools, or department stores.

2. **Make sure you have enough examples to prove your idea.** If your topic sentence is, "Books have influenced the course of history in the United States," you need several examples to prove it. If your topic sentence is "Sarah is accident-prone," you should show Sarah having several different accidents.

Notice the specific and relevant examples used in the following student paragraph.

Before prospective parents decide on the new baby's name, they should consider several important factors that could have an impact on their child as he or she grows older. For instance, names without specific gender, such as Robin, Kelly, and Chris, create confusion for teachers who are trying to schedule boys' and girls' gym classes. Master Robin is likely to find himself in the girls' gymnastic program, and Miss Kelly is likely to be named monitor for the boys' rest room. Another problem for the growing child is the tine, old family name that other children can distort in name-calling or teasing: Cosmos, Angel, or Elmer. Names that would seem perfectly suitable for a newborn child are ludicrous when the child is fifty years old. Bambi may seem to be a darling name for a newborn, but Grandma Bambi is an incongruous image. Names usually associated with notorious or outrageous persons should be avoided; Adolph Hitler Smith would spend most of his life defending himself from the abuse of his peers and the disapproval of society. A child who was given a common name that is spelled differently will spend countless hours throughout life correcting report cards, registration forms, and anyone who asks his or her name for official forms. Mari, Alyce, Jonn, and Tym are examples of common names spelled uncommonly. Prospective parents should remember that of all the things they give their children, the only thing they will keep all their lives is a first name. Accordingly, the greatest care should be taken when choosing a name for a baby.

Regina Sandor

Many students ask, "How many examples should I use?" There is no definite number, but you should use enough to ensure that your reader will understand your purpose clearly and completely. For paragraphs of 250 to 300 words, three to five good examples are usually sufficient, but it is the quality of the examples you select that will determine whether or not the reader accepts your main idea.

USING GOOD EXAMPLES

If you want to make a point effectively, then you must choose examples that are both **specific** and **relevant.** Suppose, for example, you were writing a paragraph to prove that some of the laws that have been passed in Massachusetts seem ridiculously funny in today's world. Examples such as the following (taken from Barbara Seuling's *You Can't Eat Peanuts in Church and Other Little-Known Laws,* as are the other laws referred to in this section) would be appropriate:

According to an old law of Truro, Massachusetts, a young man could not get married until he had killed either six blackbirds or three crows.
It is illegal to eat peanuts in church in Massachusetts.
In Massachusetts, it is an infraction of the law to lounge around on bakery shelves.
To take a bath in Boston, you must have a doctor's written prescription.

The following two examples, however, would **not** be effective:

Massachusetts has a ridiculous law about church.
Massachusetts passed some funny laws about getting married and taking a bath.

These would not be effective because they are not specific. They are relevant—that is, they pertain to the controlling idea—but they are vague. Now take a look at the following examples:

Singing out of tune in North Carolina is against the law.
In Gary, Indiana, it is illegal to attend the theater within four hours of eating garlic.
Salt Lake City, Utah, has a law against carrying an unwrapped ukelele on the street.

These examples would not be effective either because, although they are quite specific, they are completely irrelevant: not one of these examples refers to a **Massachusetts** law.

To take a bath in Boston, you must have a doctor's written prescription.

Notice how a skillful writer uses specific and relevant examples to illustrate his controlling idea:

It is a miracle that New York works at all. The whole thing is implausible. Every time the residents brush their teeth, millions of gallons of water must be drawn from the Catskills and the hills of Westchester. When a young man in Manhattan writes a letter to his girl in Brooklyn, the love message gets blown to her through a pneumatic tube—*pfft*—just like that. The subterranean system of telephone cables, power lines, steam pipes, gas mains, and sewer pipes is reason enough to abandon the island to the gods and the weevils. Every time an incision is made in the pavement, the noisy surgeons expose ganglia that are tangled beyond belief. By rights New York should have destroyed itself long ago, from panic or fire or rioting or failure of some vital supply line in its circulatory system or from some deep labyrinthine short circuit. Long ago the city should have experienced an insoluble traffic snarl at some impossible bottleneck. It should have perished of hunger when food lines failed for a few days. It should have been wiped out by a plague starting in its slums or carried in by ships' rats. It should have been overwhelmed by the sea that licks at it on every side. The workers in its myriad cells should have succumbed to nerves, from the fearful pall of smoke-fog that drifts over every few days from Jersey, blotting out all light at noon and leaving the high offices suspended, men groping and depressed, and the sense of world's end. It should have been touched in the head by the August heat and gone off its rocker.

E. B. White, "Here Is New York"

EXERCISE IVb
Suppose you are writing a paragraph about laws that have been passed specifically to protect the rights of animals. Put a check mark before the relevant examples.

_____ 1. It is illegal for a dog to come within ten feet of a fire hydrant in Sheridan, Wyoming.

_____ 2. In Topeka, Kansas, it is illegal to worry a squirrel.

_____ 3. In Natchez, Mississippi, it is against the law for elephants to drink beer.

92

A kiss can last no more than one second in Halethorpe, Maryland.

_____ 4. In Connecticut, the law states that if you are a beaver, you have a legal right to build a dam.

_____ 5. In Nebraska, sneezing in public is prohibited.

_____ 6. Mules are prohibited from going into saloons in Lourdsburg, New Mexico.

_____ 7. In Colorado, the law upholds a dog's right to one bite.

_____ 8. In Rumford, Maine, it is against the law to bite your landlord.

_____ 9. It is unlawful to mistreat a rat in Denver, Colorado.

_____ 10. All citizens of South Carolina are required to carry guns with them to church on Sunday.

_____ 11. In California, picking feathers from a live goose is illegal.

_____ 12. It is illegal for monkeys to ride buses in San Antonio, Texas.

_____ 13. On Market Street in San Francisco, the law requires that elephants must be kept on a leash.

_____ 14. A kiss can last no longer than one second in Halethorpe, Maryland.

_____ 15. It is illegal for a donkey to sleep in a bathtub in Brooklyn, New York.

Which of the above laws would provide good examples for a paragraph about laws that have been passed to place restrictions on animals?

EXERCISE IVc
In the following paragraph, underline the irrelevant sentences and write their number on the line below.

(1) In my opinion, the German shepherd is the best all-round breed of dog in the world today. (2) There are several reasons for this. (3) First, German shepherds are quite adaptable; with a good diet and adequate exercise, they can exist anywhere. (4) You should always feed them only once a day, and a mixture of meat and dry food is preferable. (5) Daily brushing is also a must.

(6) Another reason why shepherds are best is that they are so intelligent. (7) They are quick to follow orders, and a well-trained shepherd can be trusted in most situations. (8) Dobermans are also smart, but they are kind of flaky too. (9) One that I know turned on his own master, but that was probably because the dog was locked in the cellar all day. (10) Labradors are obedient too, but they are sort of dumb about other things like being responsible. (11) Shepherds also have fantastic temperaments. (12) They really enjoy family living and are great with little children. (13) They are steady and dignified—not like those little toy poodles that yap constantly because they are so neurotic. (14) The reason for this is that these poodles were bred down from the standard size, and the part that shrank most was their brains. (15) The big poodles are really good dogs, but they still can't compare to the shepherd. (16) Finally, the shepherd is naturally protective; he will protect to the death his home and human family. (17) He is better than any burglar alarm, although some of those new alarms which are sensitive to vibrations are really slick. (18) They are simple to install and almost 100% reliable. (19) A shepherd can always sense danger and quickly gives warning well in advance of a stranger's arrival. (20) These are only a few reasons why I feel that the German shepherd is a "super" dog. (21) Anyone who wants to purchase one should always deal with a reputable breeder, and there are many things to be considered when selecting a pup.

THE EXTENDED EXAMPLE

Several examples are usually more convincing than one, as in the case of Jan's attempts to discourage Betty from going out with George; but sometimes you can illustrate an idea with one extended example—if it is a thorough, detailed example containing enough information to explain your point clearly. The writer of the paragraph that follows, for example, uses both methods to illustrate the "new technique of wholesale murder" which developed during the bootlegging wars of Chicago in the days of Al Capone.

First, he cites several examples to support his point, but then he uses one longer, more detailed example:

Series of Brief Examples

One of the standard methods of disposing of a rival in this warfare of the gangs was to pursue his car with a stolen automobile full of men armed with sawed-off shotguns and submachine guns: to draw up beside it, forcing it to the curb, open fire upon it—and then disappear into the traffic, later abandoning the stolen car at a safe distance. Another favorite method was to take the victim "for a ride": in other words, to lure him into a supposedly friendly car, shoot him at leisure, drive to some distant and deserted part of the city, and quietly throw his body overboard. Still another was to lease an apartment or a room overlooking his front door, station a couple of hired assassins at the window, and as the victim emerged from the house some sunny afternoon, to spray him with a few dozen machine-gun bullets from behind drawn curtains. But there were also more ingenious and refined methods of slaughter. Take, for example, the killing of Dion O'Banion, leader of the gang which for a time most seriously menaced Capone's reign in Chicago. The preparation of this particular murder was reminiscent of the kiss of Judas. O'Banion was a bootlegger and a gangster by night, but a florist by day: a strange and complex character, a connoisseur of orchids and of manslaughter. One morning a sedan drew up outside his flower shop and three men got out, leaving the fourth at the wheel. The three men had apparently taken good care to win O'Banion's trust, for although he always carried three guns, now for the moment he was off his guard as he advanced among the flowers to meet his visitors. The middle man of the three cordially shook hands with O'Banion—and then held on while his two companions put six bullets into the gangster-florist. The three conspirators walked out, climbed into the sedan and departed. They were never brought to justice, and it is not recorded that any of them hung themselves to trees in remorse. O'Banion had a first-class funeral, gangster style: a ten-thousand-dollar casket, twenty-six truckloads of flowers, among them a basket of flowers which bore the touching inscription, "From Al."

Frederick Lewis Allen, Only Yesterday

Conclusion

A paragraph that explains needs a good conclusion, but it should not end with an example. You begin with a controlling idea, provide examples to clarify it, and then conclude in a way that implies, "Look reader, now that I have explained everything to you, you should be convinced that I know what I am talking about." Try to be a bit more subtle, however; a restatement of your controlling idea, once it has been fully explained, will accomplish the same purpose. It will remind your reader of the main idea and summarize the examples you have given.

Notice how the conclusion in the following paragraph reaffirms the topic sentence.

A reputation that took years to build can be destroyed in minutes. A man has devoted forty years of his life to his job in a bank. He has given faithful and loyal service. One day he takes two hundred dollars of the bank's money home. The man is branded a crook, an embezzler. He is fired from his job; he is forever disgraced, and possibly threatened with prison. Who remembers the forty years of good service? Again, a man who is a loving husband and a kind and provident father for twenty-five years becomes infatuated with a girl. He takes her out. When his wife and children learn of this, he becomes an outcast. The twenty-five good years are forgotten. A spectacular case of more than sixty years ago proves that one misstep can blast forever a carefully built reputation. In the years following World War I, the national craze for baseball grew wilder and wilder. Fans crowded into stadiums. Stars swelled into heroes. Of all the teams, the Chicago White Sox were the best, with the best pitchers, runners, and teamwork. Then, in 1919, the Sox threw the World Series. People took their baseball very seriously in those days, so this crookedness gave them an ugly shock. After the scandal hearings, the guilty players were too frightened of mobs to leave the courtrooms. One of the guilty players, considered the best before Babe Ruth, was Shoeless Joe Jackson. As Jackson left the hearing, a youngster called out to him, "Say it ain't so, Joe." Even though the remark has remained as a wistful part of the American language, the scandal was, unfortunately, true. The Sox were wiped out as a team and the individual members barred from organized baseball and the baseball Hall of Fame. Baseball itself came perilously close to extinction. Reputation

is, indeed, a fragile thing. It takes years to build but only a moment to lose.

1. What examples could you give to show how various animals adapt to their environment?
2. What do you consider the most exotic places in the world?
3. Which twentieth-century discoveries do you consider the most important?

ASSIGNMENT
Select one of the following for a paragraph developed by examples.

1. Think of someone you know quite well. Select a particular habit or characteristic—recklessness, absentmindedness, chronic lateness, wearing mismatched clothes—and develop a paragraph through the use of examples.
2. After studying the sentence section of this chapter, write a paragraph developed by three subtopics supported by specific examples. You might consider such experiences as buying a car, going on a vacation, studying for a test, learning to drive, or buying Christmas presents.
3. Try writing a paragraph in which you illustrate an old proverb such as "Honesty is the best policy."

SENTENCES

The Use of Subtopic Sentences

When you are offering a series of examples in support of your topic sentence, it is often helpful to group the details under subtopic sentences. Each subtopic sentence provides a main point in support of your topic sentence by introducing one aspect of the controlling idea you are developing. Frequently, words similar to those used to express the attitude in the topic sentence may be used in the sub-

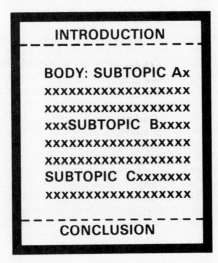

INTRODUCTION
- - - - - - -
BODY: SUBTOPIC Ax
xxxxxxxxxxxxxxxxxx
xxxxxxxxxxxxxxxxxx
xxxSUBTOPIC Bxxxx
xxxxxxxxxxxxxxxxxx
xxxxxxxxxxxxxxxxxx
SUBTOPIC Cxxxxxxx
xxxxxxxxxxxxxxxxxx
- - - - - - -
CONCLUSION

topic sentences to remind the reader of the controlling idea as you develop it more fully.

Each of these subtopic sentences has a controlling idea, too, just as your topic sentence does. Sometimes it is useful to make an outline using your subtopics. If you take the topic sentence plus the subtopic sentences, you have your paragraph in skeleton form. To develop that paragraph, you need to provide at least one good example to support each of the subtopic sentences.

Suppose you are given the opportunity to write about anything you want, providing that you support your main idea with examples. Here is a simple formula for writing such a paragraph:

1. Select your controlling idea—a subject plus an attitude.
2. Write down a clearly worded topic sentence containing that controlling idea.
3. Select **three** main points to support your topic sentence. These three main points are subtopics.
4. Think of **at least one** good example to clarify and explain each subtopic.

Here is how the formula might work. Suppose you choose to write something about your father. In thinking about your father, you might, for example, remember his sense of humor. Thus, your topic sentence might be "My father has a keen sense of humor."

Next, you consider the main points of his "keen sense of humor." You might, for example, find that these three main points could be expressed in these subtopic sentences:

1. He loves to tease my mother.
2. He constantly jokes about our neighbor.
3. He can even joke about his own misfortunes.

Then your examples can be used to support your subtopics, as in the following paragraph.

My father has a keen sense of humor. For one thing, **he loves to tease my mother.** Now Mom never learned to drive until she was forty, and she never has had any luck with cars. In fact, she bumps into all kinds of innocent things, like mailboxes and fireplugs and lamp posts. Dad always says that there is a god of cars who hates women that learn to drive at forty. Also, **Dad constantly jokes about our neighbors.** We once had a shortsighted neighbor (a strange ranger with a peculiar bump on the side of his head) who frequented the neighborhood tavern. His name was Dodge, or something like that, but Dad always called him "Diogenes" and kidded him about staggering into the wrong house at night. Dad always claimed that Diogenes got the bump on his head from trying to crawl into bed with Mrs. Dickenson, a dignified widow who lived up the street. Dad's humor never fails him; **he can even joke about his own misfortunes.** One of his favorite stories concerns the time he worked at a blacksmith shop when he was sixteen. His pants caught on fire, and he got a painful burn, but he was too ashamed to go to the hospital because he didn't have any underwear. Over the years, Dad's rugged sense of humor has carried us all through the good times and the bad.

Examples should follow a sensible pattern. Decide which of your examples should be listed first and which should come later. Then try to arrange them in a logical order which moves smoothly toward your conclusion.

A useful principle to apply in arranging examples is that of **climactic order.** Climactic order calls for arranging your supporting points in the order of increasing importance. Thus, wherever possible, you would save your most important point or most vivid example for the end.

Suppose you wanted to write a paragraph about your college. Your first idea might be: "I like my college." After limiting and refining your idea, you might come up with a topic sentence such as: "I chose Griffith College for several reasons." Now, the reasons become your subtopics.

TOPIC SENTENCE: I chose Griffith College for several reasons.
SUBTOPIC A: The college is close to my home.
SUBTOPIC B: The college is less expensive than other schools are.
SUBTOPIC C: The faculty is excellent.
SUBTOPIC D: Most of all, the college has a fine program for my major.

Now all you have to do is support or prove each of the subtopics with a sentence or two, and your paragraph is complete. Using subtopics often helps you to organize your paper and to avoid extensive rewriting. It also helps you to get your idea across clearly to your reader.

STEPS IN WRITING A PARAGRAPH WITH SUBTOPICS

Choosing a Topic

Choosing a topic for a paragraph developed by examples often requires only listening to your own remarks or those of your friends. Carol walks into the class, slams her books down on the desk, and says, "He drives me up a wall." Bob, ecstatic over being given the car for a week, says, "My mother is a saint." You, happy over the midterm grades just received, say, "I enjoy going to school here." Any one of these remarks could be rewritten as a topic sentence and developed into a paragraph with examples.

Getting the Examples

Suppose you ask Carol who "drives her up a wall" and how "he does it." He, she says, is her Spanish teacher. As you question Carol, she mentions many things about her Spanish teacher that annoy her.

Jingles change constantly	Dresses outrageously
Refuses to answer questions	Talks in a monotone
Gets off the subject	Insults students
Chain-smokes in class	Mimics students' accents
Clears his throat often	Paces constantly

| Comes late | Never finishes the lesson |
| Listens to only the brightest students | Has no compassion for the slow learner |

explaining with examples

Organizing the Paragraph

As you look at the list of examples, you find that some of the examples clearly go together; they can sensibly be grouped. "Jingles change constantly," "chain-smokes in class," "clears his throat often," "paces constantly," and "dresses outrageously" are all personal habits. "Gets off the subject," "talks in a monotone," "never finishes the lesson," and "refuses to answer questions" all refer to teaching techniques; "mimics students' accents," "comes late," "listens only to the brightest students," "insults students," and "has no compassion for the slow learner" concern his attitude toward students.

Making an Outline

Once you have grouped your examples in this way, you are ready to make an outline using subtopic sentences. Subtopics can help you develop a unified, coherent paragraph. Each new subtopic sentence provides primary support for your topic sentence by introducing another feature of your controlling idea. Usually you will put last the most important subtopic (in this case the most annoying). Here are the subtopics arranged from least to most important, that is, in **climactic order.**

A. He has annoying personal habits
B. His teaching techniques are not good.
C. His attitude toward students is terrible.

As you look at the subtopics, you notice that while *B* and *C* are constructed alike, *A* is a little different. The subject in *A* is *He* (the teacher), but the subjects in *B* and *C* are the things that annoy you. For a better outline, you change *A* to "His personal habits are annoying." You then revise your topic sentence and you have an outline that will make writing the example paragraph easy.

TOPIC SENTENCE: Although most teachers care about their students and try to create a good atmosphere in the classroom, I don't think my Spanish teacher does. I hate to go to that class for several reasons.

A. First, his personal habits are annoying.
B. Second, his teaching techniques are poor.
C. Most of all, his attitude toward students is terrible.

EXERCISE IVd

Try writing subtopics for each of the following sentences:

1. The members of my family find different ways to make me happy.
2. My sweetheart has a great personality.

3. _____ is my favorite subject for several reasons.
4. My last vacation was the best one I ever had.
5. Although often maligned, television does provide valuable public services.

**THE UNDER-
DEVELOPED
PARAGRAPH**

Consider the following underdeveloped paragraph on William Faulkner's writing; it has only a topic sentence and three subtopic sentences:

> William Faulkner is a difficult writer to understand. For one thing, he has a very difficult writing style. His characters are also difficult to understand. Time is often confusing so that it is difficult to keep track of when things happen in his stories.

A well-developed paragraph generally requires both **primary** and **secondary** support. Subtopic sentences that directly support the controlling idea provide the **primary support.** However, other sentences are needed to provide the **secondary support** to illustrate or clarify your main supporting points. It is this secondary support that puts flesh on the bare bones of your paragraph and develops it fully enough to show your readers exactly what you mean.

Notice the development in the revised version of the paragraph on Faulkner. Here each subtopic is developed.

> Until you become familiar with his style, William Faulkner's fiction presents several difficulties. For one thing, he often writes in long, complex sentences which seem to run on almost endlessly. Faulkner seems reluctant to put a period on paper until he has set down every last detail that a character senses. A good example of this trait can be seen in the opening passage of his short story, "Barn Burning." As for Faulkner's characters, mostly small-town Southerners or poor dirt farmers, they too are as tortured as his writing. Writhing with inner tensions, they display a rough violence that is in sharp contrast to the peaceful setting of flowering verbena and creaking wagons drawn by lop-eared mules. In the action of the story, time often shifts with baffling swiftness. The reader frequently finds the past suddenly pulled into the present and long-ago events reenacted in the minds of the characters as the story progresses. Certainly, there is no denying the difficulties that confront the Faulkner reader, though the reading does become easier as you become more familiar with his style.

EXERCISE IVe
Read the following paragraph, a student's early draft.

> My employer, Harry Kramer, or Uncle Harry, as I prefer to call him, has been the most influential man in my life. Because he has given me important guidance, I have been able to make many sound decisions on financial and social problems. With his help, I have been able to set a code of morals and standards to live by. He has shown me the importance of all the little things in life that I always took for granted. I have been inspired by him to realize that I have an unlimited amount of potential and that only I can control my destiny. It was he who encouraged me to go back to school, and now I can see how important an education is. With his help, I have gone from a boy, confused and without direction, to a respectable young man with many goals. The influence that Uncle Harry has had on me has changed my entire life. *Matthew Boyd*

After rereading his work, the writer decided that the paragraph was underdeveloped. He really had only a topic sentence, five subtopic sentences, and two final sentences that formed his conclusion. Develop each of his subtopics with two or three sentences of specific supporting detail to make a well-developed paragraph.

TOPIC SENTENCE
My employer, Harry Kramer, or Uncle Harry, as I prefer to call him, has been the most influential man in my life.

SUBTOPIC A
Because he has given me important guidance, I have been able to make many sound decisions on financial and social problems.

_____
_____
_____
_____
_____

SUBTOPIC B
With his help, I have been able to set a code of morals and standards to live by.

_____
_____
_____
_____
_____

SUBTOPIC C
He has shown me the importance of all the little things in life that I always took for granted.

_____
_____
_____
_____
_____

SUBTOPIC D
I have been inspired by him to realize that I have an unlimited amount of potential and that only I can control my destiny.

_____
_____
_____
_____
_____

SUBTOPIC E

It was he who encouraged me to go back to school, and now I can see how important an education is.

_____

_____

_____

_____

_____

CONCLUSION

With his help, I have gone from a boy, confused and without any direction, to a respectable young man with many goals. The influence that Uncle Harry has had on me has changed my entire life.

WORDS

The Glaring Errors

Frequently, a big obstacle the beginning writer must overcome is his or her own bad habits of speech. Misused words and expressions do more than offend the sensitivities of frustrated English teachers; they give the reader a bad impression of the writer—so read this section carefully. You might recognize some glaring errors that are part of your writing and speaking habits.

Some glaring errors make an inexperienced writer appear ignorant or stupid. If the reader gets this impression about the writer, he or she will not be interested in the writer's ideas, no matter how good they are. Some of the glaring errors can be eliminated rather easily.

DOUBLE NEGATIVES

Never use the double negative: two *no*'s make a *yes*.

INCORRECT: I don't got none. [This means that you *do* have some.]
CORRECT: I don't have any.
        I have none.
INCORRECT: My teacher doesn't know nothing. [This means that he *does* know something.]

CORRECT: My teacher doesn't know anything.
My teacher knows nothing.

INCORRECT: I don't have no time for games. [This means that you *do* have time for games.]

CORRECT: I don't have any time for games.
I have no time for games.

IT'S AND ITS **Don't confuse *it's* with *its*.** *It's* = it is. *It's* is a contraction like *don't (do not)* or *didn't (did not)*. The apostrophe replaces a letter that is omitted. You use many of these contractions in your speech every day: "Let's go to the movies" obviously means "Let us go to the movies." "I shouldn't go" obviously means "I should not go."

Its = belonging to it (the possessive). Like other possessives, such as *his*, *hers*, and *theirs*, *its* does not use the apostrophe to show ownership: "The dog ate its bone." "The ship lost its rudder."

INCORRECT: Its time to go to class.

CORRECT: It's time to go to class.

INCORRECT: My car lost it's wheel.

CORRECT: My car lost its wheel.

**MISUSED
WORDS** **Do not misuse words.** Using words improperly implies that you are uneducated, that you do not know the rules of **standard** usage, which are established by the majority of educated people. Avoid the use of **nonstandard** words and expressions in all your college writing, unless you are quoting dialogue or repeating a humorous anecdote.

Watch for the following words, which are often misused.

already/all ready
Already means "by this time, before the time mentioned." "The sun had *already* begun to set."
All ready means "all prepared, completely ready." "The fans were *all ready* to cheer for the home team."

altogether/all together
Altogether means "wholly, completely." "We are not *altogether* satisfied with his explanation of how the money was spent."
All together means "all in one place." "They were *all together* in one room."

all right/alright
All right means "acceptable, correct, satisfactory." "The tax experts said it was *all right* to take the deduction."
Alright is not standard English and should not be used.

amount/number
Amount refers to bulk items or a quantity that cannot be counted. "The *amount* of grain India received was not enough to prevent widespread starvation."

Number refers to something that can be counted. "There is a large *number* of people at the banquet this year."

less/fewer

Less is used with items that you can weigh or measure. "*Less* grain than was needed was sent to India."

Fewer is used with items that you can count. "There are *fewer* people at the banquet this year than there were last year."

almost/most

Almost means "close to, nearly." "He *almost* lost the election; *almost* half the voters stayed at home."

Most means "the majority or nearly all of a group." "*Most* of the workers refused to cross the picket line."

NOTE: Do not use *most* in place of *almost*. "He went to look for work most every morning" is incorrect.

awhile/while—both in the sense of a period of time

Awhile is an adverb. "If you will wait *awhile*, I'll go with you."

While is a noun. "We were invited to sit down for a *while*."

NOTE: *While* is also used as a subordinate conjunction, but it should be used this way only in the sense of time. "While the music played, they danced together" is correct, but "While I like chop suey, Harry likes sukiyaki" is not. In this case the correct sentence would be "Although I like chop suey, Harry likes sukiyaki."

real/really

Real means "actual, in existence." "The danger was not imaginary; it was all too real."

Really is an adverb (often overused) meaning "extremely." "We were really exhausted from the hike."

NOTE: Never use *real* in place of *really*.

then/than

Then is usually an adverb meaning "a particular time." "It was then that he decided to change his job." "The cow then took a huge mouthful of grass."

Than is a conjunction generally used to introduce the second member of a comparison. "My brother is three years older than I." "I like nothing better than a bowl of warm grits on a chilly winter morning."

alike/unlike/not alike/unalike

Alike means "in the same way or manner." "All men should be treated alike under the law."

Unlike means "different or dissimilar." "America, unlike England, does not have a royal family."

Not alike also means "different or dissimilar." "Sally and Jane are not alike in the ways that they dress."

Unalike is nonstandard and should not be used.

who/that/which

Who is a relative pronoun used to refer to a person. "The boy who lives next door is my best friend."

That and *which* are relative pronouns referring to animals or things. "The horse that won the race was a two-to-one favorite." "This jacket, which is my favorite, is beginning to show some wear."

through/threw/thru

Through is a preposition that indicates passage from one side to another, indicates between parts of, or is a synonym for *finished.* "The bird flew through the window." "Tarzan swung through the trees." "He was through with his work."

Threw is the past tense of *to throw.* "The President threw the first baseball of the season."

Thru is a nonstandard variation of *through* and should not be used in college writing.

NOTE: Do not confuse *through* with *thorough,* which means "fully, completely, or perfectly done." "The painters did a thorough job on our house."

allot/alot/a lot

Allot means "divide, distribute." "The state will allot the funds for our new park."

Alot is nonstandard and should not be used. "I liked her alot," for example, should be "I liked her very much."

A lot is most commonly a piece of land. "There is a lot near us that we would like to buy."

from/than

From, instead of *than,* should be used to indicate discrimination or distinction. "Carl's ten-speed is different than mine" is incorrect. Correct sentences are "Carl's ten-speed is different from mine" or "Carl's ten-speed differs from mine."

infer/imply

To *imply* is to hint or suggest; you imply something to someone. "The newspaper articles imply that the mayor is a crook."

To *infer* is to arrive at a conclusion, to conclude; you infer something from evidence. "We can infer from the testimony of the witness that the mayor is a crook."

The following words and phrases are often heard conversationally or in street language, but to use them in college writing is a glaring error.

you'uns	nowheres	was you
theirselfs	we was	themself
that there	hisself	this here
youse	y'all	them there
ain't	these here	

In addition, watch for these nonstandard words, phrases, and expressions.

could of/would of/should of/had of
Incorrect: I wish I had of gone.
Correct: I wish I had gone.
Incorrect: I could of gone swimming.
Correct: I could have gone swimming.

off of/in back of
Incorrect: He fell off of the house.
Correct: He fell off the house.
Incorrect: The garage is in back of the house.
Correct: The garage is behind the house.

had ought/hadn't ought
Incorrect: He hadn't ought to have said that to me.
Correct: He ought not to have said that to me.
             He should not have said that to me.

at
At is usually unnecessary at the end of a question.
Incorrect: Where is she at?
Correct: Where is she?
NOTE: In the following example, *at* **is** necessary at the end of the question:
"What on earth are you staring *at*?"

them/them there
Do not use *them* or *them there* before a noun.
Incorrect: Them apples will make great cider.
Correct: Those apples will make great cider.

went and/go and/try and
Do not use *went and, go and,* or *try and;* they are often used incorrectly.
Incorrect: We went and saw the movie.
             I will go and see who is at the door.
             You could try and do it alone.
Correct: We went to see the movie.
           I will go to see who is at the door.
           I will see who is at the door.
           You could try to do it alone.
NOTE: The following example is correct because two separate actions are in-
      tended: "We will go to the fire and do our best to help the victims."

we was/you was/they was
Do not use *we was, you was,* or *they was.*
Incorrect: We was eating our dinner when the phone rang.
Correct: We were eating our dinner when the phone rang.

he don't/she don't/it don't
Do not use *don't* when *he, she,* or *it* is the subject.
Incorrect: She don't look like a heavy drinker to me.
Correct: She doesn't look like a heavy drinker to me.
        She does not look like a heavy drinker to me.

good/well
Do not use *good* as an adverb; use *well.*
Incorrect: She drives the car real good.
        The engine ran good after the tune-up.
Correct: She drives the car quite well.
        The engine ran well after the tune-up.
NOTE: *Well* can be used as an adjective meaning "in good health."
He was not well this morning; in fact, he had to leave work early."
Good is used correctly as an adjective in the following examples:
I feel good.
The lawn looks good to me.
The steak is good.
His health is good.

bad/badly
Do not use *bad* as an adverb; use badly.
Incorrect: The engine runs bad.
        He scored bad on his test.
Correct: The engine runs badly.
        He scored badly on his test.
Bad is used correctly as an adjective in the following examples:
I feel bad.
The fish smells bad.
It looks bad for our team.

learn/teach
Do not use *learn* when you mean *teach.*
Incorrect: No one in the family could learn him any English.
Correct: No one in the family could teach him any English.
        He could not learn English from anyone in the family.

Finally, be alert to words that change according to their use in the sentence. For instance, some words change their form when they change from singular (*man, mouse*) to plural (*men, mice*). Pronouns change their forms for gender (*he, she, it*). Those are obvious. Not quite so obvious are the changes in form to indicate the use of the pronoun. Note the following examples:

STANDARD: *I* am the captain of the team. [subject]
        John and I are team captains. [subject]
NONSTANDARD: *John and me* are team captains. [subject]
STANDARD: *He* is the champion. [subject]
        He and I are winners. [subject]

NONSTANDARD: *Him and me* went to the game. [subject]

STANDARD: The ball hit *me*. [object]
          The heat floored *him and me*. [object]

NONSTANDARD: The teacher told *he and I*. [object]

STANDARD: Between *him and me* there is no argument. [object of preposition]

NONSTANDARD: Between *he and I* . . . [object of preposition]
          Between *him and I* . . . [object of preposition]

STANDARD: Send the memo to *him and me*. [object of preposition]

NONSTANDARD: Send the memo to *he and I*. [object of preposition]

Who changes its form, too, depending on its use in the sentence.

STANDARD: *Who* is at my window? [subject]

STANDARD: *Whom* do you mean? [object]

NONSTANDARD: *Who* do you mean? [object]

STANDARD: To *whom* are you writing? [object of preposition]
          Whom are you writing to? [object of proposition]

NONSTANDARD: *Who* are you writing to? [object of proposition]

EXERCISE IVf
Cross out the incorrect words or phrases and write the correct form below each
sentence.

1.   He could of refused to accept the award.
     have
     _____

2.   *almost* Most half of the students failed the last exam.
     _____

3.   Those books don't have no pictures in them.
     _____

4.   Who did you get the call from?
     _____

5.   We were not altogether when the dam broke.
     _____

6.   The supervisor called Fernando and I into the office.
     _____

7.   The amount of students registering this year is less than registered last year.
     number
     _____

8.   An alligator will sometimes eat it's own offspring.
     _____

9. Its so dark in this room that I can't hardly see.

_____

10. Susan looked badly because she was real sick.
_____ bad _____ really _____

EXERCISE IVg
Cross out the incorrect words or phrases and write the correct form on the line following.

1. She bakes a cake real good.

_____

2. Jack hadn't ought to treat Sally that way.

_____

3. How many of you'uns are going to the game tonight?

_____

4. They were already to go on vacation.

_____

5. I must pull myself all together before tonight.

_____

6. There was a large amount of people at the fair.
_____ number _____

7. The Valenzuelas invited my wife and I to their housewarming.
_____ me _____

8. I think it's alright if he smokes pot.

_____

9. Whom was that masked man?

_____

10. My father is going to learn me how to drive.

_____

11. It doesn't belong to me; it belongs to them guys.
_____ those _____

12. Where is she sitting at?

_____

13. While he is intelligent, he still gets failing grades.

_____

14. When I was younger, my tastes were much different then my father's; than I changed.

_____

15. I think the way she did it was real cute.

_____

CHAPTER V

comparing and contrasting

ORGANIZATION

One of the best ways to make a subject interesting and informative is to develop it by means of a comparison or contrast. **Comparison** shows **similarities** between persons, places, things, ideas, or situations. **Contrast** does just the opposite: it points out the **differences** between persons, places, things, ideas, or situations. Whether you organize material for a comparison or for a contrast, your methods are essentially the same.

Two Basic Methods for Organizing Comparison/Contrast
First Method
If you let A and B stand for the two things being compared, then you compare them point by point. Every time you say something about A, you also say something about B—right in the same sentence or in the sentence immediately following.

111

POINT BY POINT METHOD	BLOCK METHOD
TOPIC SENTENCE	**TOPIC SENTENCE**
BODY: ABABABABA BABABABABABABA ABABABABABABAB BABABABABABABA ABABABABABABAB BABABABABABABA ABABABABABABAB BABABABABABABA	BODY: AAAAAAAAA AAAAAAAAAAAAA AAAAAAAAAAAAA AAAAAAAAAAAAA BBBBBBBBBBBBB BBBBBBBBBBBBB BBBBBBBBBBBBB BBBBBBBBBBBBB
CONCLUSION	**CONCLUSION**

Second Method

If you let *A* and *B* stand for the two things being compared, then you can use the block method in which you tell all about *A*, then tell all about *B*. Thus you discuss *A* in a block and *B* in a block.

Keep in mind that these two patterns need not always be followed rigidly, but they do provide the clearest patterns for developing a comparison or contrast.

Topic Sentence

The topic sentence of a comparison or contrast paragraph is of primary importance because the writer's purpose **must** be clearly defined. Your topic sentence, therefore, should identify both items (subjects) to be compared or contrasted and tell the reader exactly what you are going to say about these items (attitude). Again, remember to narrow your topic sentence so that your purpose is clear to the reader and so that you can prove your topic sentence with specific details.

There are several things to remember as you write a topic sentence for a comparison/contrast paragraph. First, remember that you have two subjects, and your topic sentence must be carefully worded to show not just the attitude but also the kind of comparison or contrast you are going to make between the two.

Second, you must have some sort of point to make beyond a simple description of the two things you are comparing. Suppose that as the subject for your paragraph you decide to choose two pets. You might see, for example, that the sharp difference between Tuffy the pup and Hector the cat makes a good subject for a paragraph of contrast.

Now suppose that your first attempt at writing a topic sentence is this:

Our pup, Tuffy, is different from our cat, Hector.

comparing and contrasting

Such a topic sentence is poor because it lacks any real point. What you need to do is sharpen your topic sentence. For example, you might revise the topic sentence to read like this:

The difference in temperament between our pup, Tuffy, and our cat, Hector, is a constant source of amusement.

Now you have given a point to your topic sentence and can go on to develop a paragaraph based on the amusing differences between the two pets.

Third, a very close relationship exists between the topic sentence and the supporting details in a comparison or contrast. The whole meaning of a paragraph of this type hinges on the strength of the topic sentence. A vague topic sentence, one that is not specific, will cause the paragraph to fall apart. Usually, your controlling thought is expressed only once—and that **must** be in the topic sentence. In the body of the paragraph, then, the emphasis is on explanatory details which support the controlling idea.

Fourth, you must create reader interest with your topic sentence and hold it with vivid, specific details. To hold interest, avoid such overused topics as these:

College is different from high school.
Big dogs are harder to care for than small dogs.

These topics have been written about so often that almost anything you have to say will already be well known or generally accepted.

In choosing a subject, you might use a personal experience such as one of these:

My new steady is very different from my last one.
My mother and dad are very much alike.

Make sure the attitude in your topic sentence is specific.

Or you may examine some of your personal preferences:

comparing and contrasting

TV could never replace the movies for me.

English classes have always been exciting for me whereas math classes remain a bore.

Or you might investigate some topic that interests you and get facts from the library to support it:

The Communist and Fascist forms of government, although supposedly opposites, are really very much alike.

EXERCISE Va

Which of the following topic sentences would work for a comparison or contrast paragraph?

_____ 1. The movie version of *Jane Eyre* is far less complex than the novel.

_____ 2. The police have a difficult job.

_____ 3. A turkey is a better buy than a chicken.

_____ 4. Buying a home is a good investment.

_____ 5. Before the renovation, our town was deteriorating rapidly; but since the renovation, our town has a new face and a new spirit.

_____ 6. Taxes in the United States are not nearly so high as they are in most European countries.

_____ 7. Sociology is a fascinating subject.

_____ 8. Juvenile delinquents come from all classes of society.

_____ 9. Marijuana is less harmful than alcohol.

_____ 10. Jobs for teenagers are scarce these days.

Body

SELECTING DETAILS

Once you have decided on a good topic sentence, list all the points of comparison or contrast that you can think of as quickly as you can. This scratch outline enables you to jot down possible details while they are fresh in your mind. Next, review the scratch outline and eliminate any points that are irrelevant or unimportant. Save only the best. Then investigate the subject to find other points of comparison or contrast. Now organize your details in a logical sequence, making sure that you have no irrelevant details.

EXERCISE Vb

Eliminate the irrelevant sentences from the following paragraph. Underline the irrelevant sentences and list their numbers on the line below the paragraph.

(1) The lot of the American writer and that of his Soviet counterpart is a study in contrast. (2) For the American writer, dissent and criticism of the system is often a ticket to the best-seller list. (3) For the Soviet writer, criticism

of the state may well mean a ticket to oblivion or a Siberian labor camp. (4) The horrors of life in the slave labor camps has been graphically described by a number of Soviet writers. (5) The American writer frequently uses exaggeration and distortion either to glamorize the abnormal or to ridicule the norms of our society. (6) If the Soviet writer, on the other hand, fails to glorify the Communist system, he may find that his works will never appear in print. (7) Some Soviet writers, of course, enjoy all the comforts that the state can offer, including a comfortable city apartment and a dacha or country home. (8) While there are at least a few American writers who have chosen to promote the Marxist view and glorify Communism, any Soviet writer who chose to praise Western democracy and individual freedom might find himself hounded by the secret police. (9) The ruthlessness of the Soviet secret police is well known. (10) Perhaps the real proof of the difference between the American and the Soviet writer lies in the fact that no American writer is put in prison for his political views, but hundreds of Soviet writers have died in the slave labor camps of Siberia.

Look again at the two basic patterns of organization for the comparison/contrast paragraph. If you go back to the Tuffy and Hector contrast, you may choose either of two methods.

First Method

If you use the first method, the point-by-point comparison, every time you say something about Tuffy, you need to say something about Hector. You might, for example, point up the contrast at the outset by telling your reader that Tuffy is a

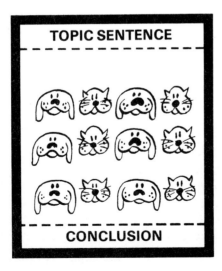

wooly, ball-of-fire pup of mixed breed and that Hector is a languorous, dignified cat of near-Persian ancestry.

Topic sentence: **Subject** (Tuffy and Hector) and **attitude** (amusing differences).

Every time you say something about Tuffy, you say something about Hector, either in the same sentence or in the sentence immediately following.

The concluding sentence would reinforce the controlling idea of amusing differences between the two.

With the first method, your comparison (pointing out likenesses) or contrast (pointing out differences) is made immediately.

You show one (*A*) and then the other (*B*). Thus, the basic organization of your paragraph looks like this:

I. Topic sentence
II. Development
A/B _____
_____ A/B _____
_____ A/B _____
_____ A/B _____
_____ A/B _____
III. Conclusion

Second Method
In the second, the block method, you put all of your material about Tuffy in the first part of your comparison/contrast and then put all of your material about Hector in the second half of your paragraph.

Topic sentence (same as first)

All about Tuffy _____

_____

_____ /*

All about Hector _____

_____

_____

Concluding sentence

* Note that the second method requires an explicit transition, a linking word or phrase, to join the two parts of the discussion.

Here are examples of transitions you might use.

Hector, on the other hand, ... etc.
As for Hector, ... etc.
Unlike Tuffy, Hector ... etc.
Hector, on the contrary, ... etc.
While Tuffy ..., Hector ... etc. (While Tuffy whizzes in blurred circles with a stolen sock, Hector simply looks on with half-closed eyes, disdainful of such puppy foolishness.)

In this method, your basic organization will look like this:

I. Topic sentence
II. Development
(subtopic one) AAAAAAAAA
(subtopic two) BBBBBBBBB
III. Conclusion

When deciding whether to use the point-by-point or block method, you should consider the merits of each. The point-by-point method is desirable when you want to emphasize detailed similarities and differences; you show them immediately to your reader by pairing one with the other. The block method, on the other hand, allows you to concentrate on one aspect at a time, giving the reader a full picture before crossing over to the other aspect of the comparison or contrast.

The method you choose, of course, depends on your purpose. The choice should not be random but should depend on exactly what you want to say. Generally, if you have a lot of details or information that is difficult to remember, the point-by-point method is preferable. On the other hand, if you have fewer or less specialized details, the block method is probably better.

Suppose you were going to contrast the Volkswagen and the Toyota, using the following points:

overhead cam	versus	pushrods
disc brakes	versus	drum brakes
rack and pinion steering	versus	recirculating ball steering

fuel injection	versus	carburetor
independent rear suspension	versus	live axle
rear-wheel drive	versus	front-wheel drive

These points are so technical that the average reader might forget what you said in a block. Therefore, point by point would be better in this case.

Look at the following paragraph contrasting a novel and the movie made from it. Because four rather specialized points are made in the topic sentence, here, too, point by point is preferred.

Although the novel *Tom Jones* and the movie made from it are both classics of their times, they differ widely in plot, setting, characterization, and theme. Both the novel and the movie focus on the same main plot, the love affair between Tom Jones and Sophia Western. However, in the novel, a half dozen or so vigorous subplots weave around the Tom and Sophia story, whereas in the movie, only the love affair is important. The setting of the novel, written in 1749, is a broad sociological world in which society is a thwarting force on the destinies of the characters. Society at all levels is corrupt; there is no legal or social protection for anyone not in the establishment. Wealth and social position alone assure survival. However, the movie version, made over 200 years later, portrays that eighteenth-century world only as a lovely background. In the novel, the characters tend to be types, as the names testify. Tom Jones is symbolically named to represent the ordinary young man, just as his guardian, Squire Allworthy, represents the good man, and Sophia Western stands for the typical young woman of Western civilization. In the movie version, however, since the love affair is the main interest, the personalities of Tom and Sophia are individualized. The theme of the novel presents life as a conflict between individuals and society in which men can win only if they have soft hearts and hard heads (instead of the all-too-frequent reverse). The theme of the movie presents life as a dance of young lovers on the trim lawns of England's green and pleasant land. Although both the movie and novel are satisfying works of art, the movie is a simple, rosy romance in contrast to the complex, grim, but funny realism of the novel.

Now look at the same basic idea, the contrast between a novel and the movie made from it, with a somewhat more general controlling idea. In this case, the block method may seem clearer.

Although the novel *Tom Jones* and the movie made from it are both classics, they differ widely in their effect on their audience. In the novel, the main plot is the love affair between Tom Jones and Sophia Western, but a half-dozen or so vigorous subplots weave around the Tom and Sophia story. Because of the numbers of characters in these many plots, the setting of the novel (written in 1749) is a broad, sociological world in which society is a thwarting force on the destinies of the characters. Society at all levels is corrupt; there is no legal or social protection for anyone not in the establishment. Wealth and social position alone assure survival. The reader, following the fortunes of Tom and Sophia, is equally caught up in the grim, violent, funny world of the eighteenth century. That world is at least as important as the characters, for their symbolic names testify that they are sociological types. Tom Jones represents the ordinary young man, and his guardian, Squire Allworthy, represents the good man. Because Tom, the squire, Sophia, and many minor characters are types, they keep the reader's attention focused on the controlling idea that life is a conflict between individuals and society. In that conflict the individuals lose unless they are softhearted and help each other and are hardheaded about their practical affairs. The movie version of the novel, made more than 200 years later, delights the viewer with a simple, rosy romance. Tom does suffer through some violent experiences with brutal soldiers, oversexed women, conniving relatives, and unjust courts, but there is never any doubt in the viewer's mind that he will—narrowly—escape. Since the love affair is so important in the movie, the characters deepen and become individualized. In the movie, they are not representative types but a glorious young man and woman with distinct personalities. The eighteenth-century world they live in certainly is not faultless, but generally the faults are played down or made amusing. The setting is not sociological environment but largely a quaint and lovely background. In this world, the reader knows that the course of true love will at last run smoothly. The movie presents life as a dance of young lovers on the trim lawns of England's green and pleasant land. Although both the novel and the movie version are satisfying comedies, the audience finds the novel realistic and thought-provoking but the movie romantic and endearing.

Which of the two paragraphs do you think is better? Do you think your preference is based on the method used?

The two following student paragraphs are good examples of the point-by-point method of development.

The majority of the people who watch television automatically associate character with actor; that is, people assume that the actor possesses the exact personality and qualities of the character whom he portrays. This could not be further from the truth, as is illustrated in the situation of Larry Hagman, who portrays the evil villain, J.R. Ewing, on the popular television series, *Dallas.* In actuality, Larry Hagman is a very kind, gentle man with a terrific sense of humor who touches everyone who comes in contact with him. J.R., on the other hand, is an evil, conniving oil tycoon who would easily stab his brother in the back in exchange for more power and money. Hagman has been a happily married man for the past twenty-five years. He feels that women should have equal rights, especially in marriage, in contrast to J.R. Ewing, who mistreats his wife terribly, chases women just for the challenge, and feels that women are only objects of possession. On television, J.R. is a high-class businessman who constantly wears very expensive tailored suits, whereas Larry Hagman, who is actually down-to-earth and fun-loving, frequently dresses in outlandish costumes ranging from a gorilla suit to a British policeman's uniform. Indeed, the character-actor assumption has no real value when associated with actor Larry Hagman and that character whom people "love to hate," J.R. Ewing.

Valerie Battalini

Realizing that good study habits are necessary for above average grades, I have drastically changed my old, disorganized method of studying to a more efficient system of study. With an ever-increasing work load, I have found it essential to organize both my time and my materials. For instance, with my old system of studying, I did not collect the various reference books, notebooks, and writing instruments that I needed to prepare for an exam. I would often leave my study area five or six times in an hour to search for a book that I needed desperately. My new study habits, on the other hand, include gathering every item I will need before I sit down to apply myself fully to the task at hand. Before, when I studied, I sat in a dimly lit room with loud rock music blaring in my ear or the television set tuned to my favorite program. However, with my new system of study, I sit in my well-lit kitchen with only the hum of the refrigerator to distract me, and I resist any urge to turn on the radio or TV. Sometimes, using my old system of study, I would sit for hours on end trying to get all of my studying accomplished. As a result, I would become bored and irritable. My mind would wander, and I would get angry at my teachers for assigning so much work—never realizing that it was I who made studying much harder than it actually was. Therefore, into my new study habits, I incorporated what I call a "goal and reward system." When I sit down to study, I establish a goal to accomplish in a particular amount of time. Then, if I satisfactorily attain my goal, I reward myself by listening to the radio or watching television for a half hour. Although I find it difficult at times to resume studying, I am reminded that if I achieve my goal, then my half-hour reward will be waiting for me. Finally, with my old study habits, I did not allot myself enough time to study for an exam—especially one that would encompass a great quantity of lecture notes. I would often wait until the last minute and then bombard my brain with a lot of material in a short span of time. Frequently, I would find myself in a state of panic because there was just not enough time to learn everything. Now I begin my studying well in advance of exams to allow time to absorb the material without a lot of strain on my nerves. This also helps me feel more confident when I go to take the exam. My new, more efficient method of studying includes none of the flaws found in my old study habits, and, as a result, my grades are improving.

Kim Strama

The next two student paragraphs are good examples of the block method.

In several ways, I am a notably different person today than I was three years ago. Three years ago, I was a rebel without a cause; I felt lost and desperate. In fact, I allowed my hair to grow until it reached my shoulders to display my rebelliousness. I was a thin teenager and wore contact lenses because I felt self-conscious wearing glasses. I was a shy and withdrawn person with very few friends. Also, I often felt sorry for myself and had little self-respect. I disliked people in general and authority in particular, and I was suspicious of anyone who was friendly toward me. Although I was shy, I had a quick and volatile temper; I exploded at the slightest insult. As a result, I was frequently involved in fisticuffs. Seeking escape, I was occasionally drunk or "high" on drugs. Today, on the other hand, I am a mature person, and I know which direction my life is headed. I am a short-haired conformist, and I wear glasses rather than contacts because I feel people should accept me for my personality and not for my appearance. Today, I make an effort to get involved with people, and, consequently, I have many friends. Furthermore, I feel that the world owes me nothing, and I try to make the most out of life. I am proud of my accomplishments and have resolved to improve myself in areas where I have previously failed. I respect authority now, and I attempt to be friendly toward anyone I happen to meet. In addition, I spend my free time in sports. I play football, baseball, basketball, and golf. I also enjoy table-tennis, billiards, and swimming. In summary, I have changed considerably. Today, I am nearly opposite to the person I was three years ago.

Dan Kleber

Students who have Mr. Brown and Mr. Smith are immediately aware of the difference in the lecturing manner of each teacher. Mr. Brown has a pleasant voice, which helps hold the interest of the students. He pronounces clearly in a rhythmic pattern, emphasizing key words. His moderate tone and inflected words make his lectures interesting. Mr. Brown also adds humor to his subject, and he welcomes questions from students who don't understand the material. He takes his time and explains slowly. He tries to make sure that his students understand a concept before he moves on to something new, and he is very enthusiastic about his subject. Mr. Smith, on the other hand, has a different tone, pronunciation, expression, and attitude from Mr. Brown's. He has a booming voice which commands rather than teaches, and sometimes it is hard to understand him because he runs his words together. His lectures are not as interesting as those of Mr. Brown either, because Mr. Smith speaks in a boring monotone. He also hates to be interrupted; feeling that he must cover everything, Mr. Smith teaches every class in a serious, determined mood. Thus, as the above points illustrate, the lectures of Mr. Brown and Mr. Smith are quite different.

Sue Pectovic

Whether you use the point-by-point method of comparison/contrast or the block method, make sure that your paragraph is balanced. Don't tell more about one half of the comparison/contrast than you do about the other.

Conclusion

The most effective conclusion for a comparison/contrast paragaraph is usually a final sentence which reinforces the controlling idea. In a paragraph about Tuffy and Hector, for example, you might conclude with a final sentence such as this: "If you could see Tuffy and Hector together, you could scarcely help laughing at the contrast between these two household playmates."

QUESTIONS FOR DISCUSSION

1. What difference is there between the way girls are brought up and the ways boys are brought up?
2. What effect do these differences in upbringing have on the way in which men and women behave?
3. Which is the weaker sex? What evidence can you give to support your answer?

ASSIGNMENT

Write a paragraph developed by comparison or contrast. Decide which kind of development, point-by-point or block, suits your subject better and then use this method throughout your paragraph. You may get a useful idea from the topics listed below. Remember, what you compare is not the most important thing. What is important is that you have some significant basis for your comparison or contrast.

Your hometown and another town or city

Discipline by your mother and your father

Two vacations

Two types of pets

Two rooms in your house

Drunk and sober

Two close friends

A book and a movie of the book

Two of your instructors

A book and its television version

Two methods of working off aggression

SENTENCES

Agreement of Subjects and Verbs

As you learned in Chapter I, the most important part of any sentence is the actor-action team—the **subject** and **verb.** Unfortunately, however, many writers do not realize that a subject and verb cannot work right as a team unless they are coordinated properly. In order to write good sentences, you must first understand that subjects and verbs have to agree in **number.**

Read the following sentences aloud:

The whole house smell like dead fish.
Bob are handsome.
Three blue spruce trees grows in her back yard.
Tom and his wife seldom speaks to strangers.

Do these sentences sound right to you? If they do, then you had better pay close attention to this section because each of the sentences above contains a serious error: the subject and verb do not agree in number. Verbs, like subjects, can be singular or plural. If you use a singular subject, then you must use a singular verb; if you use a plural subject, then you must use a plural verb.

What do singular verbs look like? When the subject is one place, one thing, or one person other than *I* or *you,* you add an s to a verb in the present tense to get a singular verb—one that you can use with a singular subject.

Jim plays football.
The engine sputters.
Dodge City looks like a tourist trap.
Mark stud*ies* every night. (If a verb ends in *y,* drop the *y* and add *ies.*)

If the subject of a sentence is plural (refers to two or more), then **do not add an s to the verb.**

Jim and Ed *play* football.
The engines *sputter.*
These places *look* like tourist traps.
Mark, Beth, and John *study* every night.

NOTE: As the examples above illustrate, you can refer to two or more things with one plural word (*they, engines, places*) or with two or more singular words (*Jim and Ed*).

Frequently, the form of the verb changes if the subject changes. For example:

I *am* eating pie.
He *is* eating pie.
You *are* eating pie.

Note that only the subject has any effect on the verb form:

They *are* eating steak and potatoes.
They *are* eating a chocolate cake.
They *are* eating before they go to the movies.

You may substitute a pronoun for any noun if this helps you decide whether a subject is singular or plural.

Singular	**Plural**
I	we
you	you
he/she/it	they

My dog (she) chases squirrels.
Not all dogs (they) chase squirrels.
The keys (they) of the old piano were a dirty yellow.
An elaborate dinner (it) with three fine wines was John's idea of a perfect evening.
The child, the cat, and the dog (they) go down the street together.
Neither Sean (he) nor Judy (she) is going to the picnic.
The class (it—as a single unit) agrees with the professor.

SPECIFIC PROBLEMS IN SUBJECT-VERB AGREEMENT

Identifying the True Subject

Since the verb form depends on the subject, you must

1. Identify the true subject.
2. See that the verb agrees.

Singular subjects call for singular verbs and plural subjects call for plural verbs. Don't be confused by nouns or pronouns that come between the subject and the verb.

The worst *feature* of these roads *is* the potholes.
       SUBJECT   VERB

A *line* of ragged and hungry children *waits* at the gate.
  SUBJECT   VERB

The *risk* to the workers *seems* unreasonably high.
  SUBJECT   VERB

The *repetition* of similar sounds *stirs* the emotions.
    SUBJECT   VERB

The words *roads, children, workers,* and *sounds* are plural, but they do not affect the verb form.

Using a Plural Verb with Compound Subjects

When two or more subjects are joined by *and,* they form a plural subject and require a plural verb.

My *cousin* **and** *one* of her classmates *are* going to Los Angeles.
The company *president* **and** his *secretary* *were* on the plane.

The exception to this rule occurs when the two subjects joined by *and* form a single unit.

Macaroni and cheese is quite nutritious.
White tie and tails is the correct dress.

Using the Correct Form with False Compounds
When the subject is followed by a phrase like *in addition to, as well as, accompanied by, together with*, these expressions do **not** take the place of *and*. They do **not** form a compound subject.

The *mayor,* as well as all of the council members, *is* going to attend the ceremony.
The *President,* accompanied by his aides and advisors, *is* scheduled to arrive tomorrow.
The *players,* as well as the coach, *are* elated by the victory over the Saints.

The phrase between the subject and the verb, often set off by commas, does not affect the verb form.

Using the Correct Form with Collective Nouns
Some of the more common collective nouns are *team, jury, class, committee, crew, gang, flock, family.* These collective nouns take singular verbs when the group acts as a unit.

The *jury is* ready to bring in its verdict.
The *class is* working on a practice test.
The *family is* gathered around the Christmas tree.

A plural verb should be used only when the sense of the sentence is plural, when it is clear that you mean the individual members and not the group.

A *flock* of geese *were* landing, one by one, on the still surface of the pond.
The *committee were* taking their seats. (Logically, they cannot all take the same seat.)

Using Nouns of Measurement, Weight, Time, or Money
Plural nouns that indicate a unit of measurement, weight, time, or money usually take a singular verb.

A thousand *bushels is* a poor yield.
Ninety-seven *dollars is* too much to pay.
Three hundred and sixty *pounds is* a mighty big man.

Using the Correct Verb Form in Sentences Beginning with Here, There, and Where
In sentences beginning with *here, there,* and *where,* the verb must agree with the subject that follows it.

Here *are* the *papers* Jim completed.
There *goes one* of Fleigel's trucks.
Where *are* those three *welders?*

Using the Correct Form with Other Inverted Sentences
There are other types of sentences in which the subject follows the verb.

Standing on the shelf *were* a model *plane and* a toy control *tower.*
Somewhere under the eaves *is* a giant hornets' *nest.*

Using the Correct Form with Correlative Conjunctions
Following are the commonly used correlative conjunctions: either . . . or, neither . . . nor, not only . . . but (also), not . . . but, / . . . or . . . .
　　　When compound subjects are joined by correlative conjunctions, the verb agrees with the nearer of the two subjects.

Either the patrolmen or the *sergeant is* responsible.
Neither the warden nor the *guards were* prepared for a riot.
Not only the scouts but the *scoutmaster was* completely confused.
The parents or the *child is* sure to suffer.

Using the Correct Form with Indefinite Pronouns
The following pronouns take singular verbs:

one	anyone	everyone	another	many a one
each	anybody	everybody	each one	anything
either	someone	nobody	another one	everything

Each of the girls *has* a good job.
Somebody has left the lights on.
Everybody in the whole class *has* a different opinion.

The indefinite pronouns *some* and *none* may be **singular or plural,** depending on the sense of the sentence.

None of the fathers *were* as tall as their sons.
None of the young workers *was* ready to take that job.
Some of the fish *were* bullheads.
Some of the meat *was* quite tender.

Using Singular Nouns that Are Plural in Form
The following nouns, though they look plural, always take *singular* verbs:

mathematics	politics	statistics
physics	civics	measles
economics	news	molasses

The following nouns always take *plural* verbs:

comparing and   pants   glasses   riches
contrasting   scissors   trousers   binoculars

EXERCISE Vc
Cross out the incorrect verb form in the following.

1. The weather (seems/seem) warmer now.
2. The clowns in this class (is/are) going too far.
3. Franco and one of his friends (was/were) in a wreck.
4. The covering on both the old chairs (need/needs) to be replaced.
5. Manuel and Alfredo (is/are) going stag to the dance.
6. Twenty-six dollars (is/are) is my total pay for the week.
7. Someone (has/have) taken my book.
8. Either Eileen or Ernestine (gets/get) the highest grades in this class.
9. Both John and his mother (looks/look) tired.
10. Everyone (sees/see) things differently.

EXERCISE Vd
Cross out the incorrect verb form in the following.

1. Either a wolf or wild dogs (was/were) killing the lambs.
2. Neither the girls nor their mother (was/were) at home.
3. Either of the plans (sound/sounds) sensible to me.
4. Too many parties or his own laziness (have/has) kept him from getting a promotion.
5. Not only the patrolmen but also the captain (was/were) taking bribes.
6. Standing at his desk (was/were) two of the welders.
7. Each of the twins (was/were) expected to graduate with honors.
8. A pile of dirty, oil-soaked rags (were/was) heaped in a corner.
9. My aunt and one of my cousins (is/are) going to Las Vegas.
10. Clearly stated in the letter (was/were) my qualifications for the job.
11. Joe and I (have/has) parties all the time.
12. She (wear/wears) the same necklace every day.
13. You (teach/teaches) me to swim, and I'll (teach/teaches) you to play pool.
14. The subject of Joe's papers (is/are) always football players.
15. My assignment for last Wednesday (was/were) two exercises and one paragraph.
16. Two exercises and one paragraph (was/were) due last Wednesday.
17. There (is/are) a dog barking in the alley.
18. There (was/were) three dirty ashtrays on the table where I ate lunch.
19. My mother, father, and sister (has been/have been) sick for almost a week.
20. My brother (see/sees) three movies a week.

EXERCISE Ve

Correct all errors in subject–verb agreement by drawing a line through the incorrect verb form and writing the correct form above it.

1. The cause of all the squeaks and rattles were the rusty fenders.

2. Seven-eighths of the area are under water.

3. There was fishing, swimming, and water skiing.

4. All the women, as well as Mr. Pecksniff, is expected to prepare the feast.

5. Each of those wild horses are ready to kick down the fence.

6. Although well-worn, the clothing of most of the people were neat.

7. The cattle rustler, together with all his cohorts, were corralled in the saloon.

8. Neither the chickens nor the farmer's wife were aware of the skunk in the hen-coop.

9. There is only a cedar chest and a piano left to be auctioned.

10. My two sisters and one of my nieces still lives in the house on Gramercy Street.

11. Results could be disastrous if the Secretary of Defense or high officials in the Pentagon makes that kind of mistake.

12. The best part of the whole show were the dancing bears.

13. Either coyotes or a puma were killing the lambs.

14. The whole team were happy over the tie with Bradford High.

15. There exist not a single reason for granting their request.

Agreement of Pronouns and Antecedents

If pronouns could talk, they would probably have a lot to complain about. People constantly misuse them. Even after proofreading, many writers (and speakers) overlook errors in pronoun usage, but using pronouns correctly is not difficult if you just keep this guideline in mind:

A pronoun must agree in number, gender, and person with the word that it refers to (its antecedent).

Here are some examples.

My *sisters,* Marie and Antoinette, said that *they* hated pumpkin pie; so Mom said, "Let *them* eat cake."
Alan said that *he* had just read a good definition of a class reunion: an excuse to get together to see who's falling apart.
As soon as it spotted the hunter, the *deer* vanished.

127

In the third example, the pronoun *it* comes before *deer*, the noun that it refers to. You can place a pronoun before or after its antecedent **as long as the antecedent is clear.**

SOME SPECIAL PROBLEMS IN PRONOUN-ANTECEDENT AGREEMENT

The Indefinite Antecedent

If your antecedent is indefinite—*anybody, anyone, somebody, someone, everybody, everyone, nobody, no one, each, either, neither, a doctor, a steelworker, the average businessperson,* and so on—then you need a singular pronoun. For example:

Everyone should have the right to live his life the way *he* sees fit.

This particular precept of pronoun-antecedent agreement (the use of the singular male pronoun to refer to an indefinite third person) needs to be more fully explained. Obviously, a mother, a daughter, a sister, a girlfriend, a grandmother, or a great aunt also has the right to live her life the way she sees fit, so women, as well as men, are included in the term *everyone.* Yet the sentence refers to living *his* life the way *he* sees fit. To many people, using a male pronoun to refer to persons in general seems illogical. Unfortunately, however, the alternative of using both the male and female pronoun forms every time you want to refer to an indefinite third party can weaken your writing. For example, an otherwise simple textbook explanation could become quite cumbersome and confusing:

When writing a narrative paragraph, the student should arrange the details of *his* or *her* narrative in chronological order. *He* or *she* should also narrow *his* or *her* subject to a single significant event and use the simplest past tense to relate *his* or *her* story to *his* or *her* reader. The student should also make sure that *his* or *her* narrative is unified. *He* or *she* should not include details that do not relate to *his* or *her* main point.

Can you imagine reading a whole book like this? If, on the other hand, you are making a brief statement, or if you are using an indefinite antecedent only a few times in your paragraph, then there is nothing wrong with using both the masculine and feminine pronouns. For example, you might begin a paragraph with the following topic sentence:

When I was a child, my father taught me that everyone has the right to express his or her opinions, but now that I am older, I realize, sadly, that my father himself never had the courage to express his own convictions.

Sometimes you can avoid the indefinite antecedent problem altogether by using a plural antecedent ("All *citizens* have the right to express *their* opinions"), but this alternative will not always work. You can't simply eliminate indefinite antecedents from your vocabulary. Traditionally, the pronouns *he, him,* and *his* have included both male and female, all humankind. Keep in mind, though, that one of the most important ideas in this book is that vivid, specific,

128

concrete language helps to create interesting, worthwhile writing. If you have many problems with indefinite antecedents, you are probably using too many pronouns and too many general, nonspecific words altogether.

The Missing Antecedent

Unless the antecedent is clear, a pronoun is meaningless. For example, "*She* witnessed the murder" means nothing to the sheriff until he knows who *she* is, so watch out for sentences such as the following:

WRONG: The whole softball team apologized, but *she* was too angry to listen. *Who* was too angry to listen? The sentence should include a specific antecedent for she.

CORRECT: The whole softball team apologized to *Mrs. Nelson,* but *she* was too angry to listen.

CORRECT: The whole softball team apologized to the *coach,* but *she* was too angry to listen.

WRONG: In Ireland, they say that Dingle Bay is a piece of heaven on earth.

CORRECT: The Irish say that Dingle Bay is a piece of heaven on earth.

The pronoun *it* is the one most likely to have the missing antecedent. Many writers use *it* so frequently that they forget they are using a pronoun. Consequently, they make errors like the following:

He got sick and died of *it*. [Of what? Pneumonia? Jungle rot?]
He got shot and *it* is in him yet. [What is in him yet?]

NOTE: In some commonly accepted sentences such as "It is raining," *it* has no antecedent and needs none.

The Vague Antecedent

Another problem is the use of *this, that, these,* and *those* without a specific antecedent.

WRONG: Steven would never deceive anyone about anything, and *this* is one of his most appealing qualities.

CORRECT: Steven would never deceive anyone about anything, and *this uncompromising honesty* is one of his most appealing qualities.

The Ambiguous Reference

Ambiguous means capable of being interpreted in more than one way; thus, if you use a pronoun that could logically refer to more than one noun, you have an ambiguous reference.

AMBIGUOUS: Bert told Ernie that he should marry Miss Piggy. [*Who* should marry Miss Piggy? Bert or Ernie?]

CLEAR: Bert said to Ernie, "You should marry Miss Piggy."
Bert suggested that Ernie marry Miss Piggy.
Bert said to Ernie, "I should marry Miss Piggy."

If you make a practice of placing a pronoun as close as possible to the word it refers to, you can decrease the chances of having an ambiguous reference:

AMBIGUOUS: Adam was arguing with the gardener about what type of snake *he* found under Eve's apple tree.
(The reader doesn't know whether *he* refers to Adam or to the gardener.)

CLEAR: *Adam* argued that the snake *he* found under Eve's apple tree was a copperhead, but the gardener insisted that it was a water moccasin.

CLEAR: Adam and Eve's *gardener* said that *he* found a copperhead under the apple tree, but Adam insisted that it was a water moccasin.

CLEAR: Adam was arguing with the gardener, Lucifer Temptowski, about what type of snake Mr. Temptowski found under Eve's apple tree.

EXERCISE Vf
Correct the errors in pronoun–antecedent agreement in the following sentences. If the sentence is correct, mark C at the end of the sentence.

1. Watching Jon's friends move my piano made me nervous because I thought that someone was going to hurt their back.
2. In my opinion, a person who votes for a candidate just because they agree with them on only one issue is a menace to democracy.
3. Randy arrived twenty minutes late for his job interview, and when they asked him to discuss his assets, he unwittingly replied, "I'm always very punctual."
4. None of the consumer advocates succeeded in getting their case past the Court of Appeals.
5. It's too cold to go swimming today.
6. Tonto told the Lone Ranger that he couldn't afford to buy a new horse.
7. The defendant fainted when the jury presented its verdict.
8. The members of the "Stamp Out Smut Society" announced that it had issued its last warning to the town's "wayward librarian."
9. Father Murphy's description of the new school superintendent was quite clear and succinct; he described Mr. Wimp as "the southern end of a horse going north."
10. Everyone who reads Robert Peck's novel, *A Day No Pigs Would Die,* says that they found themselves moved to laughter and to tears.
11. Each of Pamela's poodles had their own plot in Burbank's largest pet cemetery.
12. They say that time heals all wounds, but it doesn't always work that way.
13. Neither the teacher nor the student was willing to compromise his principles.
14. My oldest son is a nurse at one of the best hospitals in the country, and this is what my youngest son wants to do.

15. You can't teach a child to play a musical instrument if they really don't want to learn.
16. It doesn't matter how hard I study, I still can't get it.
17. Each member of Poland's Solidarity Union had to register their name in the Communist Party Headquarters.
18. In New Guinea, they say that the natives can endure a tremendous amount of pain.
19. Roberta suspected that Mr. Dempsey was a city boy when he asked her for "an implement with which to extract nails."
20. Although it was not supposed to be painful, my nose surgery turned out to be an excruciating experience.

INCOMPLETE AND ILLOGICAL COMPARISONS

In everyday conversation you frequently hear such statements as these:

It is just too hot.
Suzy is such a pretty girl.
The Ewings are so wealthy.

These are incomplete comparisons.

1. In writing, avoid the words *so*, *such*, and *too* unless you complete the comparison.

   INCOMPLETE: We had such a big dinner.
   COMPLETE: We had such a big dinner *that I didn't even want breakfast the next morning.*
   INCOMPLETE: It is such a pretty little cottage.
   COMPLETE: It is such a pretty little cottage *that I have often dreamed of living there.*

   NOTE: If no comparison is intended, replace the *so*, *such*, or *too* with *very*, *extremely*, or *exceedingly*.

   INCOMPLETE: Suzy is so pretty.
   COMPLETE: Suzy is extremely pretty.

2. Do not omit words necessary to make a comparison clear and exact.

   INCOMPLETE: Ruth works as hard, if not harder, than her husband.
   COMPLETE: Ruth works *as* hard *as* her husband, if not harder.

3. Avoid thoughtless or illogical comparisons.

   ILLOGICAL: His salary was lower than a janitor.
   COMPLETE: His salary was lower than a janitor's salary.
   COMPLETE: His salary was lower than that of a janitor.

131

ILLOGICAL: The Sahara is larger than any desert in the world.
COMPLETE: The Sahara is larger than any other desert in the world.
COMPLETE: The Sahara is the largest desert in the world.

EXERCISE Vg
Rewrite the following sentences to make them clear and complete.

1. They were such good friends and found life so peaceful in the country.

   _____

2. Dr. Wilkerson was too much of a scholar.

   _____

3. Because of her experience, she deserves a more responsible position.

   _____

4. I'm glad the garage Mr. Pottle built for us is not like any of our neighbors.

   _____

5. Like many other leaders, his greed and thirst for power led to his downfall.

   _____

6. The cheetah is faster than any animal.

   _____

7. Harold is such a handsome man, and I am so fond of him.

   _____

8. John is as bright, or brighter, than his brother.

   _____

9. Mary has a personality like an angel.

   _____

10. The World Trade Center is taller than any building in New York.

   _____

WORDS

Metaphor and Simile

One of the important ways in which we are able to understand new things or new ideas is to compare these new and unknown things to other things and ideas that we do know. Language helps us to do this by a device known as a **metaphor**—a variety of comparison, usually made in very few words, which lights up our understanding. The characteristics of a good metaphor are that it creates an image and that it is imaginative (notice the similarity of those two words) and that

**He manipulated the faculty like puppets
on a string.**

it is not worn out by overuse. Metaphors are sometimes divided into two kinds,
simile and metaphor. Sometimes both kinds are simply known as metaphors.

A **simile** says that one thing is *like* another—"A is like B." A **metaphor**
says that one thing **is** another—"A is B."

A simile makes its comparison with words such as *like, as,* and *than:*

Her hair hung down her pallid cheeks *like* seaweed on a clam.
We spend our years *as* a tale that is told.
How sharper *than* a serpent's tooth it is to have a thankless child.
He manipulated the faculty *like* puppets on a string.

NOTE: Not every comparison is a simile. For example, if you say that the
city of Sao Paulo is like New York City, you have made a comparison, but no
simile is involved. On the other hand, when the poet says, "My love is like a réd,
red rose," he isn't making a literal comparison. He certainly doesn't mean that his
sweetheart has long, prickly stems.

Remember that to be a simile, a comparison must make an image; it must not merely attempt to convey information but must aim to deepen understanding through imagination.

In a metaphor, the comparison is implied rather than expressly stated. The metaphor, in effect, goes one step further than the simile; instead of saying that something is "like" something else, it implies that something **is** something else.

Yesterday *is* but a dream.
Our doubts *are* traitors.

When Snoopy climbs on top of his doghouse and proclaims: "Happiness is a warm puppy," he is using a metaphor. A metaphor is a comparison of two things in a **non**literal sense. The literal meaning of a word is its strict dictionary meaning—exactly what the word denotes. For example, Snoopy could have used the literal meaning of happiness and said:

Happiness is the quality or state of being delighted, pleased, content, or glad.

but it wouldn't have had the same effect as

Happiness is a warm puppy.

By using the positive connotation of a "warm puppy" instead of the denotation of happiness, Snoopy creates a feeling of happiness. Who could feel anything but happy when he pictures himself snuggling up with a cute, little, soft, warm puppy?

Metaphors can add vividness to your writing. They can conjure up an image in a very few words. (That's why poets use them so much.) However, there are several things you must beware of in using the metaphor:

1. Make sure your metaphor is clear.
    There will be little chance for error in the simile, "She was quick as a cat"; but if you use the metaphor "She was a cat," your readers may get a different image than quickness. One may think of sleekness or gracefulness. Another may get the image of a gossip whose tongue is sharp, or of a hissing, clawing monster.
2. Don't mix your metaphors.
    Although often amusing, mixed metaphors do not give a clear picture to the reader. If, for example, on describing a solitary and desolate wilderness, you use ". . . where the hands of man have never set foot," the reader will respond—but with laughter. If you say, "Like a cougar stalking its prey, he ran around like a chicken with its head cut off," you have certainly given the reader a confused picture.
3. Don't be afraid to try the extended metaphor.
    The comparison does not have to be completed in a few words. Perhaps your whole paragraph will be based on the metaphor. For example, you might have as your topic sentence "From his throne high in the loftiest tree in the forest, the eagle surveys his realm." Then you can write your entire paragraph by comparing the eagle to a king.

Cliché

A metaphor that has been used over and over again is called a **cliché**. You will want to use metaphors in your paragraphs, but the surest way to bore your audience is to fill up your writing or your speech with clichés. These worn-out phrases no longer create an image or carry meaning. Notice that clichés are phrases, not single words. Although a single word may be ill-chosen for a particular use (because it is inaccurate or vague or too general), a single word at least escapes the curse of being a cliché. The word *snow*, for example, always creates an image, but *white as snow* has been used so many times that it no longer stimulates the imagination.

Clichés generally fall into one of the following three categories:

1. Worn-out quotations, like *home sweet home*, *birds of a feather*, *you can't keep a good man down*
2. Overused combinations of words, like *at this point in time*, *last but not least*, *blushing bride*, *have a nice day*
3. Worn-out metaphors, like *pretty as a picture*, *good as gold*, *sly as a fox*

Since these threadbare metaphors are the most boring of all clichés, you must make every effort to avoid them in your writing. This isn't difficult to do once you become aware of them.

Here are a few examples:

burn your bridges behind you
turn a cold shoulder (*or* turn over a new leaf)
like water over the dam
pouring money down a rat hole (*or* down the drain)
as bald as an egg (*or* a billiard ball)
as dumb as an ox
as playful as a kitten
as drunk as a skunk (*or* a fish *or* a hoot owl)
as fresh as a daisy

See how many you can add to the list.

EXERCISE Vh
Read the following metaphors. Tell which are effective. If the metaphor is not effective, explain why it is not.

1. He was as effective as a blind umpire.

_____

2. He was as dangerous as a bull in a china shop.

_____

3. We must iron out these tangles.

_____

4. She was as graceful as a newborn colt.

_____

5. The new treasurer is a bottleneck that must be sidestepped.

_____

6. It is as welcome as an F in math.

_____

7. He wolfed down his dinner.

_____

8. He strained at the leash.

_____

9. He was a beaver about his work.

_____

10. He lifted his feet and put them down like a dog walking in water.

_____

11. The modern cop is a savage with Mace replacing the spear.

_____

12. Communism is a hyena sitting back on its haunches watching warily from a safe distance until the democracies destroy themselves.

_____

EXERCISE Vi
Use a dictionary to find the literal meanings of the italicized words. Then write your own explanation of each word by using a metaphor.

EXAMPLES

war

Literal: War is a major armed conflict between nations or between organized parties within a state.
Metaphor: War is hell.

frustration

Literal: Frustration is the feeling that one has been "prevented from achieving a goal or gratifying a desire."
Metaphor: Frustration is knowing the answer to the last essay question but having only five minutes left to finish the test.

1. *marriage*

Literal _____

Metaphor _____

2. *divorce*

Literal _____

Metaphor _____

3. *happiness*

   Literal _____

   Metaphor _____

4. *loneliness*

   Literal _____

   Metaphor _____

5. *greed*

   Literal _____

   Metaphor _____

6. *death*

   Literal _____

   Metaphor _____

7. *love*

   Literal _____

   Metaphor _____

8. *vanity*

   Literal _____

   Metaphor _____

9. *security*

   Literal _____

   Metaphor _____

10. *freedom*

    Literal _____

    Metaphor _____

EXERCISE Vj
Improve the following sentences by rewriting them to eliminate all the clichés.

1. Peg will never be ready in time for the party; she's as slow as molasses in January.

   _____

2. Uncle Frank always tries to be funny, but his jokes are as old as the hills.

   _____

3. No wonder Nancy's husband weighs 300 pounds; he eats like a horse.

   _____

4. I could feel myself getting nervous; my head was as warm as toast, and my hands were as cold as ice.

_____

5. My boss probably thinks that I'm as nutty as a fruitcake because she always manages to walk into my office when I'm talking to myself.

_____

6. If you think you're going to get any money from him, you're barking up the wrong tree.

_____

7. Even though Pete sometimes acts like he's dumb as a doorknob, he's really as sly as a fox.

_____

8. Although my grandfather is 90 years old, his mind is still as sharp as a tack.

_____

9. Papa thinks that Matthew is as cute as Christmas and as good as gold.

_____

10. Someone forgot to put the cheese back into the refrigerator; it's as hard as a rock.

_____

EXERCISE Vk
Underline all clichés in the following paragraph. Then rewrite this paragraph without using any clichés.

Variety is the spice of life, and my husband, Gene, is living proof. Gene is as strong as a horse. You should see him when he gets mad; his face turns as red as a beet, and he seems as brave as a lion and as fierce as a tiger. Sometimes, though, he can be as gentle as a dove, but trying to get him to help me with the housework is like pulling teeth. He's always as hungry as a bear, but he refuses to help me with the dishes; he becomes as stubborn as a mule. He finds more excuses than Carter has liver pills. He claims that he's as busy as a beaver and has a million things to do. I think he has his fingers in too many pies, but I can't tell him anything. Talking to him is like talking to a brick wall; he gets madder than a hatter and makes me feel that I'm about as dumb as an ox. Then, quick as a wink, he'll start purring like a kitten and tell me that I'm the apple of his eye. All of a sudden, he's the true-blue, one-in-a-million husband, and I'm sitting on top of the world looking at the skies through rose-colored glasses; so, married life may not be a bowl of cherries, but don't knock it until you've tried it.

dividing and classifying

ORGANIZATION

Division and classification are essential as we attempt to make sense out of the world around us and the people in it. By the time you get to college, classification affects many areas of your life. For example, you may be classified as a Protestant, Catholic, or Jew; as a Democrat, Republican, or Independent; as an English major, biology major, criminal justice major, or some other. Sooner or later, almost every bit of usable information about you is recorded according to some classification, including sex, marital status, educational level, annual income, home ownership, credit standing, number of dependents, and many other categories.

In your writing, often the best way to explain an object, process, or idea is this:

1.   Break it down into parts (division)
2.   Arrange these divisions according to some sensible pattern (classification)

For example, a textbook for a college course in law enforcement might explain a pre-trial process through a chronological (time) division which breaks down into five steps: (1) arrest, (2) booking, (3) detention or release, (4) formal accusation, and (5) preliminary hearing. Each step, in turn, would then be discussed. An auto mechanic's handbook might explain the principles of an internal combustion engine by dividing the operation into its four parts—intake, compression, power, and exhaust—and then show the reader how each part relates to the whole.

Classification, then, is a process of bringing order out of confusion by breaking down a general topic into its component parts. (It's an intellectual parallel to sorting the clothes after you take them out of the dryer.) By sorting out the parts of the whole, you create a logical order.

There may be a variety of principles that determine what categories you decide upon for your order, but all you have to do is decide which principle you are going to use and stick to it. It is your created order, and the only rule you must follow is to be consistent.

For example, look at some of the ways you could divide the members of a college football team. You can separate them:

> by when they are in the game
> > offensive team
> > defensive team
> > special teams
> > > kickoff
> > > punt
> > > punt return
> > > goal line stand
> > > kickoff return
> > > short yardage
> by positions (offensive)
> > linemen
> > backs
> > ends or flankers
> by ability
> > first team
> > second team
> > scrubs
> by seniority
> > four-year men
> > three-year men
> > two-year men

You could, of course, divide them by height, weight, high school teams, scholastic ability, or any number of things. Just be sure that all members of the group are included and that you do not switch categories.

Classification is very closely related to outlining, which is also a process of making order out of confusion. Suppose you wanted to write an article on the main types of churches in your community. You might classify them this way:

TYPES OF DEVELOPMENT	TYPES OF EXPOSITION	PARTS OF A PARAGRAPH
1. DESCRIPTION 2. NARRATION 3. *EXPOSITION	1. DEFINITION 2. COMPARISON 3. CONTRAST 4. EXAMPLE 5. ETC.	1. TOPIC SENTENCE 2. BODY 3. CONCLUDING SENTENCE

I. Christian
  A. Catholic and Orthodox
    1. Roman Catholic
    2. Greek Orthodox
  B. Protestant
    1. Methodist
    2. Baptist
    3. Presbyterian
    4. Episcopalian
    5. Lutheran
II. Jewish
  A. Orthodox
  B. Conservative
  C. Reform

Or you might classify them by number of members. Any of various methods of classification might suit your purpose, but, again, you should stick to one method.

You frequently go through the process of classifying before you begin to write. Suppose you are trying to decide how to write your next English assignment. In your mind, you would go through the various methods of development you are now familiar with. Instead of a hodgepodge of possibilities, you can classify the kinds of development we have studied into description, narration, and exposition. You can further subdivide exposition into definition, comparison and contrast, example and illustration, and classification and division.

As you have worked through this textbook, you have repeatedly seen the parts of a paragraph classified as topic sentence, body, and conclusion. Such classifying helps you understand the organization of a good expository paragraph.

You have also repeatedly seen the three areas into which this study of English is divided and classified: (1) organization, (2) sentence, and (3) word.

Topic Sentence

Like all topic sentences, the topic sentence for a paragraph of division and classification must have a clear subject and attitude. In addition, it must indicate the areas and the number of categories into which you are going to classify your topic.

Which of the following topic sentences imply clear divisions or classifications?

Public speakers fall into three categories: the assured, the anxious, and the indifferent.

I am convinced that the Toyota Land Cruiser is more rugged than the Jeep CJ5.

My boyfriend has a unique definition of love.

EXERCISE VIa

Which of the following sentences would be appropriate for a division and classification paragraph?

_____ 1. The average college freshman today must divide his or her time among at least three different roles.

_____ 2. Migrant workers are very poorly paid.

_____ 3. There are three different kinds of students at our school: the brain, the regular guy, and the goof-off.

_____ 4. Writing a good paragraph requires four distinct processes.

_____ 5. Food stamp programs are wasteful.

_____ 6. A person's life can be divided into five distinct stages, but one is far more important than the others.

_____ 7. Church is an uplifting experience for many people.

_____ 8. Customizing a car involves working with the body, the engine, and the interior.

_____ 9. The winter of 1980–81 is one to remember.

_____ 10. Many factors determine success, but the most important is being in the right place at the right time.

Body

If you want your paragraph of division and classification to be clear, follow these guidelines:

1. Make sure the classification is logical and consistent.
2. Arrange the body in logical order (the horse goes before the cart).
3. Explain each part of the body fully.

LOGICAL CLASSIFICATION

Classification should be useful and informative. You must have a single, logical basis for your division and classification. Be sure that all members of the group are included and that you do not switch categories. The following classification of a football team is illogical:

defensive backs
defensive linemen
letter men

Don't put the cart before the horse.

Letter men does not fit here because it is based on a different category—experience and ability—but the other two are based on the position played.

LOGICAL ORDER

The purpose of division and classification is to give the reader a better understanding of the process, concept, or object that is being examined. Breaking a concept down into its component parts will not help the reader understand that concept unless you show how each part relates to the whole concept. In order to do this, you must present the parts in a logical order. If you are explaining a procedure, take the reader from the first step to the last step; don't present the first step, then the last step, then all of the steps in between. If you are explaining the job requirements of a registered nurse, begin with the least important requirement and proceed to the most important requirement. If you are explaining the structure of the human brain, classify or divide the different parts of the brain in some sort of logical order, such as according to function—from the least important section to the most important section—or according to location—from the front of the brain to the base.

ADEQUATE DEVELOPMENT OF EACH PART

To be adequately developed, a paragraph of classification and division must do two things. First, the classification must include all members of the group. If you are explaining about different kinds of drivers, be sure that you identify and thoroughly explain each kind. Second, each member of the group must be discussed at approximately the same length as all the others. Don't classify some drivers as "defensive" and describe them in one sentence if your other types are discussed in five sentences.

Make sure that the body of your classification and division paragraph includes **all** the members of the class and that each division has a **fair share** of the development.

The following paragraphs were written by students in a freshmen English class.

143

In the first example, notice that, although the paragraph is lengthy, it is unified and consistent.

Since first bursting forth on the music scene more than twenty years ago, Bob Dylan's songs have gone through four major and distinct changes: (1) social consciousness and protest songs; (2) angry, cynical "attack" songs; (3) simple songs of life and love; and (4) religious songs of God, lifestyles, and the hereafter. In the early 1960's, he was an inspired poet who had an extraordinary gift for writing with overpowering authority, simplicity, and beauty. His songs were original, penetrating, and full of images, and they forced people to think. His voice was harsh, but he sang with such urgency and emotion that he was called the voice of his generation. His songs were about war, poverty, injustice, and discrimination, and they conveyed his thoughts with amazing intensity and feeling without using the usual clichés or meaningless slogans that so many other songs did. In 1965, he abandoned the civil rights and conventional protest songs and turned to rock n' roll. His songs were mean, spiteful, angry, and full of vengeance, hatred, scorn, and resentment. Instead of accompanying himself with the acoustic guitar and harmonica, he used an electronically amplified guitar, along with two additional guitarists, a drummer, an organist, and a pianist. The songs captured the frustrations and turbulence of the times and left a deep, lasting impression on most of those who heard them. Following a near fatal motorcycle accident, marriage, and fatherhood, Dylan's music changed again: he returned to the acoustical guitar and wailing harmonica. His new songs showed a reversed outlook on life, a basic feeling of being glad to be alive. They were songs of pleasure, pain, love, and frustration, and they were no longer defensive. There was now tenderness where there was previously contempt. They were sung with a softness and mellowness instead of the previous sneering and snarling; he had turned his attentions from the world without to the world within. In the late 1970's, he got divorced and became a born-again Christian. His songs were now full of preachings and subtle accusations toward mankind in general. The songs are a plea to humanity to "clean up its act" before it is too late. The music has changed to a gospel sound, but the singer's brilliance still shines through. Dylan's music now reflects a new dimension of an old attitude, and since he thrives on changes, there will undoubtedly be much more to come.
Judy Dunham

Another kind of classification divides the body of the paragraph into clear steps according to a time sequence. In the following example, the student uses this form of classification with a humorous twist.

If you ever decide that you would like to be eaten by a shark, you need only follow several basic steps. First, choose a deserted beach with no record of previous attacks. Then, wait for a moonlit night so that the shark can see you plainly from below the surface of the water. Now that you are certain of being a good target, dive in and swim out into deep water. Next, splash the water with your hands and feet; this will bring the hungry fish in close to take a look at its potential snack. (It is preferable to have a few cuts or open wounds bleeding freely in the water.) The dinner bell has now been rung. Make sure that you are alone, so that once the shark starts to nibble, it won't be deprived of its meal by someone who is pulling you to safety. The last step consists of simply lying back and waiting; the shark won't be long in coming.
Joe Aversa

Another frequent use of classification is to show characteristics of a type. In the following student example, the writer classifies three dominant characteristics of an avid basketball player.

The avid basketball player can be identified by three basic oddities that set him apart from the crowd around him. First, the hooping fanatic will have long, gangly arms which drag on the ground and cause brushburns on his fingers. Many times such a person has cried out, "Ow, you're stepping on my fingers!" This is not an oddity in itself, but when you consider that the injured basketball player is standing straight up, you get an idea of just how long his arms are. Second, our erstwhile slam-dunker has a tendency to chase people who move around him. This can often be noted at a bus stop. An executive may be late for a meeting, and to make up for lost time, he dashes from his office and bolts for the bus entrance. Like a well-toned sprinter, the roundballer darts after him and takes a defensive stance at the curb, preventing the dazed executive from entering the bus. After a confusing five seconds of briefcase slapping and sidestepping, our red-faced hero realizes where he is and begs off muttering, "Sorry, man, you want the foul?" Third, a true hoopster reacts to anything vaguely resembling a basketball. This final item may be the most humorous to a nonplayer, but it is also the most important aspect of a basketball player's nature. While sitting at the breakfast table, do *not* simply hand the hooper a grapefruit. You must call him by name and say, "Here, this is a grapefruit. Would you like it?" I cannot begin to tell you how important it is to emphasize the word "grapefruit," or else you may end up with a ceiling full of yellow mush. If you detect any of these three symptoms in yourself, do not abandon hope, because recognizing the fact that you may be a "jay-buster" is the first step in treating the affliction. On the other hand, you could go with the flow. You may not be accepted socially, but you will be a killer on the court. You must decide which is more important.

Thomas Drop

The following brief paragraph by a noted author further illustrates the use of division and classification.

There are roughly three New Yorks. There is, first, the New York of the man or woman who was born here, who takes the city for granted and accepts its size and its turbulence as natural and inevitable. Second, there is the New York of the commuter—the city that is devoured by locusts each day and spat out each night. Third, there is the New York of the person who was born somewhere else and came to New York in quest of something. Of these three trembling cities the greatest is the last—the city of final destination, the city that is a goal. It is this third city that accounts for New York's high-strung disposition, its poetical deportment, its dedication to the arts, and its incomparable achievements. Commuters give the city its tidal restlessness; natives give it solidity and continuity; but the settlers give it passion. And whether it is a farmer arriving from Italy to set up a small grocery store in a slum, or a young girl arriving from a small town in Mississippi to escape the indignity of being observed by her neighbors, or a boy arriving from the Corn Belt with a manuscript in his suitcase and a pain in his heart, it makes no difference: each embraces New York with the intense excitement of first love, each absorbs New York with the fresh eyes of an adventurer, each generates heat and light to dwarf the Consolidated Edison Company. *E. B. White, "Here Is New York"*

Conclusion

Don't forget that your classification paragraph needs a conclusion. Don't leave the reader's mind focused on the last part of the topic that you classified, but rather on the topic as a whole, on the controlling idea presented in your topic sentence. For example, if you are analyzing the different ways to drive a snowmobile—sitting position, kneeling position, and standing position—then don't conclude your paragraph with a sentence about the standing position; conclude it with a statement that ties the paragraph together, such as, "The position that you choose will depend upon driving conditions." To use a sentence such as, "The standing position is also good for traction," would not conclude the paragraph. It would only conclude **one part** of the paragraph. Remember that a paragraph consists of three parts: topic sentence, body, and **conclusion.** Look at the last sentence in each of the student paragraphs presented in the previous section. Do you think that they are good conclusions? Do they conclude the whole paragraph or just one part of the paragraph?

Here is the basic outline for a paragraph of division and classification:

Topic sentence: North Carolina consists of three distinct regions, sloping from west to east.
1. The high, cool mountain region of the west includes the Blue Ridge and Great Smoky Mountains.
2. The central plateau, known as the Piedmont, comprises the industrial heart of the state.
3. The sandy coastal plain slopes gently eastward from fertile farmlands to the tidewater and the Outer Banks.
Conclusion: In one long slope from the Appalachians to the Atlantic, North Carolina falls into three distinctly different natural regions.

Questions for Discussion
1. From courses you have taken and textbooks you have read, what other examples of division and classification can you cite?
2. How do zoologists, botanists, geologists, and ornithologists make use of division and classification?
3. How many different ways can you classify Americans? (The first twenty ways should be easy, but try for forty or fifty.)

Assignment

Write a paragaraph of division and classification, making sure that your topic sentence clearly announces what you are going to explain and that your development supports all parts of your topic sentence. Include with your paragraph an outline showing its structure. You may want to use one of the following subjects.

Types of	Chronological division of	Spatial division of
drivers	storm	kitchen or living room
bosses	church service	your campus
baseball fans	studying for a test	department store
Christmas gifts	preparing for a wedding	playground
sweethearts	choosing a pet	basement

SENTENCES

The sentences in a division/classification paragraph, as in any paragraph, are not separate islands of thought. They are parts of a whole which must be linked together through various devices. The most important unifying device is the topic sentence itself. Every sentence in the paragraph needs to be clearly related to the controlling idea. Furthermore, the sentences must be arranged in some sequence to provide the reader with an ongoing progression of thought. You need an orderly and sensible pattern of development to take your reader with you.

Imagine, for a moment, that each supporting detail is one step in a staircase which you have carefully constructed for the reader. The reader begins at the top, where she receives the controlling idea, and cautiously descends toward the bottom. At each step, the reader gains another level of insight about your controlling idea. When she reaches the bottom, the reader should be fully aware of your purpose—if you have built a good stairway. What would happen, however, if your stairs were shaky—or if some did not fit—or if some were missing? The reader would probably become distracted and stumble; as a result, she might forget some details, or even the controlling thought. This would force her to return to the top and start all over again. A poorly constructed stairway of details not only wastes the reader's time, but also makes her frustrated and angry with you, the writer. She may eventually give up in disgust, climb onto the bannister, slide to the bottom, and forget the whole thing. You cannot afford to let this happen!

Even though your details are presented in a logical order, the problem of **smooth** passage from top to bottom still remains. It is your job to keep the reader from becoming distracted. You want her to devote full attention to the information you are trying to convey. This smoothness is called **continuity.**

A paragraph is said to have good continuity when ideas are smoothly linked together. The linking process is called **transition,** and the bridges between ideas are called **transitional devices.** The proper use of transitional devices can make you a better writer.

1. They help to clarify meaning by bridging the gap from one idea to the next.
2. They help to keep the reader from becoming distracted or disoriented; he or she is able to follow more clearly what you are saying.
3. They help your style to become smoother; it will flow more easily and your writing will not be choppy.

```
┌─────────────────────────────┐
│ UNIFYING DEVICES            │
│ 1. ENUMERATION              │
│ 2. PRONOUNS                 │
│ 3. CONNECTING               │
│    WORDS                    │
│ 4. REPETITION               │
│ 5. PARALLEL                 │
│    STRUCTURE                │
└─────────────────────────────┘
```

How to Make Your Paragraph Stick Together

Some of the devices that aid unity and continuity in the development of the paragraph are (1) enumeration, (2) reference of pronouns, (3) use of transitional words and phrases, (4) repetition of key words and phrases, and (5) parallel wording.

Let us examine these devices more closely.

ENUMERATION Using words such as *first, second, third,* or *then, later, finally* serve to guide the reader in step-by-step fashion through the development of the paragraph. Such devices are especially helpful in a paragraph providing specific information or giving explicit instructions to the reader.

The following passage illustrates how enumeration can aid paragraph unity and coherence.

We human beings have certain basic needs that are so much a part of our natures as to be almost universally recognized. *First,* we have physiological needs directly related to survival and self-preservation. . . . *Second,* we have a need for security, including the desire for safety, stability, and some sense of order. . . . *Third,* we have a need for love and belongingness. . . . *Fourth,* we have a need for esteem, including not only self-respect, but also the desire for attention, dignity, and appreciation. . . . *Fifth,* we have a need for self-actualization or self-fulfillment. . . .

Note: Never use *firstly, secondly, thirdly.*

When one is writing on technical subjects or giving explicit instructions, numbers are frequently used to ensure clarity and precision, as in the following example.

These, then, as every student pilot learns, are the four forces that act on an airplane in flight: (1) weight pulls it down, but (2) lift of its wings holds it up; (3) drag holds it back, but (4) pull of the propeller keeps it going.

Note: The numbers in parentheses do not change the other punctuation. Numbers, however, are not ordinarily used in the paragraphs you write in freshman composition class.

PRONOUN REFERENCE   Using pronouns such as *he, she, it, these, we, those,* or *they* to refer to a subject named in a previous sentence helps to unify the paragraph.

The following passage shows how the repetition of the pronoun can unify a paragraph: *We* carries the idea of *us as a people* throughout the paragraph.

Something will have gone out of *us as a people* if *we* ever let the remaining wilderness be destroyed; if *we* permit the last virgin forests to be turned into comic books and plastic cigarette cases; if *we* drive the few remaining members of the wild species into zoos or to extinction; if *we* pollute the last clean air and dirty the last clean streams and push our paved roads through the last of the silence, so that never again will Americans be free in their own country from the noise, the exhausts, the stinks of human and automotive waste, and so that never again can *we* have the chance to see ourselves single, separate, vertical, and individual in the world, part of the environment of trees, and rocks, and soil, brother to the other animals, part of the natural world and competent to belong in it.   *Wallace Stenger,* The Sound of Mountain Water

CAUTION: Pronoun reference must be clear and consistent.

1. The noun that the pronoun represents must be given first. Do not start out with *this, that, they, it, he,* or *she;* the reader will not know to whom or to what the pronoun refers.

2. The pronoun must agree in number with the noun to which it refers. If the noun is *child,* then you must use a singular pronoun, *he* or *she* — not *they.* If the noun is *people,* you must use a plural pronoun, *they* — not *he* or *one.*

3. The pronoun must be consistent in class or person with the noun to which it refers. If the noun is *motorist,* the pronoun you must use is *he,* not *you* or *we.* If the noun is *company,* the pronoun you must use is *it,* not *he* or *they.* Be sure to avoid inconsistent shifts in pronoun reference.

INCONSISTENT: Each student at this college must pass freshman English. They can't graduate if they don't.

Do not use a pronoun until you have identified the subject.

149

CONSISTENT: Each student at this college must pass freshman English. He can't graduate if he doesn't.

dividing and
classifying

INCONSISTENT: A middle-income family cannot afford the tuition. They don't qualify for financial aid.

CONSISTENT: A middle-income family cannot afford the tuition. It doesn't qualify for financial aid.

INCONSISTENT: John has no one to support except himself. You don't need a big income.

CONSISTENT: John has no one to support except himself. He doesn't need a big income.

TRANSITIONAL WORDS AND PHRASES

Transitional words and phrases serve as pointers to guide the reader in much the same way as road signs guide the motorist. Words and phrases such as *of course, as a result, on the other hand, nevertheless, however,* and *consequently* direct the reader along the course of development from topic sentence to conclusion.

Words and phrases like *in the morning, later, afterwards, next, in the evening, at last,* or *finally* show progression or changes in time. Leaving out such words can be very confusing to your reader. Consider the following:

The party was a real blast; it didn't break up until 3:00 A.M. I made some coffee and toast, but that didn't help my headache at work.

Unless you include some transition before the second sentence, the reader will not know **when** you made the coffee. However, if you insert *at daybreak*, the reader will stay with you:

The party was a real blast; it didn't break up until 3:00 A.M. At daybreak, I made some coffee and toast, but that didn't help my headache at work.

Any contrast or shift in thought should be clearly marked for the reader. You do not say "I like ham, *and* I hate eggs." You need a word that shows contrast here.

I like ham, *but* I hate eggs.
I like ham; *however,* I hate eggs.
I like ham; *on the other hand,* I hate eggs.

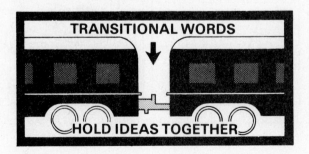

You can also show a concession by use of transitional words.

Although I failed the test, I passed the course.
Even though I like dogs, I hate that terrier.

If you want to show simple addition, use *and, also, again,* or similar words.

She bought the car, *and* she paid for it in cash.

If you are going to illustrate a point, tell your reader what you are doing. Before you tell the story or give the illustration, use the expression *for example.*

He was a real delinquent. *For example,* he once was arrested for having broken forty-three street lights.

Read this paragaraph. What is wrong with it?

He was a delinquent in many ways. His mother loved him. He was a truant. He was arrested for breaking street lights. He stole a car. He was a bully in the school. He was intelligent. He made poor grades. His mother was worried and hurt. She never let him know. She was there. She believed in him. She let him know it. He never felt deserted. She stood behind him. He reformed. A mother's love paid off.

Now see what happens when transitional words are included:

Although he was a delinquent in many ways, his mother *still* loved him. *Even though* he *often* skipped school and was *once* arrested for breaking street lights, his mother kept right on loving him. *At one time,* he even stole a car. *In addition,* he was a bully at school, and *although* he was intelligent, he *still* made poor grades. *Even though* his mother, *of course,* was worried and hurt, she never let him know. She was *always* there. She believed in him, *and* she let him know it. He never felt deserted *because* she always stood behind him. *Finally,* he reformed. A mother's love, *in this case,* paid off.

Isn't this clearer? See what the addition of a few transitional words can do.

TYPES OF TRANSITIONAL WORDS AND PHRASES

TO SHOW ADDITION: *and, moreover, furthermore, in addition, also, again.*
TO SHOW CONTRAST: *but, on the other hand, however, yet, nevertheless, on the contrary.*
TO SHOW SIMILARITY: *likewise, in the same way, in like manner, similarly.*
TO SHOW EMPHASIS: *in fact, indeed, certainly.*
TO SHOW CONCESSION: *granted, even though, although, though.*
TO INTRODUCE AN EXAMPLE: *for example, for instance, that is, in other words, in particular.*
TO INTRODUCE A RESULT: *thus, therefore, consequently, hence, then.*
TO INTRODUCE A CONCLUSION: *in summary, in conclusion, finally, in short.*

Paragraph unity is often aided if you repeat key words and phrases that keep the central idea before the reader.

In the following paragraph, notice how the three key words are repeated throughout the paragraph.

The large **size** of the human **brain** evolved in response to the development of *cultural information*. A **big brain** is an advantage when dealing with such *information*. **Big-brained** individuals were able to deal more successfully with the *culture* of their group. They were thus more successful reproductively than their **smaller-brained** relatives. They passed on their genes for **big brains** to their numerous offspring. They also added to the accumulating store of *cultural information*, increasing slightly the premium placed on **brain size** in the next generation. A self-reinforcing selective trend developed—a trend toward increased **brain size.**

Paul R. Ehrlich, The Population Bomb

**PARALLEL
WORDING**

Repeating the sentence pattern, especially the verb form, may add both clarity and emphasis to the paragraph.

The two following paragraphs use parallel structure effectively to make their point clear.

The policeman against environmental deterioration must be the powerful Department of Population and Environment. . . . It must be carefully insulated against the forces that will quickly be aligned against it. **It is going to cost** industry money. **It is going to cost** municipalities money. **It is going to** hit a lot of us where it hurts. **We may have to** do without two gas-gulping monster cars per family. **We may have to** learn to get along with some insect damage in our produce. **We may have to** get along with much less fancy packaging of the goods we purchase. **We may have to** use cleaners that get our clothes something less than "whiter than white." **We may have to** be satisfied with slower coast-to-coast transportation. Such may be the cost of survival. Of course, **we may also have to** get along with **less** emphysema, **less** cancer, **less** heart disease, **less** noise, **less** filth, **less** crowding, **less** need to work long hours or "moonlight," **less** robbery, and **less** threat of war. The pace of life may slow down. **We may have more** fishing, **more** relaxing, **more** time to watch TV, **more** time to drink beer (served in bottles that MUST be returned).

Paul R. Ehrlich, The Population Bomb

Note how the parallel grammatical structure, especially the *who* clauses, adds clarity and force to the following passage:

It is not the critic **who** counts; nor the man **who** points out how the strong man stumbled, or where the doer of deeds could have done them better. The credit belongs to the man **who** is actually in the arena, **whose** face is marred by dust and sweat and blood; **who** strives valiantly; **who** errs and comes short again and again; **who** knows the great enthusiasms, the great devotions; **who** spends himself in a worthy cause; **who,** at the last, knows in the end the triumph of high achievement, and **who,** at the worst, if he fails, at least fails while daring greatly so that his place will never be with those timid souls **who** know neither victory nor defeat.

Theodore Roosevelt, "While Daring Greatly"

(For more about parallelism, *see* Chapter VII.)

Underline the key words that are repeated in the following paragraph.

The Japanese imports on the shelves of our appliance stores and the Japanese cars on American streets and highways testify to the amazing productivity of the Japanese worker. As long-held myths about Japanese workers have faded, solid information has emerged concerning the efficiency and productivity of Japanese workers. For one thing, the Japanese worker is among the best educated and most highly skilled in the world today. And once he enters the labor market, the Japanese worker usually stays with one company until the day he retires. No doubt, the low rate of job hopping and absenteeism significantly contributes to the Japanese worker's productivity. To the typical Japanese worker, the company is not just the place where he punches in and out; his whole life is bound up with it. He identifies with the company—its prosperity is his prosperity—and the company, in turn, looks after him, provides him security, and gives him a sense of belonging. Even the social life of the Japanese worker is centered around the company he works for; he is a member of the company family, and to it he gives his loyalty. This total system of company and employee relationships may be viewed as paternalism; yet it accounts, in large measure, for the high productivity of the Japanese worker.

EXERCISE VIc
Underline all examples of parallel wording in the following paragraph.

Although it is not easy to get on your feet and speak out before a group for the first time, once you do, you have taken a big step forward. Once you summon the courage to step forward and speak out, each succeeding effort will be a little easier. Perhaps you have felt that there were times when you should have spoken out but didn't; once you do, you will feel a sense of relief and some degree of pride. Getting on your feet for the first time may take a determined push on your part, but once you give yourself that shove, you may be surprised by your own ability. Keep in mind, of course, that able speakers didn't develop their ability by silently warming a seat; they started by heeding the impulse to speak out. So must you. Once you do speak out—no matter how hard it may seem that first time—you have taken an important step toward self-fulfillment.

EXERCISE VId
Put the following sentences in logical order so they will form a coherent and well-organized paragraph on what to look for when examining a used car. Transitional devices as well as spatial order should provide clues to the proper sequence. Indicate the order by writing the sentence numbers in the sequence you decide is best.

(1) Once under the hood, check hoses, belt, fluid levels, and oil. (2) Next, observe all the possible rust problem areas, especially fenders, headlight brackets, and rocker panels. (3) Someone else should watch the lights while you operate them. (4) First, walk slowly around the car and look for any undulations (waves) in the surface which might suggest that major body work has

been done. (5) Finally, beware of excessive exhaust smoke; this may indicate the need for an engine overhaul. (6) Once you are satisfied that the body is sound, carefully inspect the interior for general cleanliness, wear, and abuse. (7) Also, be sure the battery is secure and free from corrosion. (8) There are several things to check carefully before test-driving a used car you're thinking of buying. (9) Before getting out, check the mileage to see if it seems realistic in terms of the car's overall condition. (10) Now try the doors, hood, and trunk lid for proper fit; also check for cracks or chips in the windshield. (11) Listen for unusual noises in the engine or muffler system. (12) Finally, inspect the tires to see if they are excessively worn or mismatched. (13) Now, with the ignition on, try lights, wipers, turn signals, and all accessories. (14) Now have someone start the motor and rev it up. (15) Watch for signs of water leakage on the floor and dashboard. (16) The last step before driving is to look under the hood. (17) Following these steps will not guarantee that you get a good buy, but you should have a chance.

EXERCISE VIe
Rewrite the following paragraph, putting in the transitional words and phrases needed to improve the continuity. Be careful that you do not change the meaning of the paragraph.

I was accepted and started work. My experience had been derived chiefly from books. I was not prepared for the difficult period of adjustment. I soon became discouraged with myself and so dissatisfied with my job that I was on the point of quitting. My employer must have sensed this. He called me into his office and talked to me about the duties of my position and the opportunities for advancement. I realized that there was nothing wrong with me or the job, and I decided to stay.

WORDS

Look-Alike or Sound-Alike Words
Many words are misused because they look alike or sound alike. Here are some of the troublesome words.

accept/except   *Accept* means "to take or receive"; do not confuse it with *except,* which shows exclusion or omission.

A good hostess will *accept* all gifts graciously.
They invited everyone *except* Bill.

adapt/adopt   *Adapt* means "to become accustomed to or to adjust to." *Adopt* means "to take on or to accept something."

When you live in the jungle, you learn to *adapt* to the environment.
After they *adopted* a child, they agreed to *adopt* a calmer lifestyle.

advice/advise   *Advice* is a noun, a thing; one gives or takes it. *Advise* is a verb, an action word that means "to recommend or inform."

It is easier to give *advice* than to accept it.
Her lawyer may *advise* her not to sign the contract.

affect/effect   *Affect* means "to influence."

John's job promotion did not *affect* his competence, sad to say.

Effect, meaning "result," is a noun.

Failing the exam had a disastrous *effect* on Lee's final grade.

Effect is also used as a verb, meaning "to bring about or cause to happen."

The staff worked long hours to *effect* a quick solution.

capital/capitol   *Capital* refers to a city; *capitol* refers to a building.

Harrisburg, the *capital* of Pennsylvania, has the most run-down *capitol* building in all fifty states.

Capital also has the meanings (1) "wealth; the group that controls wealth"; and (2) "upper-case letter."

Dan and Vera don't have the *capital* to buy that pharmacy.
Use a *capital* C when you refer to the Washington, D.C., government building, the Capitol.

choose/chose   *Choose* is the present-tense form; *chose* is the past-tense form of *choose.*

Today we have to *choose* wallpaper to go with the slipcover fabric we *chose* last week.

coarse/course   *Coarse* means "rough or uneven."

The cement contains *coarse* gravel.

Course is a procedure or plan of action or a path.

Physics is a hard *course.*
The road followed the *course* of the river.

complement/compliment   *Complement* means "to add to or make better" as a verb and "the full quantity or amount" as a noun.

A béarnaise sauce will *complement* the flavor of the beef.
The regiment has a full *complement* of foot soldiers.

Compliment means "to praise" as a verb and "a statement of praise or admiration" as a noun.

I love to hear *compliments* about how gracefully I ice-skate.

council/counsel   *Council* refers to a group, usually one that has a governing or administrative purpose; *counsel* means "advice or warning," and a *counselor* is one who gives advice.

The town *council* meets on Tuesday.
If I had followed my banker's *counsel,* I'd be rich today.

desert/dessert   *Desert* as a verb means "to abandon"; it is also a noun used as a name for a dry wasteland.

They could not *desert* their post because the army was in the middle of the *desert.*

Dessert, the noun with double *s,* is a usually sweet last course of a meal.

The gelatin *dessert* was topped with whipped cream.

its/it's   *Its,* unlike noun possessives, uses no apostrophe. The contraction *it's,* which means "it is," uses an apostrophe (to show that a letter is left out of the contraction).

The investigating committee released *its* report.
It's a shame we have to cancel the game; but I checked the field, and *it's* squishy with mud.

lead/led   As a verb, *lead* means "to guide, conduct, or direct," and it is spelled like the noun *lead.* The past-tense form of *lead* is *led,* which is pronounced the way the noun *lead* is. As a noun, *lead* names a heavy metal.

Jeff agreed to *lead* them to the abandoned *lead* mine.
Napoleon *led* his troops across Europe.

loose/lose   *Loose,* an adjective, describes that which does not fit tightly. *Lose,* a verb meaning "to misplace," has only one *o.*

Wear *loose* clothing when you travel in hot climates.
You will *lose* your way in the swamps.

passed/past   *Passed* refers to the act of overtaking. *Past* refers to time—the opposite of *future.*

The Jaguar *passed* the Alfa Romeo on the final turn.
He has done some strange things in the *past,* but what is *past* is *past.*

principal/principle   *Principal* means "primary, the most important person or thing." In this sense it names the administrative head of a school.

A high school *principal* has the *principal* responsibility for discipline.

Principle means "rule, characteristic; moral attitude or belief."

The experiment illustrated a *principle* of cell growth.
The architect is a woman of *principle;* she wouldn't have taken a bribe.

right/rite/write   *Right* is used as a noun referring to a value or concept; it also names a direction (turn *right*) and describes correctness (*right,* not wrong).

This *right* is guaranteed by the Constitution.

A *rite* is a ceremony or ritual.

Human sacrifice was part of a religious rite among the Aztecs.

Write means "to inscribe letters, words, or symbols on a surface for the purpose of communication."

Being able to *write* well should be a goal of all college students.

sight/site/cite   *Sight* refers to any visual impression. *Site* refers to location. *Cite* means "to recognize or bring forward."

The first *sight* of you sent my blood racing.
The *site* for the new gym is on the south slope of the hill.
My drama teacher couldn't *cite* an example from a Greek tragedy.

there/their/they're   *There* can refer to location.

He is over *there,* behind the parade marshal.

Their is always used to show possession or ownership. *They're* is always a contraction for *they are.*

They're not planning to visit *their* relatives in Canada this summer.

to/too/two   *To* indicates motion toward, or it combines with a verb to make a verb form called an infinitive.

We went *to* town *to* buy coffee and sugar.

Too indicates extremes, more or less of some characteristic or quality than one wants. *Too* can mean "also," as well.

The soup was *too* cold, and the fish was *too* salty. I forgot the vegetables, *too.*

The number is always *two*.

One and one are *two*.

who's/whose   *Who's* is a contraction for *who is*.

Jan is the only employee *who's* never late for work.

Whose is the possessive form of *who*.

You are a person *whose* promises I trust.

Use a good dictionary to check the meaning of any words you are still not sure of.

EXERCISE VIf
Check your dictionary for the difference in the meaning between the following pairs of words.

access/excess	allusion/illusion
censor/censure	detract/distract
beside/besides	stationary/stationery
accept/except	uninterested/disinterested
peace/piece	aloud/allowed
prosecute/persecute	altar/alter
bare/bear	cereal/serial
born/borne	patients/patience
device/devise	new/knew
farther/further	lend/loan

Apostrophe to Show Possession

While some words are troublesome because they look alike or sound alike, other words are troublesome because they require the use of the apostrophe. As you have already learned, the apostrophe (') is used to indicate letters that are left out of words such as *isn't, couldn't, don't, let's*. There is another important use of the apostrophe. It is used to show possession. It stands for "belonging to," as in *John's book* (the book belonging to John) or *children's hour* (the hour belonging to children).

Following are rules for use of the apostrophe to show possession.

1.   Add an apostrophe and an *s* to show possession in singular nouns.

my mother's dress
Mary's job
the teacher's assignment
the room's atmosphere
the club's rules

2. Add an apostrophe and an *s* to singular nouns that already end in an *s*.

Charles's friend
Dickens's novels

3. Add an apostrophe without the *s* to form the possessive of plural nouns.

my brothers' wives
the players' dressing room
the students' lounge

4. Use an apostrophe and an *s* for plural nouns that do not end in *s*.

the children's book
the men's room
the group's decision

5. With compounds that are possessives, use an apostrophe for both if each word is a separate "belonging to"; use an apostrophe on the last one only if the possession is a joint one.

Henry's and Robert's jackets are both ripped.
Henry and Robert's clothing business failed.

6. Don't overlook the need for the possessive form in the following constructions using indefinite pronouns.

somebody else's problem
everyone else's house
nobody's business
anybody's opinion
in each other's way
taking one another's part

7. Don't overlook the need for the possessive form in such expressions as these.

a quarter's worth
ten dollars' worth
a day's work
three weeks' wages
forty years' labor

EXERCISE VIg
Supply the correct possessive form in the following sentences. If the sentence is correct, write C in the blank.

1. Before New Years Eve, we throw out our Christmas tree.

_____

2. Daves tie caught on fire.

_____

3. William and Marys house was redecorated.

_____

4. All of my teachers tests are unfair.

_____

5. Thomas notes are excellent.

_____

6. I spent two weeks time studying economics.

_____

7. Mr. Jones idea of fun is playing practical jokes.

_____

8. Ted and Susans skit is funny.

_____

9. I spent two hours searching for my mothers recipe.

_____

10. Charles bosses orders were to keep one weeks supply on hand for emergencies.

_____

11. After seven years effort the dam was completed.

_____

12. A nickels worth of penny candy now costs a quarter.

_____

13. Somebodys car is parked in my spot.

_____

14. Our basketball players kept getting in each others way.

_____

15. He had never done a full weeks work in his life.

_____

CHAPTER VII

defining

ORGANIZATION

Knowing how to define a term is one of the most valuable skills you can learn—not just as a student of English or math or psychology, but also as you study life. The more you learn about life, the more you realize that relationships between people are often permanently destroyed because of "misunderstandings." These misunderstandings are sometimes the direct result of one's failure to communicate his or her meaning of a word. For example, consider the case of Pam. Pam is eighteen years old. She wants to leave home and move into an apartment because her parents aren't giving her enough "freedom." Pam's parents, however, are firmly convinced that Pam is already getting too much "freedom." Obviously, Pam and her parents have different definitions of the word "freedom." Perhaps, if Pam had clearly defined what she meant by "freedom," the conflict with her parents could have been peacefully resolved. A clear, thorough definition of a term or concept at the outset of a disagreement can prevent a minor disagreement from exploding into a major war.

Limited Definitions

In writing or speaking, you often need to provide your reader or listener with at least a **limited definition.** There are several ways briefly to clarify your terms without getting bogged down in lengthy, involved explanations. Here are some ways to provide a limited definition.

SYNONYMS The easiest way to define a word is to explain it in terms of another word, a **synonym,** which means the same or nearly the same thing.

Dr. Andrews was indeed *loquacious,* an extremely *talkative* man.

You should always include a brief definition when the word or term that you use might not be understood by the reader. Also, make sure that the language of your definition is simpler than the original term. The following version would only create more confusion:

Dr. Andrews was indeed *loquacious,* an extremely *garrulous* man.

Always consider your reader's ability to comprehend what you are writing; be aware of readers' limitations, but don't insult their intelligence by oversimplifying terms or ideas that they would obviously understand.

FORMAL DEFINITIONS A brief **formal definition** should, like the synonym, closely follow the original term.

The *thesaurus,* a book that contains lists of synonyms, is a valuable tool for the beginning writer.

In this example, a short explanatory phrase, instead of a single word, defines the term *thesaurus.* Be certain, however, that your description is complete; provide enough details to explain the term clearly.

COMPARISONS Another way to define a word or term is to express it as part of a **comparison.**

When he tried to convince her, she was *immovable*—like a tree with roots extending to the center of the earth.

These are the methods most frequently used for limited definition. Other methods of definition are discussed later in the chapter.

Abstract Terms

Since formal education is primarily concerned with the communication of ideas—ideas that are often expressed in abstract terms—you constantly face the need to define, for yourself and for others, what those terms mean to you.

For example, courses in history, economics, sociology, psychology, physics, and criminal justice might require that you precisely define these terms:

These words are abstract—what they represent cannot be seen, felt, heard, touched, smelled—or weighed.

1. What is *capitalism?*
2. What is *fascism?*
3. What is *ecology?*
4. What is *motion?*
5. What is *work?*
6. What is a *neurosis?*
7. What is *prejudice?*
8. What is *integrity?*
9. What do you mean by *law and order?*
10. What do you mean by *a liberal education?*

The italicized words above are symbols for abstract or intangible things, things you cannot see or hear or touch or smell. You cannot buy an ounce of integrity or shed a pound of prejudice; you cannot extract liberal education from the blood of Harvard graduates nor put capitalism on the counter to pay for a pound of bologna; you cannot eat fascism like cornflakes or see a neurosis the way you see a striped cat. Since these words stand for ideas or concepts rather than concrete objects, you must define them if you want to communicate your meaning precisely.

Notice how Martin Luther King, Jr., defines the abstract term *power.*

Power, properly understood, is the ability to achieve purpose. It is the strength required to bring about social, political, or economic changes. In this sense power is not only desirable but necessary in order to implement the demands of love and justice. One of the greatest problems of history is that the concepts of love and power are usually contrasted as polar opposites. Love is identified with a resignation of power and power with a denial of love. It was this misinterpretation that caused Nietzsche, the philosopher of the "will to power," to reject the Christian concept of love. It was this same misinterpretation which induced Christian theologians to reject Nietzsche's philosophy of the "will to power" in the name of the Christian idea of love. What is needed is a realization that power without love is reckless and abusive and that love without power is sentimental and anemic. Power at its best is love implementing the demands of justice. . . .

> *Martin Luther King, Jr.*, Where Do We Go from Here: Chaos or Community?

Formal or Logical Definition

Here is a pattern to follow in writing precise definitions.

1. First, place the term to be defined in a class or category: for example, fascism is an economic system. This places the term in a general class; you are saying that *fascism* (the term) belongs to a limited class of things (economic systems).

2. Second, describe the principal characteristics that distinguish or differentiate the term from all others in the class: for example, fascism is an economic system in which industry is wholly controlled by the central government while ownership remains in private hands.

This pattern can be used in defining both concrete objects or abstractions:

Term	Class or Category	Differentiating Detail
Plimsoll mark	one of a set of lines on the hull of a merchant ship	indicating the depth to which it may be legally loaded under specified conditions
Orangutan	one of the anthropoid apes	having a shaggy reddish-brown coat, very long arms, and no tail
Paternalism	a policy or practice of treating or governing people	by providing for their needs without giving them responsibility, in a manner suggesting a father's relationship with his children
Neurosis	a mental or functional disorder	characterized by one or more of the following reactions: anxiety, compulsions and obsessions, phobias, depressions, disassociation, and conversion

Your basic definition, then, consists of three parts: **term** to be defined, **category** to which the term belongs, and **specific detail** which differentiates it from other terms in the category. Note that both the category and the differentiating detail must be as exact as possible; for example, don't say:

A hammer is a *thing*

instead of

A hammer is a *tool*

or

A phobia is a *feeling*

instead of

A phobia is an *anxiety*

Similarly, your specific detail must provide enough information to distinguish your term from any other term that could fall in the same category. For example, it is not enough to say that

A phobia is an anxiety provoked by some object, situation, or idea.

Many kinds of anxiety are "provoked by an object, situation, or idea." The fear of colliding with the huge Mack truck that you are trying to pass, fear of flunking next Tuesday's biology test, or fear of loneliness, are natural, momentary fears that are not phobias, yet they can all be defined as fears that are "provoked by some object, situation, or idea." Only **one** term should apply to your basic definition. If any other term can fit into your definition, then you did not include enough specific detail. The following is a better basic definition of phobia:

A phobia is an intense and irrationally fearful anxiety provoked by some object, situation, or idea that is not actually harmful.

Barbara Fried, Who's Afraid: The Phobic's Handbook

The only term that can apply to that definition is a "phobia." Defining a phobia as "an intense or irrationally fearful" anxiety that is provoked by something "that is not actually harmful" distinguishes a phobia from all other kinds of fears. Remember, if your basic definition applies to any term other than the word that you are defining, then your basic definition does not have enough specific detail. If you say that

Love is a strong feeling that one person has for another.

you are not differentiating love from other strong feelings. Think of some other terms that would apply to this definition.

Hate is a strong feeling that one person has for another.
Passion is a strong feeling that one person has for another.
Sympathy is a strong feeling that one person has for another.

How would you rewrite this definition so that it would apply only to the term "love"?

CAUTION:

defining

1. Avoid circular definitions, that is, the use of a term to define itself.

A circular definition is one that is circular.
A hay conditioner is a farm machine that conditions hay.

2. Avoid the improper use of *where* and *when*. *Where* refers to location and *when* refers to a particular time.

INCORRECT: Pruning is when you trim the ends off limbs and stems to make a plant or tree grow better.

CORRECT: Pruning is the practice of trimming ends from branches and stems to make a plant or tree grow better.

INCORRECT: The Olympics is when athletes from every nation compete for gold, silver, and bronze medals.

CORRECT: The Olympics are games in which athletes from all nations compete for gold, silver, and bronze medals.

INCORRECT: Phipps Conservatory is where you see some of the finest live floral exhibits in the country.

CORRECT: Phipps Conservatory is a place where one can see some of the finest live floral exhibits in the country.

EXERCISE VIIa

Identify the faults (using *A* through *E*) in the definitions in items 1–10. *A* = circular; *B* = inexact class or category; *C* = insufficient differentiating detail; *D* = improper use of *when* or *where*; *E* = synonym more difficult than the term to be defined.

_____ **1.** Revival is a renaissance.
_____ **2.** Saprophytic means pertaining to, or having the nature of, saprophytes.
_____ **3.** Public speaking is when you have to get up before a group and talk.
_____ **4.** Ptomaine poisoning is an acute stomach disorder.
_____ **5.** A tachometer is a thing that tells you the revolutions per minute of a revolving shaft.
_____ **6.** Polygyny is when a man has two or more wives at the same time.
_____ **7.** Microcosm is an epitome of the universe.
_____ **8.** School is where you go to learn, to gain knowledge by instruction and study.
_____ **9.** A diesel is a type of internal combustion engine.
_____ **10.** A bathtub is any tub used to take a bath in.

EXERCISE VIIb

Write a precise one-sentence definition for each of the following words; include term, class, and differentiating detail.

river	faucet	library
pistol	jeans	spoon
clown	automobile	fork

Now, with the help of your dictionary, write precise definitions for these words. Again, include term, class, and differentiating detail.

defining

dik-dik	panjandrum	folk dance
titmouse	quisling	socket wrench
mastiff	shogun	pecking order

EXERCISE VIIc
Rewrite the following basic definitions.

1. Hunger is a feeling that you have when you are hungry.

_____

2. Friendship is when you respect somebody.

_____

3. A hypochondriac is a person who is always sick.

_____

4. Marijuana is a drug.

_____

5. A test is a thing that tests your knowledge.

_____

6. A police officer is an individual who deals with the law.

_____

7. A party is where you go to have a good time.

_____

8. An egomaniac is in love with himself.

_____

9. A dictionary is a book about words.

_____

10. Prejudice is when you don't like some people.

_____

The Extended Definition

Many words represent concepts or ideas that are too complicated to be defined in a sentence; therefore, a paragraph is necessary to explain the meaning. For example, you ask your sociology teacher to define *race*. He replies, "Race, although thought of primarily as a physical and hereditary factor, is actually a social concept." If he stops his definition at this point, he has really not told you very much. It would take a paragraph for him to explain to you the definition of race. Or, if in answer to the question, "What is a radical?" your professor answers, "A radical is someone like Jerry Rubin, or Eldridge Cleaver, or Jesus, or Mahatma Ghandi," you still do not have a clear understanding of a radical unless you know what characteristics these individuals have in common.

Each of these definitions would have to be expanded before you could fully understand the meaning of *race* or *radical.* In other words, you would need an **extended definition** of each term. You already know how to write a one-sentence basic definition (term + class + differentiating detail), so once you learn different ways of **developing** a basic definition, you will know how to write a paragraph of definition. Essentially, an extended definition follows the same three-part structure common to all paragraphs:

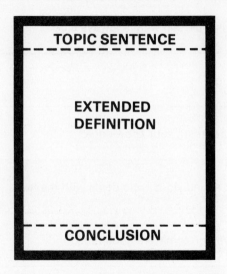

1. **Topic Sentence:** Introduction of the controlling idea in the basic definition.
2. **Body:** Development of the controlling idea through various methods of definition such as synonyms, examples, word origin, comparison, negation, and process (discussed later in this chapter).
3. **Conclusion:** Restatement of the controlling idea.

Topic Sentence

Your topic sentence will usually have as its subject the word to be defined. The attitude should be the general meaning you attach to the word.

Cultural relativity means respect for the ways of people who are different from ourselves.

Justice is rewarding or punishing a person according to his deeds.

or

An *implosion* is a more or less violent collapse inward from the vacuum effect of a drastic change in air pressure such as the low pressure at the core of a tornado.

The *hypothalamus* is the part of the brain that takes care of many of the brain's routine housekeeping chores.

These introduce the topic, but you need a paragraph to explain them.

Remember that a topic sentence needs not only a subject but an attitude toward the subject. For example, to say, "A titmouse is a small grayish bird" does not provide a usable topic sentence. To say, "Everybody has a different idea about what pornography is," or to say, "Love has different meanings for different people," is equally unsatisfactory.

A good topic sentence is one which (1) stimulates new thought about a familiar subject or (2) brings an unfamiliar subject home to us in terms of our common experience.

EXERCISE VIId

Which of the following topic sentences would be suitable for a paragraph developed by definition?

_____ 1. The policeman's job is not an easy one.
_____ 2. Prejudice is more than just a vague feeling of dislike for a group of people.
_____ 3. Fast-food chains are the fastest growing businesses in the United States.
_____ 4. A hot rod is a car that has been "souped up," "chopped down," and lovingly "customized."
_____ 5. Traveling by train is quite different in Europe than it is in the United States.
_____ 6. The meaning of the word *bully* has changed through the years.
_____ 7. What is *slang?*
_____ 8. Do not use *anxious* when you mean *eager.*
_____ 9. Television is a bore.
_____ 10. The Pittsburgh Steelers shall rise again.

Body

EXTENDING YOUR DEFINITION

Earlier in this chapter a basic definition of *phobia* was worked out. With this basic definition, you were given a general idea of the meaning of *phobia*, but you would probably find it rather difficult to carry on an intelligent conversation about phobias with that amount of information. In order for you to thoroughly understand the meaning of *phobia*, the basic definition has to be expanded. This can be accomplished in a number of ways, some of which were discussed earlier under Limited Definitions. The extended definition frequently makes use of several of the methods discussed next.

Synonyms

A synonym, as previously explained, is a word that has almost the same meaning as another word. Hence, if you are defining *phobia*, words like *dread, panic, horror,* or *hysteria* might help the readers understand the meaning, especially if they are more familiar with these words than with *phobia*.

Examples

As you have already seen, examples often help to clarify the meaning of a word. Consequently, they often come in handy in a definition paragraph. The reader will have a clearer understanding of the meaning of phobia if you provide specific examples of different kinds of phobias.

acrophobia   A morbid fear of heights: standing on a bridge, a roof, a mountain, or even a chair.
misophobia   An irrational fear of contamination: dirt, dust, germs, radiation, infection.
claustrophobia   An excessive fear of enclosed spaces: closets, elevators, automobiles, or small windowless rooms.

Word Origin

If you were defining *claustrophobia*, you could tell the reader that the word is derived from the Latin word *claustrium* meaning "lock, bar, bolt," and, later, "a shut-up place, a cell or cloister," and from the French word "phobe," meaning "fearing" or "dreading." You could also show how the meaning of a word has changed throughout the course of history.

Comparison and/or Contrast

Even though a phobia is not as serious a disorder as paranoia, being phobic about something can be compared to being paranoid, because a person who suffers from paranoia often behaves much like an individual who has a particular phobia.

FEAR OF HEIGHTS   **FEAR OF GERMS**   **FEAR OF CLOSED PLACES**

For example, a person who has a paranoid persecution complex has such an irrational obsession about being persecuted that he or she begins to see danger in harmless situations and begins to see enemies everywhere—whether they exist or not. In the same way, an individual who suffers from claustrophobia has such an irrational fear of enclosed spaces that an otherwise harmless room without windows suddenly becomes a terribly dangerous trap that will suffocate the phobic.

Negation

Sometimes you can help the reader understand what something **is** by explaining what it **is not.** For example, suppose that your reader has three different conceptions (A,B, and C) of the word that you are defining. If you show the reader that you are not talking about A and that you are not talking about B, then you have helped the reader determine the meaning of the term. Through the process of elimination, the reader narrows down her thinking to C and thus is no longer confused about other possible meanings of the term. To illustrate, you can help the reader understand the meaning of *phobia* by pointing out that a phobia is not a superstition. A person who is more comfortable walking around a ladder rather than under it for fear of incurring some future bad luck does not necessarily have a phobia about ladders. The mere fact that a person is superstitious about walking under ladders does not mean that he is going to faint at the sight of a ladder. However, if you had a severe case of acrophobia (fear of heights), the sight of a ladder might indeed set your heart pounding and cause you to become dizzy and faint.

Process

If you were trying to define a Wankel engine to someone who had never heard of such an engine, you might help him or her understand what a Wankel engine is by telling how it works. Similarly, you could help your reader understand what a psychologist is by telling what a psychologist does. You might help the reader understand *phobia* if you tell how a person acts when he or she has a phobia. According to *The Phobic's Handbook,* upon seeing or even thinking about his irrational fear, the phobic may develop symptoms of "extreme restlessness, rapid heart rate, palpitations, pains anywhere in the body, numbness, nausea, vomiting, diarrhea, weakness, dizziness, fainting, instant fatigue, inability to concentrate or remember, and an overwhelming urge to go elsewhere immediately, if not sooner."

EXERCISE VIIe
Tell what method of defining is used in each of the following.

Definitions of Man

1. Man is a two-legged animal without feathers. *Plato*
2. Man is the only animal that blushes—or needs to. *Twain*
3. *Man* comes from the Gothic *manna,* perhaps from the root word *man,* which means "to think."

anonym

4. A man is a human being, a person.

5. Man is different from the other animals in that he alone can communicate when not within sight or hearing of men. Man alone walks erect on two feet; most other animals have no free limbs. Man has an opposable thumb which allows him to pick up and hold things easily, whereas most animals have thumbs parallel to their other digits.

6. Man is not the only animal who thinks nor the only animal that communicates. He is not born with a conscience nor is he born with complicated instincts to guide his future actions.

7. Man or men can indicate things as well as people: chessman, merchantman, and Portuguese Man of War.

Definitions of Courage

8. Courage is bravery, valor, fortitude.

9. Recklessness is that appearance of courage that is not courage at all.

Pierre Van Paasen

10. It is better to live one day as a lion than a hundred years as a sheep. [Motto on the Italian 20-lire coin]

Often, an extended definition is a blend of factual information and opinion (judgment); the writer selects details that support her own point of view. One popular way to explain a term is to use an **anecdote**—a short narrative (story) which presents a situation that clarifies the term for the reader. The anecdote might be a personal experience or an imaginary situation in narrative form. In either case, it should hold the reader's interest and relate directly to the term being defined.

There are many ways to write an extended definition. Here is one student's definition of the word *euphemism*.

Define an egomaniac.

172

As I was the child of inhibited parents who were raised by even more inhibited parents, euphemisms became a part of my personal heritage from childhood through adolescence—and even continued into my adult life. When I was a small child, euphemisms were limited mostly to bodily functions. I used various inane expressions to avoid embarrassing my parents and, also, I suspect, to improve my numerical skills. I discovered the interesting fact that women in the family way were apt to acquire a little bundle of joy from the stork as a direct result of the birds and the bees. I passed from childhood into adolescence, and euphemisms were expanded to politely skirt some of life's unpleasantnesses. My great aunt took a turn for the worse, and after several months of being under the weather, God took her to heaven. Now that I am an adult, my life is filled with euphemisms which attempt either to mollify me or to deceive me. My five-year-old lacks motivation; my two-year-old is in the adventurous stage. I drive a previously owned, reconditioned car, and our spendable income is decreasing as a result of an inflationary spiral. But even with an adult understanding of the often confusing and even outright untruthful aspects of euphemisms, I still use them: in my own way, I am just as inhibited as my parents.

Kathy Curtis

DEFINING ABSTRACT TERMS

A great many technical terms have a very precise and restricted meaning, and even common terms may have a very restricted meaning when used in a specific context. For example, the words *energy, mass, velocity,* and *work,* as they are used in a physics textbook, have only one specific definition and are not open to interpretation.

With many words, however, the interpretation will vary according to the background and experience of the person using the words. What might seem like *prosperity* to a very poor person might seem like *poverty* to a very wealthy one. Thus, the meaning lies not in the words themselves but in the people who use the words. That is especially true in dealing with abstract terms such as *love, honor, beauty*—words that refer to ideas rather than tangible objects. However, to say that such-and-such a word means "different things to different people" is of no help in defining the word. And if you try to cover every possible meaning of an abstract term in a single paragraph, what you usually end up with is a list instead of a unified paragraph. What you need to do, then, is to select one particular aspect of meaning and develop that aspect as fully as possible.

Look at some of the possible ways of regarding two common abstract terms: *success* and *failure.*

SUCCESS	FAILURE
Success in school	Failure in school
Success in marriage	Failure in marriage
Success as a parent	Failure as a parent
Occupational success	Failure in a career
Political success	Political failure
Personal triumph	Personal defeat
Happiness	Unhappiness

What kind of "success" or "failure" do you intend to discuss?

Perhaps you see that success and failure can both exist at the same time: financial success may be accompanied by unhappiness and failure in marriage; political success may be accompanied by failure as a parent; occupational success is not always dependent on success in school. Does this give you some new ideas about the definition of *success* and *failure?*

Now consider the familiar word *work.* If you look up the word in any good dictionary, you will find more than twenty-five different definitions, not counting expressions such as "work up," "work over," "work off," "work in," and "work down." In addition, there are at least as many possible attitudes toward the subject of work.

Here is one person's view:

Few of us care to think of work as the central purpose of our being; yet, for most of us, it is the main cohesive element of our lives. Not only does daily work consume the major part of our energies, it is the linchpin that holds our lives together. Extended periods of unemployment can depress and demoralize even the most stouthearted of men. The man out of work soon feels purposeless and hollow. Without the demands that daily work imposes on hands and brain, he soon comes to feel useless and begins to devalue his own worth as a human being. He has lost his center of gravity. To some men, of course, work becomes an all-demanding, all-consuming fixation; we often refer to such men as "workaholics." While the workaholic is certainly not to be envied, he does at least have something that the unemployed man does not have and can find no substitute for—his work.

COMBINING FORMS OF DEVELOPMENT

In writing an extended definition, you are not limited to any one form of development. In developing an *extended definition* of *charity,* for example, you might use any combination of the methods of development previously described.

NARRATION: Tell about the work of one man or woman whose efforts exemplify true charity.

DESCRIPTION: Show the joy that a poor child gets from receiving even one small gift.

FACTUAL DETAIL: Use factual details and statistics to show how much Americans donate to charity.

EXPLANATION WITH EXAMPLES: Use examples to show how various charitable organizations help those in need.

COMPARISON/CONTRAST: Use comparison/contrast to show the difference between genuine charity and the kind of charity that humiliates and degrades people.

DIVISION AND CLASSIFICATION: Divide the people who donate to charity into various groups and classify them according to their motives for giving—guilt, pity, self-aggrandizement, love of people.

Notice how in the following paragraph the student defines *stress* through the use of comparison, examples, and process.

The word *stress,* when applied to a combat situation, has a special meaning. It can refer to physical, emotional, or mental stress or any combination of the three. Physical stress, which is probably the easiest to understand, deals with the strain placed on the body during combat. It's an enormous demand placed on the soldier's energy, and it quickly stretches his physical resources to the limit. His adrenaline flows, he can feel his heartbeat rapidly speeding up, and he becomes hyperactive with excessive strength and speed. Just as quickly, though, exhaustion sets in upon him, and all of his bumps, cuts, and bruises begin to ache. This is often accompanied by a painful headache or a severe case of the shakes due to a rapid depletion of blood sugar. It is similar to running a foot race. One starts out at a very fast pace, but in a short time, he tires, and all of his energy seems to be depleted. As one tries to continue running, he can feel every muscle in his body begin to throb. It's hard to tell sometimes where physical stress stops and emotional stress begins. Emotional stress includes fear, hate, sorrow, and even, at times, a curious form of joy. When the soldier is under duress, each of the emotions exerts its pressures upon him, sometimes causing panic or hysteria. For example, fear can be so powerful an influence that a soldier who gets caught in a fire fight can react by just starting to run, trying to escape, instead of immediately jumping for cover. He then becomes a running target for the enemy. One may wonder how joy can even be remotely connected to a combat situation, but, as all of the other pressures build up, laughter can become a form of release—a type of hysteria all its own. A man might find something funny that might be totally humorless to others and break out in a low rumbling laugh that turns into a long, rapturous convulsion. It can occur anytime, anywhere. Emotional stress in a combat situation can therefore be highly dangerous, but mental stress is probably the worst type of stress. It includes the pressures and strains caused by the mind's ability to think, to wonder, to remember, and to comprehend. It occurs when the soldier realizes that he may die or that he may not live up to what he expects of himself. It is seeing himself in a different way and wondering if he'll ever get home to live his life over and correct his mistakes. It is being responsible for another's life or perhaps many lives and living with the worry and the guilt. Mental stress can also be generated by memories of home and what mom and dad expect him to be. He may try to fulfill their expectations and crack under the strain. Poor living conditions also contribute to mental stress—in addition to the continuous presence of the nagging, unanswered question: ''*Why* am I here?'' Actually, one could take all of life's stresses, multiply them by two, and force them on an individual for an hour; then he would experience what a soldier in combat experiences in two minutes. Stress, when applied to a combat situation, clearly has a meaning all its own.   *Mark Pleshenko*

Conclusion

Your conclusion, again, should sum up your feelings about the meaning of the term in your topic sentence, which you have already proved in the body of your paragraph.

Some words mean different things to different people. *Marriage* to a young girl about to take the big step may have an entirely different meaning than *marriage* does to a bored husband celebrating his twentieth year of bondage. These words that have different meanings to different people are words rich in connotation.

Freedom may be the name of a town, a patriotic feeling, a new liberation when you leave home and begin your own life, or even a sense of relief when you break up with your steady. Perhaps you experience freedom when the 5:00 o'clock whistle blows at the mill, or you walk alone in the woods, or you wind out your car on a lonely road, or you spend a few minutes sitting alone in church.

Janis Joplin once sang in a song that "freedom's just another word for nothing left to lose." Does it mean any of these things to you—or something else?

Suggested Activity

Choose an abstract word and ask twenty people to give you their definition of the word. Try to get people of different types: young and old, rich and poor, college educated and high school dropouts, married and single. See if their definitions can be classified on the basis of any of their characteristics.

ASSIGNMENT

Write one clear, well-developed paragraph defining an abstract term. Here are some words you might use:

love	crime	trust
marriage	justice	patriotism
war	delinquent	freedom
hate	luck	punishment
education	religion	mercy
wealth	frustration	work
peace	family	equality
happiness	hope	prejudice

SENTENCES

Parallel Wording

I came. I saw. I conquered.
... of the people, by the people, for the people.
A penny saved is a penny earned.

These are examples of parallel wording, which means the use of the same word or sentence pattern several times. Parallelism is used for emphasis; it is a **repetition** used to make a strong point; it forces the reader to notice. Notice the difference between the foregoing parallels and the following nonparallels:

I came and saw the country, and then it was conquered by me and my men.
... that came from the people and was designed by them for the purpose of the group itself.
If you save a penny, it is just as if you had earned it.

Notice that the second set does not have the impact of the first because parallel wording was not used; and, therefore, the second group does not have the strength, the emphasis, of the first.

You may use parallelism in a series of words:

Our flag is *red, white,* and *blue.*

or in a series of phrases:

Harry was in trouble *with his mother, with his teacher,* and *with his girl.*

or in a series of clauses:

John ran up the steps; Susan ran down the steps; Joe stood bewildered on the landing.

CAUTION: Do not overuse parallelism. If you do, your writing becomes tiresome. Emphasizing everying is the same as emphasizing nothing.

Do not try to make nonparallel things parallel.

Jerry was a reader, a writer, a studier, and neat.

Neat does not fit the pattern and should not be included in the parallel structure. Better say:

Jerry was a reader, a writer, and a studier. He was also neat.

(Notice the change in meaning if *also* is omitted.)

Notice the parallel structure in the following paragraph.

The teacher wanted the students to study the chapter, not skim it. He wanted them to understand the rules, not memorize them. He wanted them to discuss the issues, not talk around them. He wanted them to enjoy the class, not laugh at it. The students did not seem to be able to tell the difference.

Note the pattern that prevails throughout the paragraph: "He wanted them to _____ not _____." This parallelism makes the paragraph both clear and strong.

EXERCISE VIIf
Make the following sentences parallel.

1. He was a good student: intelligent, hard-working, and he had an interest in the subject.

   _____

2. Jerry was tall, blue-eyed, and he had blond hair.

   _____

3. He decided to enroll in English Literature, Accounting II, Introduction to Business, and to take a course in art history.

_____

4. To take a walk, to go on a picnic, or meeting the gang at the swimming pool were his alternatives for this sunny afternoon.

_____

5. Harry went to the store, bought the necessary items, came home, and a sandwich was his creation.

_____

6. Martin Luther King was a great humanitarian, a great preacher, and who believed in leading the civil rights movement.

_____

7. After we choose a candidate, after we work for him, and when he is finally elected, we must keep him informed of our needs.

_____

8. I dressed carefully, arrived early, sat primly in the chair, and the boss I was waiting for never came.

_____

9. Chang Li decided that because of the money involved he would either cancel his trip to China or he would combine his trip to China with a conference in the Philippines. Another alternative would be to stow away on a plane going there.

_____

10. The professor was considered absent-minded because he often drove his car downtown and came back on a bus, often the lecture notes he brought were for the wrong class, and he sometimes lost his way going to the cafeteria.

_____

PARALLEL WORDING WITH CORRELATIVES

Elements linked by correlative conjunctions (*either . . . or, neither . . . nor, not only . . . but also, both . . . and*) should be parallel in structure.

FAULTY: Either he will win an award for his photography or his sketches.

PARALLEL: He will win an award **either** *for his photography* **or** *for his sketches.*

FAULTY: She neither has the time nor the inclination to go to card parties.

PARALLEL: She has **neither** *the time* **nor** *the inclination* to go to card parties.

FAULTY: She is not only famous for her movie roles but also in working with orphans.

defining

PARALLEL: She is famous **not only** *for her movie roles* **but also** *for her work with orphans.*

FAULTY: They hoped both to gain new members and raising money for charity.

PARALLEL: They hoped **both** *to gain new members* **and** *to raise money for charity.*

EXERCISE VIIg
Correct all errors in parallelism in the following sentences.

1. He could never decide whether to wear Western clothes or if he wanted to look like a sailor.

   _____

2. Either he is very foolish or a very naive young man.

   _____

3. The best way to combat poverty is not by setting up more government agencies but creating more jobs in industry.

   _____

4. You must present your pass to the guard both when you arrive and at the time of your departure.

   _____

5. They found that the old barn was not only large enough but also it would suit their purpose for building a theater.

   _____

6. According to his neighbors, Joe Smith was either an upstanding citizen or he must have been an artful scoundrel.

   _____

7. Either you can cash this check at your bank or send it in with your next order.

   _____

8. Both at home and when he was in the office, he had nothing on his mind but golf.

   _____

9. Mr. Johnson was not only a failure as a businessman, but as a father as well.

   _____

10. He is either plainly dishonest, or he uses notoriously poor judgment.

    _____

Correct all errors in parallelism in the following sentences.

1. Either it will snow or rain.

   _____

2. He not only works hard at school but also on his job at the foundry.

   _____

3. Your baggage will be searched both when you enter the country and at your departure.

   _____

4. Julie neither had the time nor the money to go to New York.

   _____

5. Either you can read the story in the library or at home in the evening.

   _____

6. North Dakota winters are both hard on machines and for the people who work outdoors.

   _____

7. Not only for his own sake but also when you consider the welfare of his family, he should spend less time at the tavern.

   _____

8. The man was under investigation both for tax evasion and because he had embezzled from the credit union.

   _____

9. They either came in late or I didn't see them.

   _____

10. The speech instructor asked that we be either seated before the first speaker was called or that we wait outside until the speech was concluded.

    _____

EXERCISE VIIi
Write some original sentences using the following.

1. Parallel words

He was cold, tired, and hungry.

a. _____

_____

b. _____

_____

c. _____

_____

2. Parallel phrases

Gloria enjoys going to the movies, going to Winky's, and going to basketball games.

a. _____

_____

b. _____

_____

c. _____

_____

3. Parallel clauses

John hoped that his book would be published, that it would become a best seller, and that it would be made into a movie.

a. _____

_____

b. _____

_____

c. _____

_____

WORDS

The Dictionary

Speakers, readers, and writers all depend on the **dictionary,** a reference book that contains an alphabetical, explanatory list of words. When you speak, you need to know how words are pronounced; when you write, you need to know how words are spelled. More important, however, whether you are speaking or reading or writing, you need to know the **meaning** of words because word meaning is the foundation of clear communication. All of these things the dictonary supplies.

Although pronunciation, spelling, and meaning are the things you most frequently look up in your dictionary, it informs you of many other things about a word. Look at this typical entry:

> **cun•ning** (kun′iṅg), *n.* **1.** skill employed in a crafty manner, as in deceiving; craftiness; guile. **2.** adeptness in performance; dexterity. —*adj.* **3.** showing or made with ingenuity. **4.** artfully subtle or shrewd; crafty; sly. **5.** *Informal.* charmingly cute: *a cunning little baby.* **6.** *Archaic.* skillful; expert. —*v.* **7.** *Obs.* prp. of **can**[1]. [(n.) ME. OE *cunnung = cunn(an)* (to) know (see CAN[1]) + *-ung* -ING[1]; (adj., v.) ME. prp. of *cunnan* to know (see CAN[1] (def. 6), -ING[2])] —**cun′ning•ly,** *adv.* —**cun′ning•ness,** *n.*
> —**Syn. 1.** shrewdness, artfulness, wiliness, slyness, trickery, deception. CUNNING, ARTIFICE, CRAFT imply an inclination toward deceit, slyness, and trickery. CUNNING implies a shrewd, often instinctive skill in concealing or disguising the real purposes of one's actions: *not intelligence but a low kind of cunning.* An ARTIFICE is a clever, unscrupulous ruse, used to mislead others: *a successful artifice to conceal one's motives.* CRAFT suggests underhand methods and the use of deceptive devices and tricks to attain one's ends: *craft and deceitfulness in every act.* **2.** adroitness. **3.** ingenuous, skillful. **4.** artful, wily, tricky, foxy. —**Ant. 2.** inability.

How many things does the dictionary tell you about a word?

1. "Cun•ning," the first entry, gives you two bits of information—the spelling and the way the word can be divided into syllables. (You need to know how it can be divided in case you can't get the whole word on the paper before you get to the margin.)
2. "Kun′ing" gives you the correct pronunciation of the word. The symbol (′) shows the primary stress or accent; the syllable marked with this sign is pronounced louder than the other syllables in the word.
3. The small "*n*" gives you the part of speech of the word. Thus, "*n*" tells you that the word is a noun. This information helps you to use the word correctly.
4. Next the entry gives you definitions or meanings of the word when it is used as a noun.

Who needs a dictionary?

5. "*Adj*" tells you that the word can also be used as an adjective. (This is the way *cunning* is usually used.)

6. In the dictionary entry, numbers 3, 4, 5, and 6 give you more definitions for the adjective *cunning*.

7. Before you go on, notice the "*Informal.*" before definition number 5. "*Informal.*" indicates a colloquialism used in the United States. This means the word cannot be used this way in formal speech or formal writing, but it can be used in informal or familiar conversation. (If you don't know what colloquialism means, look it up in a good dictionary.)

8. Notice also that before definition 6 you have the word "*Archaic.*" This, too, means you can't use the word in formal composition, this time because the word no longer has the meaning given here. "*Archaic*" means "from an earlier period," so definition 6 tells you what the word used to mean.

9. Next you learn the history of the word. Before you can understand the history, you may have to look up, usually in the front of the dictionary, what the abbreviations mean. "ME" means Middle English. This means the word was used in England during the period 1200-1500 A.D. "OE" means Old English, or words used in England before 1200 A.D.

10. "See CAN" tells you where you can look in the dictionary for additional information.

11. Next you are given the spelling, pronunciation, and syllabification of the other forms of the word: "cun′ning•ly," the adverb; cun′ning•ness, the noun.

12. The next entry gives you synonyms of the word—six of them. This section is useful in your writing because often you find yourself repeating and repeating a word. To relieve the monotony, you may want to use another word that means **almost** the same thing.

13. The section beginning "CUNNING, ARTIFICE, CRAFT" is the usage section of the definition. This is a very important part of a word definition. It tells you **when** and **how** to use the word. It explains the differences in meanings of words that mean almost the same thing. It helps you to use the

exact word, the word that will make what you write clear to the reader. All **good** desk dictionaries have this section; some pocket dictionaries do not.

Thirteen items of information in a few inches of type make the dictionary an indispensable reference tool.

The Dictionary as a Guide to Pronunciation

An up-to-date dictionary records the pronunciation currently used by the majority of educated people. To make use of the dictionary as a guide to pronunciation, however, you must become familiar with the **pronunciation key,** which is the system of symbols the dictionary uses in indicating pronunciation. A pronunciation key is usually found at the front of the dictionary. Many dictionaries also provide a key printed in the margin at the bottom of the vocabulary pages. Learning this key is the first step in using the dictionary as a guide to pronunciation.

With any word of more than one syllable, an important part of correct pronunciation is putting stress on the right syllables. A common fault of pronunciation is to misplace the accent or stress—to say pre-**fer**-able instead of **pref**-erable or **de**-vice instead of de-**vice.** Such errors in pronunciation can easily be avoided by paying attention to the stress marks (′) which your dictionary provides.

> **EXERCISE VIIj**
> Paying close attention to pronunciation symbols, use a standard dictionary to check the pronunciation of the following words which are frequently mispronounced:

abdomen	irrelevant	realtor
actually	irreparable	respite
athlete	library	sherbet
carburetor	mischievous	slept
comparable	nuclear	strength
genuine	picture	theater
government	political	thoroughly
handkerchief	probably	vitamin
	protein	

The Dictionary as a Guide to Spelling

If there are two acceptable spellings of a word, a good dictionary will give both and will usually indicate which of the two is preferred. Many times the reason for two correct spellings is that one is British English and the other American English. For example, American English spells this word as *h-o-n-o-r,* but British English is *h-o-n-o-u-r.* Although both are correct, if you are an American, the American spelling is preferable for you.

The dictionary also indicates whether a compound word should be spelled as one word, such as *football;* or hyphenated, such as *sight-seeing;* or two words, such as *horse race.*

defining

A good dictionary will also list the principal parts of verbs, the plurals of nouns, and the comparative and superlative forms of adjectives, but often only if these forms are irregular and so present spelling difficulties. For instance, the following irregular verb:

INFINITIVE: to occur
PAST TENSE: occurred
PRESENT PARTICIPLE: occurring
THIRD PERSON SINGULAR PRESENT TENSE: occurs

or the following irregular plural nouns:

hero – heroes
pansy – pansies
child – children
deer – deer
ox   – oxen

or the following irregular adjectives:

pretty – prettier – prettiest
bad   – worse   – worst

EXERCISE VIIk
Check in a good dictionary to determine if the following words should be written as one word, a hyphenated word, or two words. Write the correct form in the blank beside the word.

1. upperlevel _____
2. intramural _____
3. welltodo _____
4. snowshoe _____
5. showoff _____

6. skilift _____
7. markdown _____
8. selfcontrol _____
9. brandname _____
10. summertime _____

EXERCISE VIII
Check in a good dictionary to find a second correct spelling and then, if it is applicable, indicate the preferred American form.

First correct form	Second correct form	Preferred American form
theatre	_____	_____
center	_____	_____
travelled	_____	_____
cruller	_____	_____
humor	_____	_____

Write out the principal parts of the following verbs. If you are unsure of them, check a dictionary.

Infinitive	Third person singular present	Present participle	Past tense	Past participle
1. to get	_____	_____	_____	_____
2. to teach	_____	_____	_____	_____
3. to dive	_____	_____	_____	_____
4. to bring	_____	_____	_____	_____
5. to swim	_____	_____	_____	_____
6. to think	_____	_____	_____	_____
7. to steal	_____	_____	_____	_____
8. to throw	_____	_____	_____	_____
9. to drive	_____	_____	_____	_____
10. to try	_____	_____	_____	_____

EXERCISE VIIn

Give the plural forms of the following nouns.

1. alumnus	_____	6. herring	_____
2. stigma	_____	7. peony	_____
3. fish	_____	8. spoonful	_____
4. fly	_____	9. index	_____
5. appendix	_____	10. goose	_____

EXERCISE VIIo

Compare the following adjectives.

Positive	Comparative	Superlative
1. sly	_____	_____
2. well	_____	_____
3. ill	_____	_____
4. much	_____	_____
5. good	_____	_____

The Dictionary as a Guide to Meaning

Dictionaries, in the strictest sense, do not define words but record the meanings used by the majority of educated speakers and writers. That is, dictionaries are recorders rather than policy makers in the usage of words. They give their readers information concerning meaning and usage through various methods, described below.

SIMPLE
DEFINITION Suppose your English instructor uses the word *syntax* in class, and you are not sure what he means. Therefore, you look it up and find the dictionary gives as a first definition "1. orig., orderly or systematic arrangement." This does not fit into the context of your instructor's lecture, so obviously you must read on. The next item in the dictionary is "2. *Gram.* (a) the arrangement of words as elements in a sentence to show their relationship to one another; (b) sentence structure; (c) the branch of grammar dealing with this." Item 2 is clearly what your instructor was talking about.

For several reasons, it is important to read the dictionary entry all the way through and not stop at the first definition. First, as in the example with *syntax*, you might get an incorrect meaning for your purpose. Second, in all Merriam-Webster dictionaries, the first meaning is the oldest meaning and therefore might be out of date for your purpose. Finally, if you read the entire entry, you learn more about the word, which helps you to remember it.

ETYMOLOGY Etymology is the history of a word. It may be simply the **derivation** of a word, that is, the languages through which it passed before it came into modern English. The following examples show the derivation of words as given in *Webster's New World Dictionary:*

Women [ME wumman < OE wifmann, later wimman < wif, a female + mann, a human being, man . . .]

This coded information means that *woman* comes from Middle English (language of England from c. 1200 to 1500), which comes from Old English (language of England from c. 400 to 1200) and that it is a compound word made up of the words *wif* (female) and *mann* (human being). The changes indicated in ME *wumann* from OE *wifmann* and from *wifmann* to *wimman* occured because the later forms are easier to pronounce.

In the case of the word *woman*, the derivation is just through the chronological periods of English. Such words are said to belong to the "native stock" of English. Probably about 60 percent of your vocabulary comes from the native stock of words, but many others come into modern English through other languages.

discipline [ME < from OFr descipline < L. disciplina < L. discipulus]

This means that the modern word *discipline* came into our language from Middle English, which derived it from an Old French word, which in turn came from two Latin words.

Root Words

You might wonder what help it is to know that a word ultimately goes back to a Latin word. As it happens, it helps a great deal because through this information you learn that Latin words, which are our largest group from a foreign language, are divided into **roots, prefixes,** and **suffixes.** Learning these relatively few components can give you clues to the meanings of thousands of words.

Roots

Roots are the basic, central portion of words, usually a Latin noun or verb. The five Latin roots most frequently used to develop English words are the following.

Latin forms	Meaning	Root
1. facio, facere, factus, ficere, fictus	to do, to make	*fac, fect, fic*

More than 250 English words are built on this root, among them:

af**fec**t, af**fec**tion, dif**fic**ult, manu**fac**ture, per**fec**t

2. capio, capere, captus	to take, to seize, to grasp	cap, capt, cept

More than 100 English words are based on this root, among them:

ac**cep**t, **cap**able, contra**cep**tive, inter**cep**t, re**cep**tion

3. mitto, mittere, missus	to let go, to send	mit(t), mis(s)

More than 100 English words are based on this root, among them:

ad**mit**, com**mit**, dis**miss**, sub**mit**, trans**mit**

4. specio, specere, spectus	to look at, to look around	spec, spect

Almost 200 English words are formed from this root, among them:

ex**pect**, in**spect**, circum**spect**, **spec**ify, sus**pic**ion

5. duco, ducere, ductus	to take, to lead, to draw	duc, duct

Almost 100 English words are based on this root, among them:

con**duct**, e**duc**ation, pro**duct**, repro**duce**, intro**duce**

Prefixes

As you can see from the examples of the words built on Latin roots, there must be more to the word than just the root. Added to the roots are **affixes,** which are made up of **prefixes** (word parts put at the beginning of the word) and **suffixes** (word parts put at the end of the word).

defining   Among the most common Latin prefixes are the following:

Prefix	Meaning	Example
ab-, abs-	away, from	*abscond* *absent*
ad-, ac-	to, toward	*accept* *adverse*
ante-	before	*antecedent*
circum-	around	*circumstance*
com-, con-	with, together	*compare* *contrast*
contra-	against	*contradict*
de-	down, away, reversal	*deprive* *descent*
in-	not	*injustice*
in-	in, into	*intrude* *inflate*
inter-	among, between	*intermural* *interfere*
mal-	bad, wrong, ill	*maladjustment* *malefactor*
non-	not	*nonentity* *nonconformist*
post-	after	*postpone* *postmortem*
re-	back, backward, again	*recall* *recollect* *remember*
trans-	across	*transmit* *transition*

The following Greek prefixes are also common and important. Their most frequent use is in technical and scientific writing.

Prefix	Meaning	Example
a-, an-	without, not	*atheist, agnostic*
anti-	opposite, against	*anti*-climax *antagonist*
dia-	across, through, between	*diagonal* *diagnosis*
eu-	well, good	*eulogize* *euphemism*
hyper-	over, alone, beyond	*hyperactive*
hypo-	below, under, less	*hypocrite*

Prefix	Meaning	Example
para-, par-	beside, alongside of	*paramedic*
peri-	around, encircling	*perimeter*
pro-	before (in time and place)	*prologue*
syn-, sym-	with, together, like	*synonym*
		sympathy

Suffixes

These Latin and Greek suffixes are attached at the end of the roots.

Suffix	Meaning	Example
-able, -ible	having the quality, capacity, or fitness	educ*able* incorrig*ible*
-al	having character of, pertaining to	poetic*al* form*al*
-ance, -ence	action, process, quality, or state of	mainten*ance* compet*ence*
-ary	belonging or pertaining to, a place for	volunt*ary* avi*ary*
-ation	act, doing, being	consider*ation* civiliz*ation*
-er, -or	process of, one who does something	supp*er* do*er* act*or*
-ful	full of, characterized by	spoon*ful* beauti*ful*
-fy	to make	intensi*fy* modi*fy*
-ion	act or state of	tradit*ion* persuas*ion*
-ism	act, state, doctrine, or characteristic of	commun*ism* capital*ism*
-ist	one who acts, believes, works, or is skilled in	typ*ist* de*ist* dent*ist*
-ity	quality, state, degree, condition	inferior*ity* personal*ity* qual*ity*
-ive	having the quality of	addict*ive* compuls*ive* affirmat*ive*
-ize	to subject to, to make, to practice	critic*ize* penal*ize*
-less	without	form*less* bottom*less*
-ment	a state of action or being	amuse*ment*

There are, of course, many more roots and some more affixes than are given here. Indeed, it would take a whole book to discuss them all in proper detail. However, once you have the idea of searching out the word parts in the dictionary entries, you have a method for greatly increasing your vocabulary.

Histories

In addition to their derivations, many words have colorful histories showing the way some imaginative person created the word. The word *pupil*, for example, means a young student. This comes from the Latin word *pupilla*, which means literally "little dolls." It is easy to see how this term of affection was applied to schoolchildren. But how did it come to mean the *pupil* of the eye? Because some-one noticed that the eye reflects *in miniature* what it sees. Therefore, since *pupils* are little people, the term *pupil* is also applied to the organ that reflects little people (as well as other little things).

Although there are many words with such quaint or interesting histories, the real value in knowing them is that such knowledge helps you remember and develop your awareness of words. Other unusual words are those taken from proper names in mythology, or from outstanding persons in history, literature, or the sciences.

SYNONYMS One of the best ways to use your dictionary to enlarge your vocabulary and so im-prove your writing is to pay close attention to the entries that list synonyms and discuss the distinctions among them. If you read the synonyms, you may be able to vary your word choice to avoid being monotonous. Even more important, an awareness of synonyms will make your writing more precise.

The great Roman orator Quintilian said that a good writer did not try to see that the reader *might* understand but that the reader *must* understand. To guarantee that your reader understands you, you must be precise, you must choose the exact word. Since no two synonyms are identical, you must select with care the one that best suits your purpose.

Notice the following entry from *The American Heritage Dictionary*. The six synonymous words for the word *moving* all refer to definition 3, but a careful writer would not use them interchangeably.

mov•ing (moo′ving) *adj.* **1.** Changing or capable of changing position. **2.** Caus-ing or producing motion. **3.** Affecting the emotions: *a moving tale.* —**mov′ing•ly** *adv.* —**mov′ing•ness** *n.* **Synonyms:** *moving, stirring, poignant, touching, pa-thetic, affecting.* These words all refer to emotional reaction. *Moving* applies to that which calls forth any deeply felt emotion. *Stirring* stresses strong emo-tion, and is related to stimulation and inspiration. *Poignant* describes that which pierces or penetrates; it has wide-ranging application, from a grief to sar-casm and (less often) to delight. *Touching* emphasizes sympathy and compas-sion. *Pathetic* stresses pity, and sometimes mild scorn (for that which is hopelessly inept or inadequate). *Affecting* applies to anything capable of mov-ing the feelings, but usually pertains to that which inspires pity and tenderness.

In the *New World Dictionary*, the entry under *give* presents twenty definitions for the word as an intransitive verb and an additional five definitions for it as a transitive verb. Then it gives the synonyms, which also vary enough that the careful writer would not interchange them.

SYN.—give is the general word meaning to transfer from one's own possession to that of another; **grant** implies that there has been a request or an expressed desire for the thing given [to *grant* a favor]; **present** implies a certain formality in the giving and often connotes considerable value in the gift [he *presented* the school with a library]; **donate** is used especially of a giving to some philanthropic or religious cause; **bestow** stresses that the thing is given gratuitously and often implies condescension in the giver [to *bestow* charity upon the poor]; **confer** implies that the giver is a superior and that the thing given is an honor, privilege, etc. [to *confer* a title, a college degree, etc.]

LABELING

Still another way in which your dictionary helps you write precisely and correctly is known as *labeling*. If, for any reason, the use of a word is limited, the dictionary will label it to indicate what its limitations are. If no label appears, the word is correct in all usages.

Subject Labels

In most dictionaries, if you looked up the phrase *home run,* you would find the label *Baseball.* The word *homeostasis* is labeled *Physiology.* Such labels appear for many words in business, law, finance, sciences, and other fields.

Usage Labels

The labels *obsolete* and *archaic* indicate that the words are limited by **time.** For example, the word *ere,* meaning "before," you would probably find marked archaic and so would not use it.

The labels *dialect* and *provincial* indicate that the words are limited by **geography.** For example, the word *cornpone* you would find marked *Dialect, southern U.S.A.*

Other labels indicate the level of **formality** at which the word is appropriate.

1. *Colloq.* means correct for speech but probably too informal for writing. For example, "*picky* [colloq.] fussy"
2. *Slang* means limited to informal speech and often limited to a specific group. For example, "*hooch* [slang] alcoholic liquor"
3. *Substandard* means limited to *uneducated* speech. For example, "*you'uns* [substandard] you, you all"

NOTE: Your dictionary will never let you down if you use it with care. However, such care includes reading the introduction to discover on what bases levels of usage are determined and what terms are used to identify them.

Types of Dictionaries

O.E.D. The most complete and authoritative of dictionaries is *The Oxford English Dictionary*. This many-volumed dictionary is a monument of scholarship, which gives you a detailed history of every word it lists. It is far too complete for everyday use, but it is a reference book you need to know about when you must have a full knowledge of any given word. Almost all college libraries have this on their reference shelves.

UNABRIDGED DICTIONARIES Unabridged dictionaries, too, are usually found only on library shelves. The best known of them is *Webster's Third New International Dictionary of the English Language*. It has 450,000 entries with complete definitions and many illustrations of the various uses of a word. (Many people prefer the older second edition because it offers more guidelines for usage than does the third edition.)

DESK DICTIONARIES The most useful type of dictionary for your everyday use is a desk dictionary. A good, up-to-date dictionary has from 100,000 to 155,000 entries with full discussions of the listed words.

From the many desk dictionaries available, here is a short list of popular editions:

Webster's New World Dictionary, Second College Edition, Cleveland: Simon & Schuster, 1980.

The American Heritage Dictionary of the English Language, New College Ed. Boston: Houghton Mifflin, 1978.

The Random House Dictionary of the English Language, College Ed. New York: Random House, 1975.

Webster's New Collegiate Dictionary, 8th ed. Springfield, Mass: G. & C. Merriam, 1976.

Funk and Wagnalls Standard College Dictionary, New York: Funk and Wagnalls, 1975.

EXERCISE VIIp
Look up the derivation (history) of ten of the following words. Can you explain how or why the meaning has changed?

bedlam	haberdasher	sandwich
body	hospital	sarcasm
bonfire	jazz	savor
bully	knight	spoon
center	lorgnette	symposium
courtesy	miasma	table
dilapidation	moonshine	verge
distaff	nice	villain
garbage	portly	whiskey
gossip	salad	window

EXERCISE VIIq

Look up the following words in a good desk dictionary to find their structural parts.

	Word	Root	Prefix	Suffix	Meaning
1.	elucidate	_____	_____	_____	_____
2.	perennial	_____	_____	_____	_____
3.	anthropology	_____	_____	_____	_____
4.	synthesize	_____	_____	_____	_____
5.	hagiography	_____	_____	_____	_____
6.	telescope	_____	_____	_____	_____
7.	photophobic	_____	_____	_____	_____
8.	hydrogen	_____	_____	_____	_____
9.	eugenics	_____	_____	_____	_____
10.	protoplasm	_____	_____	_____	_____

EXERCISE VIIr

For the words listed below, find the proper nouns from which they came.

1. to pander _____

2. ohm _____

3. titan _____

4. ampere _____

5. watt _____

6. venereal _____

7. mentor _____

8. pasteurize _____

9. vulcanize _____

10. psyche _____

EXERCISE VIIs

Look up the following words in a good desk dictionary and find the synonyms. Read these synonyms carefully and then make up sentences using the word and each of its synonyms in a way to reveal the different shades of meaning among them.

1. defend   3. explain
2. noise   4. difference

194

5. recover	**8.** change
6. talkative	**9.** new
7. ruin (verb)	**10.** hairy

EXERCISE VIIt
On one page of a desk dictionary, the following words appeared from eight different sources other than the expected English and Latin.

hag, meaning "marsh" from Scottish
Hagar, a proper name, from Hebrew
Haggadah, traditional Jewish literature, from Hebrew
haggard, means "gaunt," from Old French
haggis, meaning "a kind of stew," from Scottish
hagio, prefix meaning "saint," from Greek
haik, meaning "an outer garment," from Arabic
hail, meaning "to greet," from Old Norse

Choosing a page at random, read through it to see how many different sources of words you can find on it.

CHAPTER VIII

explaining with facts

ORGANIZATION

As you have seen, there are various ways of supporting your controlling idea. One of the most effective ways is to collect factual details and organize them to develop your topic sentence. This method follows the standard paragraph organization: introduction, body, and conclusion.

In the 1950's a successful police series, "Dragnet," began on TV. It was quite popular, and viewers loved to imitate Detective Sgt. Friday, who at some point during each program, would intone, "All I want is the facts, M'am—just the facts." Once Sgt. Friday got the facts, he solved the case. Once your reader gets the facts, he will probably be convinced that you know what you are writing about and believe what you say. Facts are effectively used to strengthen any written presentation.

What is a fact?

A fact is a piece of information that can be verified (proved to be true or not true).

How is a fact used in this kind of paragraph?

A writer whose purpose is to inform can select key details (facts) to support the controlling idea.

Why is it important to use facts whenever possible?

A fact provides correct information to the reader. Once a careful reader sees that you are using solid facts to support your controlling idea, he or she will be more willing to accept what you have to say.

How can one tell what is a fact and what isn't?

The Difference Between Fact and Judgment

A **fact** is something that actually exists—in other words, something that can be verified. For example, "When John became a father, he stayed home every weekend for three months to baby-sit"; or "During John's first six weeks as a father, he arose at five o'clock every morning." If you can't prove that something happened or that it exists, then what you have is not a fact; it is probably a judgment. A **judgment** is a more general statement, like an opinion, a conclusion. For example, "John's lifestyle changed drastically when he became a father." Note that you can't even begin to form a judgment about John's lifestyle until you know the facts—the specific changes in John's lifestyle. When the judgment is a generalization, that generalization should be based on facts. Without facts to support them, judgments may be merely prejudice (*pre-judgment*). Here are some examples that illustrate the difference between fact and judgment.

FACT: Sherry wine is produced in both California and New York. (An encyclopedia or a reliable handbook on wines can prove that this is true.)

JUDGMENT: The *best* sherry wine is produced in New York State. (There may be differences of opinion on this view.)

FACT: Frank demolished three cars last year.

JUDGMENT: Frank is a *reckless* driver.

FACT: In addition to providing the B complex vitamins, spinach is also a source of vitamin A and vitamin C.

JUDGMENT: Spinach is *good* for you.

FACT: I got an A on my last psychology test.

JUDGMENT: My last psychology test was *easy.*

Notice how the words *best, reckless, good,* and *easy* imply judgment on the part of the writer, whereas a sentence such as "Sherry wine is produced both in California and New York" reveals no particular feeling.

You develop a paragraph with factual details by using **facts** to explain a controlling idea which is a general statement, a judgment, or an opinion. Before you begin to write a factual detail paragraph, therefore, you must first be sure that you understand the difference between a fact and a judgment.

Even if a factual statement is wrong, it is still a factual statement; that is, it can be proved right or wrong. "Our auditorium seats 950 people" is a factual statement even if the auditorium seats only 800, because you can prove the statement is incorrect. "Our auditorium is large" is a judgmental statement because you can't prove that an auditorium is "large" or that it isn't. "Large" and "small" are general words that express the view of the writer or speaker. Thus, it is the words used that make a statement factual or judgmental. Facts are always stated in specific terms; judgments are stated in general terms. In factual statements, you will find specific names, statistics, figures, and the like.

Convincing with Facts

Some statements cannot be substantiated without facts. For example,

Lindbergh's flight was not the first crossing of the Atlantic by air.

There is no way that you can prove this statement without citing facts that show someone else flew across the Atlantic before May 20, 1927. In his book *Only Yesterday*, Frederick Lewis Allen presents several facts to prove that Lindbergh was not the first person to cross the Atlantic by air.

... Alcock and Brown had flown direct from Newfoundland to Ireland in 1919. That same year the N–C4, with five men aboard, had crossed by way of the Azores, and the British dirigible F–34 had flown from Scotland to Long Island with thirty-one men aboard, and then had turned about and made a return flight to England. The German dirigible 2R–3 had flown from Friedrichshafen to Lakehurst, New Jersey, in 1924 with thirty-two people aboard. Two Round-the-World American army planes had crossed the North Atlantic by way of Iceland, Greenland, and Newfoundland in 1924.

The most effective way to support some statements is to use **numerical facts**—statistics. For example, the following statement about the effects of the air pollution disaster in Donora, Pennsylvania, in 1948 requires numerical data for proof: "Worst hit by the smog were adults." You could cite a few examples of adult Donora residents who became seriously ill or died from the smog, but that wouldn't prove your point. It would prove that **some** adult residents of Donora were seriously affected by the air pollution, but it wouldn't prove that the adult residents were hit worse than any other Donorans. The statement could be substantiated much more convincingly through numerical facts, as the following paragraph illustrates.

Worst hit by the smog were adults. Of 100 Donorans age 20 and over, precisely 50.5% became ill from the smog; for Donorans who were younger than 20, the illness rate was half as great. ... This lower rate for the young may have resulted from their generally better health. Or the shorter lifetime of young Donorans may have favored them with less previous exposure to their town's polluted air. Whatever the reason, the study made clear that the older a Donoran was, the more likely he was to become ill in the smog. Illness affected 31% of Donorans between the ages of 20 and 24. The illness rate jumped to 55% for the 40 to 44 age bracket. Among persons 60 to 65, the sizable fraction of 63% became ill. Further, the older a person was, the more severe were his symptoms. Consider three age brackets: a younger group under age 35, a middle group between ages 35 and 54, and an older group age 55 and over. In the smog, the middle group suffered twice the severe illnesses of the younger. The older group's severe-illness rate was double even that.

Howard R. Lewis, With Every Breath You Take

Remember that specific facts are always more convincing than a series of judgments. It's easy for the reader to disagree with your opinions if they are not supported with facts, but if you back up your judgment with factual detail, your reader will find it harder to argue with you.

On a sociology examination, a student was asked to prove that primitive cultures suffer when they come into contact with advanced civilizations.

It's really tough on a primitive culture when an advanced culture moves in. The primitives can't do things their own way anymore, and they get troubled and sick and they die off. This has happened many times and in many places around the world.

The student's answer is true. However, you can't be sure that it is true because the writer has not given you any facts to check. He uses general and nonspecific terms. You would be surprised to find a paragraph like that in your sociology textbook—and your sociology professor would be disappointed to find that paragraph on your test.

Consider the following paragraph as an answer to the essay question.

Contact with an advanced civilization has virtually destroyed some primitive cultures and peoples. When the British came to Melanesia, they abolished headhunting, a major aspect of the Melanesian culture. The Melanesians lost interest in living. On one island, the number of childless marriages increased from 19% to 46%, on another from 12% to 72%. Also, in the early 1900's, the Australians began migrating from their coastal cities into the interior of the continent. As a result, the aborigines, who had lived there for centuries, virtually disappeared. Also, the population of Tahiti was decimated after the arrival of de Tocqueville and the French explorers. Our own American Indian population dropped from an estimated 200,000 to less than 30,000 during the 1800's when the white man's westward movement destroyed the buffalo. When an advanced civilization meets a primitive one, it is the latter that often suffers.

Now this paragraph may or may not convince you, but because it contains facts and not just judgments, you can check to see whether or not the statements are true.

EXERCISE VIIIa
Tell which of the following statements are facts and which are judgments.

_____ 1. Babe Ruth was a great baseball player.
_____ 2. Roger Maris hit more home runs in one season than did any other professional baseball player.
_____ 3. Algebra is difficult.
_____ 4. Seattle is the rainiest city in the country.
_____ 5. Idiots have a mental age of 0–2 years.
_____ 6. Our new recreation center holds a lot of people.
_____ 7. A penny saved is a penny earned.
_____ 8. It's fun to write paragraphs.
_____ 9. Our stadium can seat 25,000 people.
_____ 10. Last year we had a cold winter.

The Pattern of Organization

The basic organization of a factual paragraph is quite simple.

1. Topic sentence—General statement (controlling idea).
2. Body—
   First factual detail of support
   Second factual detail of support
   Third factual detail of support
   Fourth factual detail of support
   etc.
3. Conclusion—restatement of controlling idea.

Topic Sentence

The topic sentence of an expository paragraph of factual detail is a generalization which states your viewpoint, based on the particular facts you have learned about that subject. A writer chooses a subject that she has learned something about. She puts the pieces of knowledge together (and goes to find out more if she doesn't know enough); then, on the basis of these facts, she reasons through to a general statement which is her topic sentence.

For example, consider the following paragraph.

Evolved over a period of perhaps two million years, the human brain is unsurpassed as a miracle of matter. Even though it weighs only about three pounds, the human brain contains some 100 billion cells. Of these, about 10 billion are neurons, or true brain cells. Each of these neurons is a sophisticated electro-chemical processing center capable of processing thousands of bits of incoming information. By processes still not fully understood, the neuron selects and interprets incoming stimuli, extracting what is of importance for the moment, transmitting selected bits of information to other brain cells, and committing to the memory bank items of lasting importance. Some areas of the brain contain as many as 100 million of these neurons to the cubic inch, and each is connected to tens of thousands of others. Although modern computers may be able to calculate the path of a missile or the chances of a nuclear explosion far faster than any human being, no combination of computers could begin to match the miraculous complexity and subtlety of the human brain.

Beware of a vague topic sentence. For example:

Topic sentence: "The old Buick needed extensive repairs."

Your reader might immediately wonder what, exactly, you mean by "extensive repairs." Engine? Transmission? Brakes? Exhaust system? Body work?

By carefully selecting specific details to answer such questions, you can effectively develop this type of paragraph.

A topic sentence **cannot** simply state a fact, because facts are neutral; they don't have positive or negative attitudes. "Fifty-eight percent of American women work" is a fact. It makes no judgment about working women with which you can agree or disagree. Thus, it is not a good topic sentence. It contains no

The old Buick needed extensive repairs.

idea that can be developed. On the other hand, "The typical American family has been undergoing a change" is a good topic sentence because it presents a controlling idea: the family is changing. The judgment that has been made about the family in the topic sentence can then be supported with factual detail.

The typical American family—father working while mother stays home and takes care of the house and children—has been undergoing a change. From 1960–1978, the number of working women increased from 37.8% to 50.1% of the female population aged sixteen years and over. The majority of American homes in 1978 included working women. There were 8.2 million families maintained by single women in 1978, and 1.3 million of these women had never been married. The total number of female-maintained households increased by 2.7 million from 1970–1978. Also, the number of homes with unrelated persons living together has increased as young people postpone marriage yet live together away from parents. Between 1970 and 1978, the number of single men increased by 4.6 million and the number of single women by 3.3 million. In addition, both husbands and wives are wage earners in an increasing number of homes. In March of 1978, 47.6% of all wives were looking for a job or already were working. And 52.9% of all mothers with children under eighteen years of age were in the labor force. We can no longer state that the typical American family is one in which the father works while the mother stays at home.

Information Please Almanac, *1980*

EXERCISE VIIIb
See if you can find the controlling idea in the next two bodies of factual detail. Then construct an appropriate topic sentence for each paragraph.

In Buffalo, New York, six persons were hospitalized with "cardiovascular collapse" after they ate blood sausage which contained excessive amounts of nitrite, used to maintain the color in the sausage. In New Jersey, two persons died and many others were critically poisoned after eating fish illegally loaded with nitrite. In New Orleans, ten youngsters between the ages of one and a half and five became seriously ill after eating wieners or bologna over-nitrited by a local meat-processing firm. One wiener that was obtained later from the plant was found to contain a whopping 6,570 parts per million of nitrite, whereas the federal limitation is 200 parts per million. In Florida, a three-year-old boy died after eating hot dogs with three times greater nitrite concentration than the government allows. And in Washington, D.C., a man died after eating pure nitrite mistakenly marketed as "Spice of Life Meat Tenderizer," which he accidentally sprinkled on food.

Jacqueline Verret and Jean Carper, Eating May Be Hazardous to Your Health

Controlling   Idea: _____

_____

Topic   Sentence: _____

_____

According to a Massachusetts Institute of Technology study, the airline fatality risk has dropped by more than half in the past fifteen years. Putting this into numbers, the chances of being killed on an airline flight in the United States are one in 2,599,000. This means that a person would have to live 3,560 years and make two flights per day just to use up all of his chances. However, it has been only recently that the fatality statistics have made a substantial drop. In 1980, according to a January 1981 government report, there were twenty accidents involving major U.S. air carriers. This was the smallest number of accidents per year in the last two decades. Nineteen eighty was the first year in U.S. aviation history that there were no fatal airline accidents, and only fourteen persons died because of airline-related incidents. This figure sharply contrasts with the average of 258 deaths that prevailed throughout the 1970's. The Federal Aviation Administration is responsible for this sudden decline in accidents. The F.A.A., through their accident prevention program, intends eventually to eliminate all aviation accidents. As a result, the F.A.A. has adopted a new ground avoidance system in all airliners, and they are presently working on a new collision avoidance system. The F.A.A., by utilizing the advanced technology available in the United States, has made these developments possible. Since the technology is greater in the United States, it is about four times safer to fly within this country than on any international flight. Because of the development and increased use of the new safety equipment, the airline industry is becoming safer each year.

Todd Daczkowski

Controlling   Idea: _____

_____

Topic   Sentence: _____

_____

EXERCISE VIIIc
Check the following topic sentences that could be developed by facts. Underline the word or words that indicate fact or judgment.

_____   1.   "Masterpiece Theater" is a wonderful TV program.

_____   2.   "Dallas" is a popular TV program.

_____   3.   Japanese-Americans are good citizens.

_____   4.   Japanese-Americans have a low crime rate.

_____	5.	Cars are expensive to buy, to run, and to repair.
_____	6.	More people are going to college now than ever before.
_____	7.	Tony Dorsett is a great running back for the Dallas Cowboys.
_____	8.	Hunting is immoral.
_____	9.	Pets are a big business in the United States.
_____	10.	Many people in the United States do not take advantage of their right to vote.

Body

The body of the paragraph consists of the specific details necessary to develop the controlling idea adequately. As you select the facts for the body of your paragraph, you must apply these common sense tests:

1. Be sure that you have **sufficient facts.** The number of facts you use will depend on your subject and purpose. You may elaborate on several factual details and discuss them fully, or you may feel that your controlling idea requires many supporting facts to make it convincing. Regardless of how many facts you use, your main concern is completeness. Have you presented enough facts to support your controlling thought fully?

2. Be sure that you have **relevant facts.** Choose only those facts that relate directly to your purpose. A fact that distracts your reader by introducing something new does a poor job of convincing. Relevant, specific, interesting facts which stick to the point can hold your reader's attention and help the reader to focus directly on your main idea.

EXERCISE VIIId

Irrelevant details have been added to the following student's factual paragraph. Underline the sentences that do not pertain to the paragraph's controlling idea, and then list these irrelevant sentences by number on the line below the paragraph.

(1) Foreign countries have many different laws and regulations regarding a legal abortion. (2) Denmark has legalized abortion up to the seventeenth week of pregnancy, but under the Italian penal code, performing or consenting to an abortion is punishable by two to five years' imprisonment. (3) I think that this is probably because there are a lot of Catholics in Italy. (4) In Switzerland, abortion is permitted when pregnancy is dangerous to the physical and mental health of the mother and when there is reason to believe that the child will suffer birth defects. (5) Bulgaria and Czechoslovakia limit abortions to women having valid medical or social reasons, while the Soviet Union, Rumania, and Hungary permit them only within a certain number of weeks after conception. (6) It is interesting to note that most of the doctors in the Soviet Union are women. (7) Perhaps they are more aware of the dangerous psychological effects of abortion on women. (8) In Sweden, under the new Abortion Act, the woman herself can decide the question of abortion prior to the nineteenth week of pregnancy. (9) Almost all Swedish laws are more liberal than those of other countries. (10) In Israel, an abortion is a crime punishable by five years of im-

prisonment—unless advance authorization makes it a legal medical act. (11) In Germany, the Abortion Reform Bill stresses that termination of pregnancy after the first thirteen weeks is illegal and can be penalized by a fine or a prison sentence of up to three years. (12) Although abortion is forbidden outright in Iraq, Lebanon, Syria, and Jordan, it is excused if done to preserve the family's (man's) honor. (13) Apparently, the women's lib movement hasn't made much progress in these Arab countries.

EXPLAINING FACTS

Even after selecting and arranging factual details, you must have more than just a list of facts. Additional supporting detail must be added to reinforce, to clarify, and to explain your factual information. It is often said that "facts speak for themselves," but this does not apply unless there is a framework of information to which the reader can relate the facts. The writer must provide sufficient explanation to ensure that the purpose of the facts is clearly understood.

In the cold, hard business world there is little room for emotional appeals and none for judgments that are not supported by facts. Where decisions are being made, reliable, convincing facts must support any proposal. If statistics help to support the facts you present, they should be correct and they should clarify, not confuse. Facts can be effectively used to support the following informative and instructional ideas:

1. My experience has shown that there are three effective ways to prevent fungus in the miniature plum tree.
2. A down sleeping bag has the following advantages over any other type.
3. Personally, I prefer the .35 Remington cartridge for hunting Pennsylvania white-tailed deer.
4. In terrain like this, a frontal assault is preferable to encirclement.
5. You must use the proper punctuation, or your reader will become easily confused.

Even the driest subjects can be made both interesting and accurate if facts are presented imaginatively. Arouse your reader's curiosity with a thought-provoking topic sentence, and *convince* the reader with facts that prove you really have something to say.

PUTTING THE FACTUAL PARAGRAPH TOGETHER

Your topic sentence is a judgment. If you write, "Babe Ruth was a great baseball player," you must support this judgment with facts.

Be careful that you don't make your judgment too general, too broad, or impossible to prove. Consider the following topic sentences.

Babe Ruth was the best baseball player that ever lived.

This would involve comparing Babe with all the other players of every position. Was he better than Ty Cobb? Grover Cleveland Alexander? Roberto Clemente? Hank Aaron? How can you prove it? Impossible.

Babe Ruth was the best athlete ever.

Again, impossible. How could you prove that a baseball player is better than a boxer or a runner or a swimmer? You can't; the judgment is too broad.

Babe Ruth was a great man.

Again, this is too broad to prove in a single paragraph. There are too many aspects of a "man" to be proved in a paragraph. Narrow your controlling idea until you have a provable judgment.

The body or development of your next paragraph must be factual. Suppose you chose the topic sentence mentioned earlier, "Babe Ruth was a great baseball player." In the body, you need facts to support this claim. You might use these:

hit sixty home runs in one year—never surpassed until season was lengthened
hit 714 home runs in his career
got 2,056 bases on balls
called his shot, a home run in 1932 World Series
earned $2,000 a week in 1932—considerably more than the President of the U.S.
pitched eight times against Walter Johnson and won six of the games, three by scores of 1–0
pitched twenty-nine scoreless innings in World Series competition—a record that still stands
led the American League in homers nine out of ten years

Conclusion

An effective conclusion is not just something tacked on to provide an ending for the paragraph. It must be warranted by the facts you have presented in the body of the paragraph. A good conclusion wraps up the discussion of the topic, leaving no loose ends or unanswered questions.

Among the effective methods of concluding a factual paragraph are the following.

1. Use a concluding sentence that restates the controlling idea of the paragraph in different words.
2. Use a concluding sentence that sums up the factual details presented in the body of the paragraph.
3. Use a concluding sentence that interprets the facts and statistics presented in support of the controlling idea.

Avoid a concluding sentence that simply repeats the topic sentence word for word.
Avoid a conclusion that is not warranted by the facts you have presented.
Avoid a conclusion that introduces a new issue or topic.

Discuss the following conclusions as possibilities for the Babe Ruth paragraph?

explaining with facts

Yes, indeed, Babe Ruth was one in a million.

Babe Ruth was an outstanding member of the human race.

The records prove Babe Ruth was an outstanding baseball player.

Standing head and shoulders above all the others who played the game is the one and only, the King of Swat, the top of the heap, Babe Ruth, a thing of beauty and a joy forever.

ASSIGNMENT

Select one of the following subjects related to the automobile. Take a clear stand—for example, "Automobile exhaust fumes spread illness and disease"—and support your stand with a fact-filled paragraph.

If a topic dealing with the automobile does not appeal to you, choose another that you feel could be well developed using facts and/or statistics. Be sure to discuss its possibilities first with your instructor.

To complete either of these two assignments, you must consult and cite *at least three* library sources for specific facts, figures, and quotations. Be sure to record the facts accurately, put all direct quotations within quotation marks, and clearly identify your sources. Information on using the works of others correctly is given in the next few pages.

1. Teenage drivers
2. Traffic deaths
3. Driver education
4. Fuel economy
5. Enforcing speed limits

6. The drunken driver
7. Car size and safety
8. The American auto worker
9. Car insurance
10. Quality in American and foreign cars

Plagiarism

Schools think of themselves as communities of learners. This common interest in learning means that there is an intense wish to **share** learning, and such sharing is ruled by a few laws that must be obeyed. To violate these rules is to **plagiarize,** to present someone else's learning as your own. This is the ultimate sin in academic life.

The first rule is that you may borrow the opinions and research of others if you wish to.

The second rule is that if you do borrow someone else's opinions or research, you **must** give credit for it.

There are two ways to incorporate the thoughts of others into your own work:

1. You may quote them directly, word for word, and place quotation marks around the quotation to show that you have made **no** changes in the original wording.

The Edwardian Age was "The name usually given the period in English literature between the death of Victoria in 1901 and the beginning of the first World War in 1914, so-called after King Edward VII, who ruled from 1901 to 1910."[1]

2. You may also **paraphrase** instead of quoting directly, putting the author's thoughts into your own language and style. This involves a complete rewriting of the original material and not just the changing of a word or two. Also, when paraphrasing, you must not change the intent or the opinions of the original source. Note the difference between the direct quotation above and the following paraphrase of the same material.

The Edwardian Age, named after King Edward VII, is the period in English literature extending from the death of Queen Victoria in 1901 to the outbreak of World War I in 1914.[1]

Remember that whether you choose to quote directly or to paraphrase, you are still using someone else's thoughts. Therefore, in both situations, you must give credit to the original source of that information.

In a single paragraph or short essay, you can usually give credit to your source informally **within** the text. Here are several ways of acknowledging your source within the paragraph itself:

1. According to Thrall and Hibbard's *Handbook to Literature,* the "Edwardian Age" is the name given to ...

2. For example, the January 1982 *Consumer's Guide* (p. 93) rates the Mazda 626 as superior to the Toyota Corolla and the Datsun 510.

3. In an address at Massachusetts Institute of Technology in June of 1981, Senator John Glenn remarked, "..."

4. In his article "The Diesels Are Coming" (*Motor Trend,* August 1981, p. 36), test driver Lars Peterson says, "..."

5. In "A Rape Victim Fights Back" (*Reader's Digest,* December 1981, p. 133), Walter Michener tells how ...

Here is a paragraph using the informal method: giving credit to your sources within the text.

Many laboratory studies are now confirming Dr. Ben F. Feingold's theory that food additives and preservatives have a devastating effect on hyperactive children. In 1973, Dr. Feingold presented preliminary observations on dietary management of hyperactive children before the Allergy Section of the annual meeting of the American Medical Association in New York. Feingold's argument is based on his clinical experiments with twenty-five children who had behavioral problems. He placed these children on his diet for six to eight weeks and diagnosed fifteen of them as responsive. His diet eliminates food that contains artificial colors and flavors and natural salicylates (substances similar to aspirin, found in various fruits and vegetables). C. Keith Connors and Charles A. Goyette, psychologists at the University of Pittsburgh, studied Feingold's diet and announced that "a simple, nutritious diet . . . will turn a problem-plagued existence into a normal life for most hyperactive children." In addition, tight double blind experiments were conducted by a Wisconsin team of psychologists on the effects of the diet. The results showed that the ten preschool children involved in the study were rated as improved by their teachers, parents, and friends. Dr. Hicks Williams, one of the Kaiser pediatricians involved in Feingold's study, stated: "Anecdotal evidence of the diet's effectiveness in certain children is overwhelming. We await scientific confirmation of the phenomenon and ultimately an explanation of its mechanism." The final study, done by J. S. Logan and W. A. Swanson, reported that a mixture of eight food dyes commonly used caused a significant inhibition of neuro-transmitter uptake in the hemagenates of a rat's brain. Although Logan and Swanson agree with Feingold's findings, they would like to see more attention given to animal or biochemical studies that might define mechanisms underlying the proposed toxicity of food dyes. Although the parents may be hindered by the time-consuming task of preparing special foods, this diet may be the long awaited answer for the hyperactive child. All of the above studies prove that Feingold's diet, which eliminates additives eaten by millions daily, can beneficially modify the behavior patterns of the hyperactive child.

Lynn Bundy

You may also give credit to your source by using a more formal method, called **footnoting.** In footnoting, credit for the source is placed either at the bottom of the page or on a separate page, depending upon the preference of your instructor. Look again at the following definition, which was borrowed from a section entitled "Edwardian Literature," in *A Handbook to Literature*, edited by Thrall and Hibbard.

Edwardian Age: "The name usually given the period in English literature between the death of Victoria in 1901 and the beginning of the first World War in 1914, so-called after King Edward VII, who ruled from 1901 to 1910."[1]

The raised numeral 1 placed *after* the passage tells the reader that you are acknowledging a borrowed thought. Your next borrowed thought would then be followed by a 2, the next a 3, and so forth. At the bottom of the page, or on a separate page, list the same numbers, in sequence. After each number, place all information that is necessary to tell the reader exactly who wrote that piece of source material and where it was found.

[1] "Edwardian Literature," *A Handbook to Literature,* ed. William Flint Thrall and Addison Hibbard (New York: The Odyssey Press, 1960), p. 162.

Always be sure to consult a composition handbook or research manual for the proper method of writing different types of footnotes. The following examples illustrate approved ways to footnote material from (1) a book, (2) a literary journal or periodical, (3) a monthly magazine, and (4) a newspaper.

[1] Ken Kesey, *One Flew Over the Cuckoo's Nest* (New York: Viking Press Inc., 1962), p. 265.

[2] James F. Knapp, "Tangled in the Language of the Past: Ken Kesey and Cultural Revolution," *The Midwest Quarterly,* 19, no. 4 (Summer 1978), 398.

[3]Lester Grundy, "Light: The Magic Decorating Ingredient," *House Beautiful,* 19, no. 2 (February 1982), 55.

explaining with facts

[4]"Congress Pro-Business, Nader Report Shows," *The Pittsburgh Press,* Sunday Edition, Section A, 17, January 7, 1982, p. 8, cols. 5–6.

Ibid., a Latin abbreviation meaning "in the same place," may be used in a footnote to refer to the book, article, or reference immediately preceding. However, it is better form to use the author's name or an abbreviated title of the work.

Here is an example of a factual paragraph using the formal method, footnoting.

There are three qualities about the cemeteries in New Orleans that I found fascinating: their unusual appearance, their vital origin, and their unique burial methods. New Orleans has practiced the present above-ground burial system since 1827. The appearance of these cemeteries suggests narrow residences with peaked roofs ranged along side streets. They are often referred to as cities within a city or "cities of the dead."[1] The tombs are often built of brick, then plastered or stuccoed to preserve the masonry. Some of the more expensive tombs are made of granite or marble, and most of the tombs are surrounded by iron gates or metal chains. Often, iron benches or chairs are arranged in front of the tombs as if the residents within are awaiting the arrival of guests. Some of the more expensive tombs have statues of trumpeting angels, marble girls in Grecian robes, Egyptian figures of men and animals, or Corinthian motifs.[2] The walls surrounding the cemeteries are six-foot brick walls with the "oven tombs," or vaults, built in. They look somewhat like filing cabinets arranged in two or three tiers. The poor can rent these vaults for a few dollars a month; however, if they fail to pay the rent, the casket is removed, and the remains and the casket are burned.[3] There are two reasons why the above-ground tombs came into existence. In the late 1700's, New Orleans buried the rich in chapels or cathedrals. The poor were buried along the riverbank in low swampy sites surrounded by ditches; the bodies were simply wrapped in shrouds or placed in cheap wooden caskets and dropped into the earth.[4] Since the water level was only two feet below ground surface, the water would pour into the gravesites as fast as the holes were being dug. Sometimes, holes had to be bored into the wooden caskets, and men would have to stand on them to force them to settle into the swampy earth. The bodies were then literally devoured by crayfish and catfish.[5] Since the bodies disintegrated so quickly, it was possible for the gravesites to be used repeatedly. Because of the cholera and yellow fever epidemics in the early 1800's, the cathedrals and churches became overcrowded. In 1827, city officials made it mandatory that all burials be above ground, and this rule initiated the burial practices that prevail in New Orleans today. The uniqueness of these cemeteries really lies in the tombs themselves. One tomb may contain as many as forty to fifty relatives spanning ten generations. It is possible for a tomb to hold this many bodies because, after a year and a day, the tombs can be reopened. The remains are then removed from the casket and deposited into a lower vault beneath or are pushed to the back; the caskets are then burned. The dust and bones of all the prior burials are mingled together, and this fact accounts for the many inscriptions on the front of the tombs. It may sound a little grim, but it works. If another relative dies before the year and a day has expired, the family can rent an "oven tomb" temporarily.[6] Above-ground burial has solved both the problems of the water-filled graves and those of the overcrowded churches and cathedrals. This method of burial may seem a little odd to us, but to the people of New Orleans it is practical and essential.

[1] Harnett T. Kane, *Queen New Orleans, City by the River* (New York: Bonanza Books, 1978), p. 295.

[2] Kane, p. 296.

[3] Kane, p. 299.

[4] Leonard V. Huber, *New Orleans, A Pictorial History* (New York: Crown Publishers, 1971), p. 118.

[5] Mary Cable, *Lost New Orleans* (Boston: Houghton Mifflin Co., 1980), p. 126.

[6] Carolyn Kolb, *New Orleans* (New York: Doubleday and Company, Inc., 1972), pp. 71, 72.

Linda Welsh

explaining with facts

SENTENCES

Modifiers

In English, words, phrases, and clauses are classified primarily according to their function. Furthermore, you can tell a good deal about the function of words by their placement within the sentence. One way of demonstrating this is through the use of nonsense words. For example, look at this "sentence":

The squazzlings gilattered the refriligs.

Even these nonsensical words can be identified by their position in the sentence: The "squazzlings" are obviosly the subject; the "refriligs" are obviously the object; "gilattered" is obviously a verb.

To demonstrate further this relationship between function and placement, you might substitute the names of two football teams for the nonsense words *squazzlings* and *refriligs*:

The Lions gilattered the Raiders.

Now, to make your meaning perfectly clear, all you need to do is to change *gilattered* to a verb that has a definite meaning:

The Lions clobbered the Raiders.

You may want to carry this experiment further with nonsense words of your own ("the wiftil twiticled through the walgy tworsted"). However, the main point is this: **you make your meaning clear to your reader not only through the words you choose but also through your placement of words within the sentence.**

Modifiers are important words in sentences because they help to make the subjects and verbs clear to the reader. "The dog," as a subject, is not as clear as "The snarling bulldog" or "The playful hunting dog."

Remember that modifiers can be

SINGLE WORDS: The *back* door . . . ,

PHRASES: The door *at your back* . . . ,

CLAUSES: The door *that is at your back* . . . .

Modifiers are confusing if:

1. They do not have a word to modify.
2. They are placed incorrectly in the sentence.

Dangling Modifiers

When modifiers have no word to modify, they are called *dangling modifiers.* They dangle because there is no word in the sentence to attach them to.

Although *swimming valiantly upstream,* the canoe was unable to reach him in time.
Reaching across the huge bay, we saw the bridge.

Since modifiers modify the word nearest them, it seems in the above sentences that *the canoe was swimming valiantly upstream* and that *we were reaching across the huge bay.*

If you put a modifier at the beginning of your sentence, it should modify the subject of the main clause (first noun in the main clause):

Swimming valiantly upstream, the *man* . . .
Reaching across the huge bay, the *bridge* . . .

You can also correct dangling modifiers by making them dependent clauses (adding a subject and a verb):

Although the *man was* swimming valiantly upstream, the canoe . . .

or by moving the modifier next to the word modified:

**Although swimming valiantly upstream,
the canoe was unable to reach him in time.**

We saw the bridge *reaching across the huge bay.*

To see if you have a dangling modifier at the beginning of your sentence, place
the modifier directly after the subject and see if the sentence is clear.

The canoe, swimming valiantly upstream, was...

You must provide a sensible "doer" of the action. Obviously, the canoe is not the
doer. If the modifier is correctly used, it can be placed on either side of the subject,
and the sentence will be clear:

Having failed the exam, *I* went home.
I, having failed the exam, went home.

EXERCISE VIIIe
Complete the following sentences by providing a sensible doer of the action:

1. While washing my car, _____

_____

2. To feel good in the morning, _____

_____

3. Having studied for six hours, _____

_____

4. After eating seven hot dogs, _____

_____

5. To escape the anger of my parents, _____

_____

6. Never having studied much in high school, _____

_____

7. By leaning far out the window, _____

_____

8. Not wanting to annoy my instructor, _____

_____

9. Having gotten into the line for tickets, _____

_____

10. While fixing my bike, _____

_____

EXERCISE VIIIf
Correct the dangling modifiers in the following sentences. If the sentence is correct, just write C in the blank.

1. Having a rusty body and a poor paint job, I had to sell the car cheap.

_____

2. The man had only one arm caused by a railroad accident.

_____

3. Before choosing a college, the transportation should be checked.

_____

4. After planting the shrubs, the rain began to fall.

_____

5. Having studied all night, I passed the test.

_____

6. To understand Mark Twain, the situation in the South at the time must be known.

_____

7. Last spring, after screaming and begging and throwing some temper tantrums, my parents allowed me to get my own apartment.

_____

8. Having seen "Jaws," my dreams became nightmares.

_____

9. Never having been lectured to before, my notebooks were useless.

_____

10. Having played basketball for five hours, my dinner was cold.

_____

Misplaced Modifiers

Modifiers should be placed as close as possible to the words they modify. They should also be placed so there is no doubt as to the words they modify.

213

214

Sometimes words can be placed in several different positions and still be clear:

On November 22, 1963, John F. Kennedy was assassinated.
John F. Kennedy, *on November 22, 1963,* was assassinated.
John F. Kennedy was assassinated *on November 22, 1963.*

Be careful to place your modifier in a position that will indicate the meaning you intend. Look at the following sentences.

Only he said that he loved my sister.
He *only* said that he loved my sister.
He said *only* that he loved my sister.
He said that *only* he loved my sister.
He said that he *only* loved my sister.
He said that he loved *only* my sister.
He said that he loved my *only* sister.
He said that he loved my sister *only.*

Note how the meaning of the sentence changes each time the position of the modifier *only* changes.

When a modifier can modify different words in a sentence, make sure you place it in a position where it will give the meaning you intend. In the following sentence, the modifier is misplaced:

They played while I was reading with the new pups in the basket.

It should be,

They played with the new pups in the basket while I was reading.

**"They played while I was reading with the
new pups in the basket."**

(Or else you have an odd place to do your reading.)

Sometimes a modifier is placed *between* two words or phrases, and the reader cannot tell which it should modify.

People who cheat on their income tax *often* get caught.

What is meant here? Must you cheat often to get caught? Or do people who cheat get caught often? Place the modifier in a position where there is no doubt, as in these revisions:

People who cheat often on their income tax get caught.
People who cheat on their income tax get caught often.

Only, nearly, and *almost* are frequently misplaced. They should **precede** the word they modify.

INCORRECT: He *only* fell ten feet.
CORRECT: He fell *only* ten feet.
INCORRECT: He *nearly* made a perfect score.
CORRECT: He made *nearly* a perfect score.
INCORRECT: He *almost* graduated with 200 credits.
CORRECT: He graduated with *almost* 200 credits.

EXERCISE VIIIg
If there is a misplaced modifier in the sentence, underline it and draw an arrow to show its proper position. If the sentence is correct, write a C beside the number.

1. My brother brought a dog into the room which is almost as big as I.
2. He only got an A in English.
3. He wrote his book about hippies in his den.
4. Charles almost ate the whole pie.
5. George had nearly a serious accident.
6. You must be vaccinated for the trip to Asia for smallpox.
7. He played tennis while we were watching vigorously.
8. I nearly searched everywhere for the error.
9. Mary sat in the car with her cat writing her paragraph for English.
10. The article contained an error which I spotted immediately.

EXERCISE VIIIh
Rewrite the following sentences so that the modifiers modify the correct word and the sentence makes a sensible statement.

1. Mary decided that she would not go on a trip at the last moment.

2. Helena jumped when her mother called as if struck by lightning.

   _____

3. No one can please the teacher who skips class.

   _____

4. How could anyone become a class president whom nobody likes?

   _____

5. Sometimes teenagers get sympathy from policemen who are on drugs.

   _____

6. Sheila, angry at her parents, decided to get help from a minister at sixteen years of age.

   _____

7. Keith decided that he only disliked Margie for her tardiness.

   _____

8. Sitting in the back row of the classroom, the lecturer could scarcely be heard.

   _____

9. George decided not to play golf as he dressed.

   _____

10. She refused to go to the store for no reason.

    _____

11. Paul was in his car with his dog driving to Texas.

    _____

12. No one is allowed to fire anyone except the boss.

    _____

13. The nurse gave the student an aspirin and told him to go home for a headache.

    _____

14. Having passed out from exhaustion, the football game went on without the star quarterback

    _____

15. He saw the germs with the microscope.

    _____

Shifts in Point of View

Awkward and confusing sentences frequently result from unnecessary shifts in **person, number, tense,** or **voice.**

NEEDLESS SHIFTS IN PERSON

SHIFT: As *you* came across the bridge, *we* could see the spire of the cathedral in the distance.

CONSISTENT: As *we* came across the bridge, *we* could see the spire of the cathedral in the distance.

NEEDLESS SHIFTS IN NUMBER

SHIFT: Each *one* has *their* directions and *know* how to get to the lodge.

CONSISTENT: Each *one* has *his* directions and *knows* how to get to the lodge.

NEEDLESS SHIFTS IN TENSE

SHIFT: The drill instructor *called* us to attention and then *announces* a fifteen-mile hike.

CONSISTENT: The drill instructor *called* us to attention and then *announced* a fifteen-mile hike.

NEEDLESS SHIFTS IN VOICE

SHIFT: Today we *discussed* medical terminology; pharmacology *will be discussed* tomorrow.

CONSISTENT: Today we *discussed* medical terminology; tomorrow we *will discuss* pharmacology.

EXERCISE VIIIi

Underline the word or words that represent a shift in person, number, tense, or voice. Then rewrite the sentences to eliminate the inconsistency.

1. Every student was asked to present their book review to the class.

    _____

2. Every night Brian goes to bed late, sleeps late, and skipped breakfast because he was late for class.

    _____

3. As we entered the store, you could see that business was very slow.

    _____

4. Celia loved her name because she thought it sounded sophisticated, but her nickname, Cel, was detested by her because it reminded her of *silly.*

    _____

5. The rear wheels were spinning and the motor was roaring, but we do manage to get to the top of the hill.

    _____

6. The entertainment committee met Thursday, and plans for the spring formal were discussed.

_____

7. The D.A. thought that whoever killed the mayor used their own belt to strangle him.

_____

8. Stella thought that the story she told the officer was more believable than those told by the other girls.

_____

9. The whole group was disturbed by the news that the president had resigned, but they decided to accept the resignation.

_____

10. As we pushed the car, you could see that we didn't have the strength to get it up the steep driveway into the garage.

_____

11. The match was exciting; the two players throw every bit of their strength and knowledge into the game.

_____

12. The movie was pleasant, perhaps a bit dull, until suddenly—in comes the monster from outer space.

_____

13. Stanley has always enjoyed bridge; he enjoys chess, and until last summer, golf was enjoyed by Stanley most of all.

_____

14. Each of the salespeople was called upon to explain their expense accounts.

_____

15. Vincent had three choices: he could go to see his girlfriend, stay at home and watch TV, and studying for the test was the third alternative.

_____

CONFUSING SENTENCES Shifts in sentence structure often lead to statements so clumsy and confusing that the only way to correct them is to completely rewrite the sentences.

> **AWKWARD AND CONFUSING:** Why doesn't the state department at least send out people who understand the language is what he wondered.

218

REWRITTEN: He wondered why the state department didn't send out people who at least knew the language.

AWKWARD AND CONFUSING: The cause of the widespread unrest in the country, which was largely the result of our misguided policy, offered little hope for a stable government.

REWRITTEN: The widespread unrest caused by our misguided policy threatened the stability of the government.

AWKWARD AND CONFUSING: It would do little good to have a college degree for a person if he or she has accomplished nothing and little to show for it.

REWRITTEN: Having a college degree does little for the person who fails to make use of his or her education.

AWKWARD AND CONFUSING: These transportation costs when ordering in large quantities the supplier may be able to absorb.

REWRITTEN: The supplier may be able to absorb the transportation cost on orders for large quantitites.

EXERCISE VIIIj

Rewrite the following sentences to express the ideas clearly and logically. Check to see that your subject–verb combination makes sense, that there are no dangling or misplaced modifiers, and that there are no needless shifts in structure or point of view.

1. She told him the chair was broken, but he sits down anyway.

   _____

2. Having had no experience with engines, his answer must have been a good guess to solve the problem.

   _____

3. His hearing eventually improved, which my aunt thinks was brought about by her prayers.

   _____

4. If a person is a genius is all the more reason why we should be willing to overlook their minor faults.

   _____

5. Any generic food that you buy that you do not care for reduces the real savings, which, after all, is the main purpose of buying generic.

   _____

6. When unsettled in mind, the mental health counselor is a good person to talk to.

   _____

7. We become discouraged quickly whenever one learns that his ideas are not appreciated.

   _____

8. I asked for ginger ale, and she gives me punch spiked with vodka.

   _____

9. The writer of this letter was born in Chicago, and Dallas has been the last place of his employment.

   _____

10. Take for example these television commercials that you see all the time, how do you know they're not rigged.

    _____

WORDS

Wordiness

When you are writing a paragraph, you should remember that effective sentences are concise. Each detail that you use should say exactly what is necessary and no more. Needless words will never improve a paragraph—and they won't **im**press your instructor; they will **de**press him. Whether you are writing a paragraph in English class or doing a term paper in biology or taking an essay exam in history or drafting a resume for the United States Steel Company, you must learn to choose precise words that say **exactly** what you mean. Writers often repeat details needlessly, or they use five or six words to say something that could have been said in one or two words.

It is easier to avoid saying too much if you recognize a few key areas where you can cut out excess words.

1. Reduce wordy phrases to a single word.

due to the fact that	because *or* since
in the event that	if
at that point in time	then
is in agreement with	agrees
at the present time	now
during the time that	while
through the use of	by *or* with
in many cases	often *or* frequently
in view of the fact that	since
in this modern day and age	today
for the purpose of	for
in spite of the fact that	despite

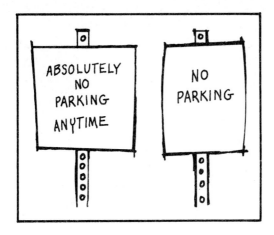

2. Eliminate redundancies, the senseless repetition of the same idea in different words.

audible ~~to the ear~~
green ~~in color~~
rectangular ~~in shape~~
~~completely~~ eliminated
adequate ~~enough~~
~~important~~ essential
7:00 A.M. ~~in the morning~~
seniors ~~in their last year of school~~

3. Eliminate the unnecessary *it.*

In the Bible it says . . .	The Bible says . . .
In the U.N. Charter it says . . .	The U.N. Charter says . . .
In the movie it shows . . .	The movie shows . . .
In the book it tells . . .	The book tells . . .

4. Eliminate some modifiers by using precise nouns, verbs, and modifiers.

The cat with the long white silky hair	The angora
The old, beat-up, rusty car	The jalopy
He clapped his hands together	He applauded
She was whiny, complaining, fault-finding	She was querulous
The boy who picked on smaller boys	The bully

5. Eliminate the timid phrase.

It seems to me
In my opinion
As I see it
It is my belief that

6. Eliminate vague and general subjects.

The sensation of pulsing, throbbing pain	Pulsing, throbbing pain
The sound of loud, cackling laughter	Loud, cackling laughter
The smell of the stale odor of cigarette ashes	The odor of cigarette ashes

7. Use actor-action sequence (active voice).

Laughter from the class next door was heard by all of us.	All of us heard the class next door laughing.
Soccer was the game played by most of the boys in the band.	Most male band members played soccer.

8. Combine sentences, clauses, and phrases.

WORDY: My favorite sport is swimming. It is fine recreation for young people and a great conditioner for people of any age.

CONCISE: Swimming, my favorite sport, provides healthful recreation for all age groups.

WORDY: I listened for the signal which would indicate that the race had begun, but the crowd with its screaming and the engines with their roaring drowned out all other sounds and noises.

CONCISE: I could not hear the starting signal because of the screaming crowd and roaring engines.

CAUTION: Although you must eliminate every unnecessary word, this does not mean that you should eliminate words necessary for clarity. Be sure *all* the words you use tell your reader something.

REDUCING SENTENCES AND CLAUSES TO VERBAL PHRASES

A **verbal** is a verb part that cannot stand alone as a verb; that is, it cannot complete a statement about the subject (see Sentence section of Chapter I). Verbal phrases, however, can often be used to replace subordinate clauses, coordinate clauses, or even separate sentences.

Study the following examples carefully.

ORIGINAL: Since the salespeople had not met their quotas, they were forced to work late every night until Christmas.

223

REVISED: *Not having met their quotas,* the salespeople were forced to work late every night until Christmas.

ORIGINAL: He was given no better choice, so he took the job cleaning auto parts.

REVISED: *Given no better choice,* he took the job cleaning auto parts.

ORIGINAL: Chavez defied the court order. He was sentenced to thirty days in jail.

REVISED: *Defying the court order,* Chavez was sentenced to thirty days in jail.
Chavez was sentenced to thirty days in jail for *defying the court order.*

NOTE: The verbal phrase may come before the main clause, after the main clause, or within the main clause, but it should be set off by commas.

Mrs. Harriman, *knowing the truth,* refused to be intimidated by the lawyer's threats.

EXERCISE VIIIk
Make the following sentences more concise without omitting information or changing the meaning.

1. I intend to pursue my studies on the graduate level in the field of English.

   _____

2. It has been brought to my attention that you are remiss in the latest payment of monthly dues.

   _____

3. There are eight students who have a desire to fill the seat of the president of the student government association.

   _____

4. I certainly enjoy camping because it gives me a great deal of fun, pleasure, and enjoyment.

   _____

5. This method is my own original creation which I figured out by myself with no help from anyone.

   _____

6. My uncle finally passed on to his eternal rest last Tuesday. His final repose and resting place is Allegheny Cemetery.

   _____

7. I am a student at the community college, I am a business major, and I am specializing in accounting.

_____

8. To enlist in the army was John's decision since other employment was not available.

_____

9. Invoking the Fifth Amendment was the method the gangster used to keep from answering the attorney's questions.

_____

10. Tom's dad was disgusted with the treatment Tom got at the hands of the baby-sitter.

_____

EXERCISE VIIII
Eliminate the deadwood from the following sentences.

1. The reason I need a full-time job is because I have to pay for my education.

_____

2. The horse, which is the one that seemed so gentle yesterday, kicked down the fence this morning and ran away.

_____

3. Because of the fact that Al stopped smoking, he gained twenty pounds.

_____

4. Attorney F. Lee Bailey, who is a well-known attorney, hardly ever loses a case.

_____

5. Many of the voters in the state of Pennsylvania feel that Governor McMurphy is an honest and truthful man.

_____

6. Peg thinks that if she does not pay any attention to her problem, it will go away.

_____

7. Elvira was given a free admission pass so she could get into the concert without paying.

_____

8. Dave did not remember to take the turkey out of the freezer.

_____

9. In this day and age people are too busy and occupied to stop and think about the meaning of life.

_____

10. The place where I go to get my car washed charges a fee of $4.50 cash money as payment to wash it.

_____

11. My favorite vacation, which I really enjoy, is driving my car to Florida beaches where it is warm and I can go swimming.

_____

12. My young son, who is a boy seventeen years old, is a pilot who can fly an airplane.

_____

13. Harry paid cash on the barrelhead for the leather jacket made of split cowhide.

_____

14. Nursing is entirely too difficult, it seems to me, to be crowded into a two-year program, and more time should be allotted to the study necessary for such a career.

_____

15. Due to the fact that I like sports, I go to sporting events and games often and many times.

_____

EXERCISE VIIIm
Reduce each of the following sentences or groups of sentences to *one* independent clause and *one or more verbal phrases:*

1. Fred was hammering away in his basement workshop. He could not hear the doorbell.

_____

2. She was allowed to date Carlos again, and Evita soon became more cheerful.

_____

3. Kathy was enraged by the newspaper story, and she wrote a long letter to the editor. She threatened to sue the paper.

_____

4. I was staring out the window at the swirling snow. I saw the car's headlights suddenly sweep across the road and disappear over the embankment.

_____

5. We knew we had played badly. We were not surprised when the coach gave us a tongue-lashing.

_____

6. Elvira stamped her foot. Then she started screaming, "I hate you! I hate you!"

_____

7. The truck came roaring down the hill. Its brakes had failed.

_____

8. After we had drawn numbers from a hat, we waited until our number was called.

_____

9. The drill sergeant marched us back and forth across the drill hall. He roared out instructions.

_____

10. He was a simple soldier. He tried to kill the enemy. He thought it was his duty to do so.

_____

CHAPTER IX

persuading

ORGANIZATION

How many times during the day do you try to influence the decisions of others, and how many times are you influenced by something yourself? "Plenty," you answer. You are referring to the fine art of **persuasion,** a process which affects most of the decisions and actions in your daily life. There are many variations of the persuasive process, but basically it is an attempt to convince, to motivate, to gain the agreement or **assent** of another individual or group.

Each day you use persuasion to fulfill your basic needs and to get along with family and friends; on a larger scale, it plays a vital part in your economic and occupational success. Persuasion is getting your son to eat his vegetables, explaining why your term paper isn't finished on time, convincing your boss that you deserve a raise, or requesting that your congressman support a particular bill. You live in an age of highly sophisticated persuasion. You are targets of persuasion; you are bombarded daily by advertising and propaganda. The motivation analyst and the propaganda expert have awesome powers that control much of

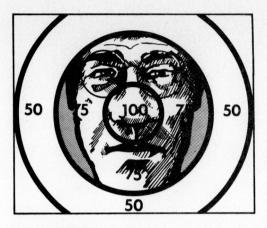

You are the target.

your life. Because persuasion can be good or bad, it is important that you learn not only to use some basic techniques of persuasion but also to be alert to how others may try to influence your thinking. Effective persuasion can work for you.

Your assignment in this unit will be to write a paragraph in which you persuade someone to agree with you on an issue about which you feel strongly. You can assume that your reader is a rational, intelligent person who is either un-committed or is slightly opposed to your point of view. This means that you have a good chance of success *if* your paragraph is effective.

Tips for Successful Persuasion

To be successful at convincing others, you must consider several things as you plan your strategy. Here are a few tips which an experienced persuader always considers in his writing.

1. **Know the type of person you are addressing.**
   a. **Don't underestimate the person's intelligence, yet be aware of his or her limitations.**

For example, everyone appreciates clear, simple language, but oversim-plification can be insulting. A request to the boss for changes in office procedure should not sound like the instructions you gave to your three-year-old son for keeping his room clean. At the same time, your new secretary, just out of Com-munity College, deserves a clearer, less complicated explanation of procedure than does the experienced secretary who has worked in your office for five years.

   b. **Try to determine which kind of convincing will work best on your reader.**

For example, a soft, subtle touch is obviously the best approach for ask-ing Aunt Matilda to sit with the kids, dog, cat, canary, and fish while you and your wife escape for a second honeymoon in the mountains. On the other hand, stronger language is needed to motivate the local dealer to complete warranty repairs on your new car, which is falling apart after four months of normal use. Threats to call Detroit and the Better Business Bureau may be the only way to get results.

2. **Know yourself.**
   a. **Display confidence and sincerity; believe in what you are saying.**

Compare these two appeals, and decide which is more effective. Explain why.

I think we need to ask the police for more protection on our street. It seems that there has been a lot of crime around here lately, and this is a very bad situation, isn't it? Maybe some of you have some ideas that might work and wouldn't upset anyone.

During the last three months we have had five muggings, one auto theft, and two burglaries on our street. Police protection has been inadequate, and the promise of increased patrols has not been kept. I propose that tonight we form a citizen's committee to attend the next council meeting to demand the protection that our tax money has already paid for.

   b. **Avoid giving the impression that you know everything or are overly impressed with your own self-importance. This can bore the reader to death.**

How would you react to this?

I am going to speak with Ralph Jones, our mayor and a close personal friend, about the crime on our street. Because of my fourteen months in the military police and six credits in psychology, I feel that my personal efforts will be much more appreciated since the rest of you may not fully understand the implications of a complex social problem such as this. I will let you know what is going to happen as soon as Ralph and I work out the details with Bud Hawkins, the police chief I went to high school with.

3. **Know what you are talking about.**
   a. **Know exactly *why* you want to persuade someone; being aware of your purpose will help you to develop a strong presentation.**

What kind of results do you think this note to a careless neighbor will get?

Dear Neighbor,
Excuse me, I'm sorry to bother you, but I think that it is your garbage can which has been spilled in my driveway for the past week. Anyway, it looks

like the can that has been sitting next to your porch, and it has your name painted on it, but I could still be mistaken. Maybe we could decide whose it is, but I don't think it is mine. I could help you clean up the mess, or ask the trash man about it. It probably isn't either of our faults. Thank you.

Your friend and neighbor,
C. Milquetoast (next door)

b. **Learn as much as you can about the subject or issue that you will discuss; lack of knowledge can weaken or destroy your efforts to convince.**

How quickly do you think the mayor will react to this citizen's plea, which contains no specific information—just vague assumptions with no factual basis?

Mr. Mayor, we are here to complain about the great increase of crime on our street. We are all concerned for the safety of our families and homes, and we hope you can do something about it. Obviously, the whole problem is caused by the kids from the project who need money for dope. It just isn't safe to walk the streets anymore, and youngsters are afraid to go out and play. We have heard a rumor that you were decreasing patrols in our area, but surely there must be enough money in the budget to give us some kind of protection. We also think that too many offenders are getting off on suspended sentences. Something must be done because we have had lots of muggings in the last year or so and all kinds of terrible things.

Topic Sentence

The main purpose of persuasion is to achieve agreement between you and your reader. Therefore, use any common grounds of agreement that you and your reader may already have. The effective persuader seeks to **identify** with the reader—to share the same vibrations—and the sooner you accomplish this, the easier your job of persuasion will be. Make the beginning of your paragraph an attempt to identify with your reader.

For example, assume that you are attempting to persuade someone that capital punishment is a necessary deterrent to crime, but you already know that he favors imprisonment and rehabilitation for all offenders. In this case, early in your paragraph mention a point on which you will both probably agree—that the citizen must somehow be protected from the habitual criminal. Once this partial agreement is recognized, the reader will probably be much more open to the reasoning that follows.

A good topic sentence helps you capture the readers' attention and interest, so that they will want to read everything you have to say. Therefore, the topic sentence should not only name the subject, but also express an attitude that stimulates the readers' interest. Remember, a topic sentence should be clear and specific. It should refer to a single subject or area of discussion. Consider the following examples:

The BMW is a much better road bike than the Perogi because it handles better, vibrates less, and has a more reliable drive train.

Only two hours of your time each month ensures that a sick child will have much needed love and understanding from someone who really cares.

persuading This office can no longer function effectively because we have only one secretary to do the correspondence for five people.

You'll love our new 380 Silver Streaker, with five on the floor, aviation cockpit, anti-quagmire four-wheel traction in three ranges, celestial roof port, and hypersonic load levelers.

You should marry me because I'm the only one who really understands you.

Once you have the reader's attention, and he or she is convinced that you have something to say, it is time to provide the details which will support your topic sentence.

Body

The support for the attitude of your topic sentence is the most important part of your persuasive paragraph. A clear purpose and knowledge of your subject are essential to the success of your effort.

1.   Always try to provide strong reasons based on facts that your reader will believe, not weak reasons based only on opinions.

Note how Sam tries to persuade George to agree with him about Joan.

SAM: You know, George, Joan is the most beautiful girl in school.
GEORGE: That's your opinion.

**Opinions without facts
don't change opinions.**

SAM: I'll bet there isn't one guy we know who wouldn't give his shirt for ten minutes of her undivided attention.

GEORGE: She doesn't turn me on at all. That phony act of hers has everyone fooled—especially you.

SAM: You just haven't got any taste, George; that woman has real class!

GEORGE: Yeah, well, Sam, nothing you have said so far has proved anything to me. In my book, she's still a loser.

George is right! Sam really has not said anything substantial. All Sam has done is pile one unsupported opinion on top of another. But what if Sam had used one or two facts as reasons to support this controlling idea:

SAM: Well, George, you remember, of course, that Joan was chosen unanimously by eight judges this spring to represent Beaver County in the Miss Teenage America Pageant.

Sam has just supplied a **fact** which George cannot dispute. He also cites an **authority** (eight judges) who think she is beautiful, too. George still disagrees, however, so Sam continues.

SAM: And don't forget, George, that there are a lot of girls here in this school, and there is plenty of competition. Why do you think Joan was chosen to be head cheerleader as early as her sophomore year? And why was she, out of twenty candidates, voted best-dressed girl by the entire student body?

Thus Sam continues to build his case, and you can do the same—by using facts to reinforce or provide validity for your opinions, beliefs, and recommendations.

2. **Always provide enough reasons to convince your reader fully, but two or three carefully chosen reasons are often better than a long list. The quality is much more important than the quantity. Persuasion should offer only as much proof as is necessary to win the reader over.**

The writer of the following paragraph has selected three good reasons, instead of a long, rambling list, to support the controlling idea:

I strongly believe that an essay test is a far more effective method of determining a student's ability to put to practical use the information and material he or she has learned in freshman composition than a multiple-choice or a true-or-false test. First, an essay test is composed of questions that force a student to put forth his or her ideas in paragraph form, which is the objective of the entire course of study in freshman composition. Second, the essay test requires the student to use many basic skills, such as proper punctuation, proper sentence structure, proper sequencing of sentences, and a smooth flow of ideas with easy transition throughout the paragraph. Finally, an essay test forces a student to think creatively—a rare occurrence in the average student. The multiple-choice and true-or-false tests, on the other hand, rarely force a student to think. The student is merely confronted with a choice of answers, and the most common method used to arrive at the correct answer is to eliminate the obviously wrong answer and choose among the others, or simply to guess. This guessing accomplishes nothing, but there is a good possibility of choosing the correct answer. In a multiple-choice test, possible answers may be so closely related to other choices that the question is ambiguous. The student benefits more from an essay test than a true-and-false or multiple-choice test.   *Peter Beach*

3. **Explain each reason fully enough so that the reader will know exactly why you think it is important. A bare list of unexplained reasons won't impress your reader. Also, think of any objections the reader might have to your point of view and include reasons with explanations that will satisfy these objections.**

How convincing is the following paragraph?

The death penalty is not the solution to the problem of serious crime. Capital punishment is simply barbaric revenge. Sometimes the wrong man is executed. Besides, the penalty is not fairly imposed. Anyway, the death penalty is not a deterrent to crime.

Now read a revised version. What are the differences between the two paragraphs?

As the crime rate increases, so do demands for the death penalty, but capital punishment does not provide a rational solution to the problem of increased crime. Putting a man to death by hanging, electric shock, or lethal injection remains a barbaric form of revenge in which the entire society participates. Besides, there is always the chance that an innocent man may be put to death; after all, that has happened a number of times in the past. Furthermore, any objective examination of the record on capital punishment shows clearly that it is usually the poor and ignorant who suffer the death penalty, not the wealthy and clever criminals. Most important of all, the idea that the death penalty is a deterrent to crime simply doesn't hold true. In states that have abolished the death penalty, there has been no consistent increase in the murder rate, nor has the murder rate declined in states that have restored the death penalty. The record provides no proof that the death penalty serves as a deterrent to crime. Whatever social and legal reforms may be needed to cut down the appalling crime rate, imposing the death penalty is not the way to solve the problem.

4. **Arrange your reasons in the most effective order for convincing; use a sequence that will best allow your reasons to relate to the controlling idea and to each other. Many successful persuaders like to save their most important reasons until last, but the arrangement can change according to the individual writer's purpose.**

Suppose, for example, that you are campaign manager for a local political candidate and that you must write an article based on the following positive attributes which he claims to possess. In what order would you list them to be most effective? (Consider the attitudes of the people and the area in which you live.)

civil rights champion
conservationist
law and order advocate
crusader for truth
labor activist
civic and church leader

  5. **A rational approach and genuine sensitivity to the feelings of your reader will convince much better than emotionalism or sentimentality.**

How convincing is this paragraph?

Smokers are vile, dirty, uncouth people who have no business walking on the face of the earth. Smoking also shows a lack of good breeding and intelligence. Anyone with any sense knows that smoking is bad for you. Just look at all the smokers who die of cancer and pneumonia every day. Also, think of all the fires that are started each year by smokers; billions of dollars are lost because of this sad defect in human character. Smoking should be banned in all public places to protect the health of decent people and little children. In addition, all tobacco products should be taxed to the extent that no one can afford them. It is time for all respectable God-fearing people to unite and wipe out this insidious social menace.

What would you do to improve it?

6. **Avoid attempts to manipulate your reader into agreeing by the use of false reasoning (fallacies) or deceptive tactics.**

FALLACIES

A fallacy is an error in reasoning, a false notion based on a mistake in logic or perception. Here are some commonly used fallacies which lead to false conclusions because they distort the logical reasoning process:

Hasty Generalization

All women are poor drivers. [Are all women poor drivers?]
The British people are nothing but a pack of snobs. [Are all British people snobs?]
Police departments all over the country are corrupt; cops really don't care about the average citizen. [What about the many cops who do an excellent job?]

The hasty generalization is a false assumption which results from jumping to conclusions about a group or issue. It is a blind, all-inclusive assumption based on too little evidence.

Ad Hominem (attack against the man)

I would never vote for Tom Smith to be township supervisor; he hasn't been to church once in the last five years. [Would his not going to church necessarily make Tom a poor supervisor?]

Byron's poetry is not fit to be read, for he led a disgusting, immoral life. [What does Byron's lifestyle have to do with his writing ability?]

The ad hominem is a false assumption used for personal attacks on individuals instead of issues; it is a distracting tactic used to trick people into making faulty judgments. Watch for this one in political campaigns.

Begging the Question (circular reasoning)

This pickup is the most rugged one on the market because our people in Detroit designed it to be rugged! [But what are the reasons why it is the most rugged pickup?]

Furthermore, my candidate is honest because he is a man of integrity! [The speaker still hasn't proved that the candidate is honest.]

In circular reasoning, the conclusion simply repeats or rephrases the beginning assumption; thus, nothing is really proven.

Polarization

West Aliquippa—love it or leave it! [This type of all-or-nothing approach offers no choice between extremes.]

Juvenile delinquency is the direct result of a breakdown in the public school system. [What about other possible reasons for delinquency?]

All manufacturing of strategic arms must stop immediately; if not, civilization is doomed. [The speaker ignores the fact that *some* arms manufacture is necessary to ensure national security.]

Polarization is a type of one-sided reasoning that is often highly emotional and offers no alternative action—nor does it allow consideration of the middle ground in any argument. Everything is either one way or the other with no consideration for the broad areas between right or wrong, good or bad.

Non Sequitur (false conclusion)

No wonder the country is in a mess; look at all those college-trained punks who are running it. [Those who attended college are not the only ones capable of poor administration.]

Is sex education really a Communist plot?

Sex education is a Communist plot to undermine the morality of our youth. [No evidence of a communist plot is given.]

John does not smoke; therefore, he will make an excellent tennis player. [John could be a lousy tennis player as well as a nonsmoker.]

A false conclusion is one that does not logically follow from the reasoning provided. This type of argument overgeneralizes, and it often indicates hasty and overemotional conclusions.

Post Hoc Ergo Propter Hoc (after this, therefore because of this)

Kay, do you know that Jack asked me out to dinner Friday night! It just had to be that new perfume I wore yesterday. [Maybe it was—maybe it wasn't.]

I attribute my 95 healthy years to the fact that I don't drink, smoke, or chase women. [What about heredity or just plain luck?]

The *post hoc* fallacy contains a misplaced cause or effect. The mere fact that one thing takes place first and another follows does not necessarily mean that the first event caused the second. The *post hoc* fallacy is also faulty reasoning because it does not state the possibility of other causes or effects.

Bandwagon (join the crowd)

Everyone knows that Judge Zink is the man for the job; become a member of his team when you pull lever 9A on November 4. [Did you ever wonder who *everyone* was?]

Join the now generation of swinging singles at Swampy Point Yacht and Racquet Club; you too can share this carefree experience already enjoyed by so many others. [Will joining the club really make you a swinger? And how do you know that everyone else likes the club?]

236

The bandwagon technique attempts to impress by the claim that everyone is doing something and that you will be left out if you don't participate. This is largely an emotional appeal and is used extensively in both advertising and politics.

Appeals Based on Biased or Incompetent Authority

Nine out of ten veterinarians agree that Stringies provides the best nutritional balance that your dog can possibly get. [Which ten veterinarians were asked for their opinions?]
If Star Body says that the Dodge pickup is the best, then that's good enough for me. [How much does a movie star really know about trucks?]

Although an appeal to an authority is not necessarily a fallacy if that authority is competent and reliable, advertisers often associate famous names with products with the hope that the consumer will be dazzled by the personality and therefore buy the product. Thus, the fallacy occurs when the authority is not knowledgeable in that particular subject.

False Analogy (illogical comparisons)

Consider the United States and Switzerland, for example. Here we are with high unemployment and high crime rates, wasting billions of dollars a year on welfare programs and defense budgets. In Switzerland there is very little crime or unemployment, and the government isn't wasting billions on welfare and defense. The country has very few natural resources, but the people live comfortably. Why can't we have a well-run economy like that of Switzerland? [Even if the claims about Switzerland are true, the analogy is a poor one. For one thing, Switzerland is only about as large as Massachusetts, Connecticut, and Rhode Island. The analogy also ignores other enormous dissimilarities between the United States and Switzerland.]
The acts of terror perpetrated by the Red Brigades are as patriotic as American colonial efforts to overthrow the British crown. [Can the wholesale murdering of innocent people be logically compared to an armed uprising in defense of basic human rights?]

An analogy is a specific form of comparison: finding similarities between two things that are normally classified under different categories. Properly used, a good analogy can provide strong support for your argument; the false analogy, however, can be misleading and deceptive. The false analogy does indeed make a comparison, but it bases the comparison on trivial similarities which ignore fundamental differences.

Rationalization (self-delusion)

Why should I buy this new suit, even though it fits perfectly, when I know that I will be fifteen pounds lighter by this time next month! [Next month? Next year? Or ever?]

A couple of drinks does not affect my driving—and one more before we go won't make a bit of difference. [Tell it to the judge.]

The rationalization is a "cop-out" that is used to avoid reality or reasonable thinking in a particular situation. Usually, rationalizations are easier to swallow than the truth. For example, there is always a student who justifies a low grade in the following manner: there was no time to study, the teacher is prejudiced, no transportation to class was available because the car is always broken down, the teacher expects too much, the student misunderstood the assignment, there is a conflict with basketball practice, and many more. All this is a substitute for the truth—that the student didn't care enough to do the work.

Even though each of the preceding examples illustrates a particular fallacy, you have probably noticed that several of them fit into more than one category. Watch for fallacies that are presented to you, and avoid using them to convince others. A discerning reader will not be fooled by fallacies, and you could be embarrassed if caught using them.

Conclusion

The persuasive conclusion can be very flexible, and it should be adjusted to what the situation calls for.

1. Perhaps your reader should be handled gently with a final appeal that is sensitive and moving.

And so I beg all of you to join with me in what may be the final opportunity to save this, our proudest natural resource.

2. On the other hand, you may decide to cover your reader with fire and brimstone and demand agreement through threats and warnings.

Finally, if you do not vacate the premises by noon on May 31, I shall have the constable evict you, forcibly if necessary, that same day.

3. In most cases, however, your conclusion will come somewhere between the two extremes: (**a**) You can summarize your main reasons, in order to emphasize how effectively these reasons support your controlling idea. (**b**) You may restate your controlling idea after having convinced your reader, point by point, that he or she should agree with you.

A sincere, direct, and strong final impression is especially necessary for the persuasive paragraph, as the following example illustrates.

In conclusion, let me again remind you, as parents, that teaching social responsibility is not completely a function of the schools. It is a process that must begin in the home and continue throughout the child's formal schooling. The teacher cannot be a parent, a policeman, a psychologist, and still be expected to teach fundamental skills. Social responsibility must be brought from the home to the classroom, and, unless this happens, learning cannot take place in our schools.

Here are two examples of effective persuasion by students.

Racial segregation of the public schools in the United States must be ended because its evil lies in the implication that skin color indicates potential. This is tantamount to saying that the color of a cow determines the quality of her milk. This premise, however, can be easily proven false. If a dairy farmer puts all his brown cows into one barn, feeds them a generous diet of silage and hay, and keeps them warmly protected from extreme weather conditions, the brown cows will produce an abundant supply of fine, sweet milk. If, on the other hand, he fences all his red cows in an open field which offers only loco weed and sourgrass as sustenance, and which provides no protection from the elements, the milk produced by the red cows, if any is produced at all, will be unfit for consumption. If the farmer then concludes that all red cows are poor producers of milk and have no place in his dairy herd, he has judged solely on the basis of color, and his conclusion is invalid. Obviously, the difference in the quality of the milk produced by the two groups of cows resulted from the farmer's uneven investment of food and shelter. Similarly, if society allows an uneven educational investment to be made in its children on the basis of color, the contributions of the deprived group will bear no relation to that group's underdeveloped potential.   *Rosemary Weber*

Hitchhiking poses a tremendous danger in the United States. Every summer, innocent vagabonds toting only a small backpack take to the highways unaware of the dangers of getting into a car with a stranger. No one can separate the potentially dangerous from the well-meaning motorist until it is too late. Most often, hitchhikers accept a lift from any stranger who appears presentable, despite repeated warnings from law officials that one simply can't judge a person by appearance alone. Consider the case of a California girl who "thumbed" a ride to school with a clean-cut, well-dressed, friendly motorist. One hour later she was found on a deserted road, severely beaten, with a 36-inch stake driven through her chest. Her assailant, who had a Jekyll-and-Hyde personality, is now in a mental institution. The ever-present risk of an accident is also frightening. In a five-month period in California, there were 441 accidents involving hitchhikers. Some of the fatalities included drivers who crashed into the rear of an automobile that had stopped unexpectedly on a busy freeway to pick up a hitchhiker. Other accidents occurred when hitchhikers accepted rides from intoxicated drivers or drivers who fell asleep at the wheel. Police and highway officials across the country have declared that violence against young hitchhikers—particularly girls—has become a major problem. For example, the most recent statistics in Los Angeles show the following crimes involving hitchhikers over a one-year period: 825 robberies (everything from picking pockets to auto theft), 292 kidnappings, 288 rapes, 101 attempted rapes, 123 sex offenses (other than rape), 146 assaults with deadly weapons, 49 beatings, 13 attempted kidnappings, and 1 murder. Also, a recent study in California reported the following conclusions: hitchhikers were involved in one out of every 160 major crimes in California, one half of all hitchhiking victims were female (even though only one out of ten hitchhikers was female), and hitchhikers were three times more likely to be the victim than the perpetrator. Despite the growing number of crimes and accidents involving hitchhikers, young people can still be seen on curbs and roadways with their thumbs up, risking their safety for a ride. Unfortunately, the hitchhiking menace will probably continue to increase unless those thumbs up become thumbs down.   *Joseph Mano*

Carefully examine the arguments below and find the fallacy (or fallacies) in each.

1. Judy's cousin Bill is visiting her this week, and she wants me to go out with him Saturday night. According to Judy, he has no interest in sports, he doesn't like to dance, and he hates beer. He sounds like a real bore. Going out with him won't be any fun at all.

2. Whenever I feel as if I'm getting a cold, I take a few grams of vitamin C, and I haven't had a bad cold in three years. I guess vitamin C really does prevent the common cold.

3. Mr. Dimsdale has been farming for over twenty years. If he says that the new pesticide isn't dangerous, then obviously it isn't.

4. A woman's place is in the home. When I was growing up, a woman never even entertained the thought of having a career. She stayed home and took care of the house and the kids while her husband went out and worked. My mother never worked and neither did my grandmother. Therefore, my wife should stay home and fulfill her proper role as mother and homemaker.

5. Tyrone never made good grades in school. He didn't like grade school, and he barely passed some of his high school courses. He must not be too bright, and he probably has a low IQ.

6. Either you believe in evolution or you believe in God; you can't have it both ways.

7. Mayor Conley's son was arrested last year for possession of drugs, and her husband has a drinking problem, so I'm not going to vote for her again.

8. Professor Morgan's courses are always packed with students, so he must not be a very tough grader. He probably gives a lot of A's.

9. Julia Clark has been on a lot of television commercials lately advertising the M & M Tax Accounting Service. It must be one of the best accounting firms in the country because Clark was an economic advisor to the president, so when it comes to money, she ought to know what she's talking about.

10. The only way to deal with a drug addict is to put him in jail and keep him there.

11. The labor unions in this country are responsible for America's spiraling inflation. They are the ones who are driving up prices. Every time they sign a contract, the public loses more purchasing power, so if it weren't for the labor unions, we wouldn't have to worry about a high cost of living.

12. Over 2 million people have already subscribed to *Quick Profits* monthly magazine, so you should subscribe right away and learn all of the easy ways to make money.

13. Six months after Ken won the state lottery, he left his wife. Money certainly is the root of all evil.

14. Harry's daughter married a policeman, so Harry will probably get all of his traffic tickets fixed from now on.

15. How can you say that Wayne Wanda is a good actor? Last year he spent a whole month in Russia, and this year he's going to visit Red China. He supports all of those radical causes like the equal rights amendment and the gay rights movement. Obviously, he's a Communist. He didn't even support the war in Vietnam. I'm certainly not going to see any of his movies.

1. What do you think Socrates meant when he said that the unexamined life is not worth living?
2. What are the fallacies you find most common in everyday conversation?
3. What persuasive strategy would you use if you knew that your readers were strongly committed to the opposite point of view?

Suggested Activity

Identify five common fallacies found in television commercials.

ASSIGNMENT

Write a paragraph of approximately 275 words in which you persuade someone to share your point of view for or against one of the following. You may need to narrow your topic to one that can be supported by a single paragraph.

REMEMBER: Proofread your persuasive paragraph carefully. Examine your reasoning and strengthen any weak links that you might find.

Television as a babysitter

Gun control

Capital punishment

One car per family

Unlimited surface mining

A ban on motorcycles

Paddling in public schools

English Composition as a required course

Legalization of marijuana

A lowered drinking age

People living together without being married

Busing as an aid to quality education

Abortion on demand

Censorship of books and movies

SENTENCES

Restrictive and Nonrestrictive Modifiers

Recognizing the distinction between restrictive and nonrestrictive modifiers is important not only for sentence structure but also for punctuation. The basic distinction is that a restrictive modifier is essential to the meaning of the sentence. A nonrestrictive modifier merely adds information to a sentence that would already be clear without it.

RESTRICTIVE: The man *who is wearing a gray pin-striped suit* is his father.

The modifying clause here, "who is wearing a gray pin-striped suit," is essential to the meaning of the sentence. It designates or points out the subject. Without it, we would not know which man was being referred to.

NONRESTRICTIVE: His father, *who was wearing a gray pin-striped suit,* met him at the airport.

The modifying clause here merely adds information to a sentence which would already be clear without it. Although it gives additional information, it is not essential to the core sentence, *His father met him at the airport.*

NOTE: The restrictive modifier, being an essential part of the sentence, is not set off by commas. The nonrestrictive modifier, however, is set off by commas because you can take it out of the sentence without changing the sentence's meaning.

RESTRICTIVE: The elm trees which are diseased will be cut down.

The writer does not mean "all elm trees will be cut down." Only the trees "which are diseased" will be cut down.

Now note how punctuation could alter the meaning completely:

NONRESTRICTIVE: The elm trees, which are diseased, will be cut down.

Here, *which are diseased* is nonrestrictive. The core sentence is *the elm trees will be cut down,* meaning all of them. The modifying clause, *which are diseased,* merely adds additional information, an explanation.

Whether or not a modifying phrase or clause is restrictive or nonrestrictive may depend on content and the writer's intention. *You must signal your intention clearly by the punctuation you use.*

The student radicals who are disrupting classes should be expelled.

Here the writer *does not* mean that all student radicals should be expelled, only that those student radicals *who are disrupting classes* should be expelled.

The student radicals, who are disrupting classes, should be expelled.

**The elm trees *which are diseased*
will be cut down.**

The punctuation changes the meaning here; clearly, the writer *does* mean that all student radicals should be expelled.

Although many fine distinctions can be made among nonrestrictive elements, the general rule for punctuation is this:

Any modifying word, phrase, or clause not essential to the meaning of the sentence should be set off by commas. (If such a modifier comes at the beginning or end of the sentence, only one comma is needed.)

Note the punctuation of the following sentences.

The suit that I bought at Taylor's is hanging in George's closet.

My suit, the blue checkered one that I bought at Taylor's, is hanging in George's closet.

Long before sunrise, at 3:00 A.M., the men were aroused for patrol duty.

During the summer of 1969, after his freshman year at Edinboro, he made his first trip to Wyoming.

The only thing to do in a case like that is to get the best lawyer you can find.

Parenthetical Expressions and Other Interrupters

Parenthetical expressions are sentence interrupters not directly connected to the sentence in which they occur. They are punctuated the same way as nonrestrictive clauses.

The Senate will, of course, have to act on the bill if it is to become law.

The mere possession of marijuana, I believe, should not be a criminal offense.

The nature of our society, according to the author, has changed irreversibly since World War II.

Interrupters that create a sharp break in thought or in grammatical structure should be set off by dashes.

He then asked the motley crowd—beggars, drunks, prostitutes, and the permanently unemployed—if they were prepared for the Second Coming.

He wrote this brilliant novel—completely broke at the time—in just sixty-four days.

A dash may also be used to set off a final word or phrase that summarizes or emphasizes the idea that precedes it.

She had everything in the world she could want except one thing—love.

Sometimes the dash can be used for a final twist or striking afterthought.

He cursed and flayed them, drove them day and night, worked them until they dropped—turning raw recruits into fighting men.

Use a dash following an initial list when it is followed by *that, this, these,*
or a similar pronoun as the subject of a summarizing statement.

persuading

Hot dogs, potato chips, mustard, onions, cherry pie, ice cream—those were
things she ate while watching television.

The waste, the callousness, the inefficiency, the mindless routine—that is
what I hate about military service.

CAUTION: The dash should be used sparingly. It should never be used
carelessly as a substitute for the comma or the semicolon.

A Punctuation Review

Throughout this book you have been learning about the importance of being
clear. You cannot be clear without correct punctuation. Notice how punctuation
alone can change the meaning of a sentence.

Turn the heat on Rocky.

Turn the heat on, Rocky.

Study for the test; on Wednesday, the tutor will be here to answer your questions.

Study for the test on Wednesday; the tutor will be here to answer your questions.

Does it make any difference where you put the punctuation mark? It
could make a great deal of difference to Rocky or to a student who wanted to pass
the test.

You should be familiar with several basic rules of punctuation:

1. Use a comma when you put a dependent clause before an independent
or main clause.

When I have to take a test, I get nervous.

2. Use a comma before the coordinating conjunction when you connect
two main clauses.

I used to hate movies, but now I'm a fan.

3. Use a semicolon between two main clauses when you do not use a coordinating conjunction.

I never eat breakfast; I never have time.

4. Use a comma between words, phrases, or clauses in a series.

Words, phrases, and clauses in a series must be separated by
commas.

245

5. Use a semicolon before and a comma after a conjunctive adverb. *conj adv.*

   I never have any money; therefore, I can never go on vacation.

6. Use a comma both before and after an adverb not used as a conjunction.

   The engine, then, will need a complete overhaul.

7. Use a comma before and after a nonrestrictive modifier.

   Non res modifier
   My brother, who is a cowboy, lives in Arizona.

8. Use a comma before and after parenthetical expressions and other interrupters.

   The book, in my opinion, is an exciting story of the West.

9. Use a dash to set off interrupters that create a sharp break in thought, etc:

   His excuse—if you could call it that—was miserable.

10. Use a comma after words of enumeration, between elements of month-day-year dates, and between elements of addresses.

    One, two, button your shoe.
    On October 31, 1980, she moved.
    Her new address is 909 Maple Lane, Oxford, MS   38655.

Additional Points in Punctuation

1. Watch out for the comma splice.

INCORRECT: The program was quite exciting, it had many scenes from combat films.
   You will have to decide what you want to do however, you should get Mr. Field's advice.

CORRECT: The program was quite exciting; it had many scenes from combat films.
   You will have to decide what you want to do; however, you should get Mr. Field's advice.

2. Don't separate subordinate elements from the main clause.

INCORRECT: I met him in Albany. Coming around the corner from the bus depot.

The air show was a big thrill for me. Because I had never seen one before.

CORRECT: I met him in Albany, coming around the corner from the bus depot.

The air show was a big thrill for me because I had never seen one before.

3. Don't put commas around restrictive modifiers.

The man *who owns the apartment building* is a retired railroad engineer.

The groups *that complain the loudest about government regulations* are also the first to call for protection from the big corporations.

4. Use a comma to separate coordinate adjectives.

It was a tall, slender, graceful tree.

She was a bright, energetic, young student teacher.

He was a thin, stooped, worn-out old man.

NOTE: Adjectives are *coordinate* if the comma could be replaced by *and*. You could say, "tall and slender and graceful" or "bright and energetic and young," but you would never say "worn-out and old man."

5. In most cases, separate introductory words, phrases, or clauses from the main clause of the sentence.

Underneath, the planks were all rotted.

Beneath the surface, hot springs bubbled and percolated.

As we drove by, the old mansion looked like the perfect setting for a horror movie.

6. In a series of three or more items, put the comma before the *and*.

We met Fred, Bill, and Tony.

An attack was launched by land, by sea, and by air.

He knew that the car was too expensive, that he didn't need such a big car, and that he was foolish for buying it.

NOTE: You are never wrong in including the comma before *and*. Leaving it out could sometimes cause doubt. For example, suppose you described a series of flags as "blue, green, purple, orange and black." Your reader might well wonder whether there were four flags or five.

Punctuate the following sentences to show whether the clauses are restrictive (necessary; no punctuation) or nonrestrictive (not necessary to the meaning of the sentence; set off by commas).

1. My Chevy which is parked at the curb is for sale.
2. All students who don't study will surely fail.
3. The shoes that I bought at Penney's are my favorites.
4. Mr. Carlson who did the stone work on the house died Thursday.
5. The test that I studied so hard for was postponed.
6. The dog that bit me has been found.
7. The Johnsons' house which cost over $50,000 is being completely remodeled.
8. Cigarette smoking which is hazardous to one's health is on the rise among teenagers.
9. Mr. Jenkins who is Terry's third attorney has given up on the case.
10. The salesman whom she had an appointment with never showed up.

EXERCISE IXc
Punctuate the following sentences correctly.

1. She selected three pins two ties a sweater and a bracelet.
2. The suspect entered the building and the detective followed closely behind.
3. Three kinds of trees in our yard are maples oaks and pines.
4. In a frantic attempt to submit his paragraph on time the student wrote all night.
5. The nation is of course under the rule of the majority.
6. Air water and noise pollution are of great concern to the environmentalists.
7. Before eating John and his wife built a roaring campfire.
8. I do not think however that I will ever learn to eat asparagus.
9. The students complained that the course was too hard the grades were too low and the teacher was too boring.
10. We are not going camping this weekend there is too much snow in the mountains.
11. Mrs. Grant a thoroughly dependable neighbor has offered to care for our cat while we are away.
12. Hanging from the gutter by his fingertips the painter shouted for help.
13. Passenger train tickets which are expensive in this country cost much less in Europe.
14. I began to doubt Martha's love surely the arsenic in my coffee was no accident.
15. Julie a dynamite girl agreed to go with me to the party but she was quite firm in her intention to stay sober.
16. A penalty holding cost Alabama fifteen yards.
17. Joe is a very poor reader it takes him three days to finish a comic book.

18. The enemy will reach the bridge by tomorrow morning therefore I suggest we act quickly while there is still time.

19. The situation was of course desperate but we decided that we must continue the journey in order to survive.

20. Joe was impatient to get to the soccer field for the match was scheduled for 2:00 P.M.

WORDS

Choices in Writing

All writing is a process of selection, of choosing one subject, one attitude, one kind of development over others. Some of this selection is almost subconscious, depending on the personality and the experiences of the writer. For example, three men look at an old house set far back on a huge, tree-shaded lawn. One man is an architect whose main interest is restoring old buildings. The second man had lived there as a child. The third man is a developer of housing projects. If these three men described this house, their selection of details would vary widely.

SLANTING

Slanting is a conscious level of choosing. In slanting, the writer wants to emphasize her attitude toward the subject—sometimes without making clear that this is her intent. (For you as a reader, it is important to be aware of slanting, so that the writer does not convince you unfairly that her attitude is correct.)

Slanting is achieved through:

1. Selection of subject and attitude.
2. Emphasis to support attitude.
3. Choice of words to support attitude.

Almost all communication has slanting to some degree. The slanting is determined by the intention of the writer, for he selects the subject and the attitude. He may choose to slant **for** something (favorable slanting), or to slant **against** something (unfavorable slanting).

POSITION

Another persuasive device is **emphasis,** the stress you put upon a word or a fact to highlight its importance. "Socrates was old but wise" emphasizes his wisdom, not his age. "Socrates was wise but old" emphasizes his age. **The position of words within the sentence changes the emphasis.** You might be trying to describe a teacher you thought strict and fair. Notice the difference as you re-arrange these two facts:

Mr. Green was a fair, strict teacher.

Mr. Green was a strict, fair teacher.

Mr. Green was fair but strict.

Mr. Green was strict but fair.

248

Perhaps the most persuasive choosing you do in writing is selecting words to support your attitude. By choosing the right word, you can, as critic I. A. Richards says, "smuggle in emotion." (Notice that even as he describes such choosing of words, he is affecting your attitude. What is your reaction to *smuggling*?)

Suppose you are describing Franklin D. Roosevelt. If you say he was an *elected official,* that is **neutral.** If you say he was a *statesman,* you are smuggling in **approval.** If you say he was a *political hack,* your choice of terms smuggles in your **disapproval.** Or again, is the dog (neutral) that is running across your yard a *mutt,* a *mongrel,* or a *cur?* These are terms of increasing disapproval which reflect your attitude toward dogs, or at least toward this particular dog. If you want to describe a romantic sunset, you might mention its *rosy glow.* If you want a sunset as a background for a murder story, you might comment on its *lurid glare.* Such slanted words reinforce your attitude and help your reader follow your thinking.

To select most effectively, you must remain aware of denotation and connotation.

> **Denotation** *is the dictionary meaning — the explicit, objective meaning of a word without any suggestions of emotional reaction.*

> **Connotation** *is implicit, subjective — the meaning that stirs emotional overtones.*

To illustrate the difference between denotative and connotative meaning, take the words *house* and *home.* Both words refer to the same object, a building where people live, but *home* suggests warmth, protection, and family affection. Thus, the word *house* could be said to be primarily denotative, whereas *home* could be said to be primarily connotative.

Consider the following groups of words:

policeman	government employee	girl
police officer	public servant	doll
cop	bureaucrat	chick
fuzz	political appointee	broad

Which words carry a generally favorable connotation?
Which words carry an unfavorable connotation?
Which words are relatively neutral?
Now consider the following two sentences.

1. The reporter *exposed* the cop's past record.
2. The reporter *presented* the *policeman's* past record.

The words *exposed* and *cop* have a built-in disapproval. The reader expects the cop's record to be bad; thus, by choosing these connotative words, you have already interpreted the facts instead of letting the facts speak for themselves. Be aware of the possible connotations of *every* word that you write.

The following are terms with a neutral meaning. That is, they have no emotional overtones; they are denotative only:

my mother	automobile
the policeman	lawyer

Now they are changed to have a connotation of approval:

my mom	limousine
the police officer	counselor

And here they have a connotation of disapproval:

my old lady	jalopy
the pig	shyster

Verbs can be connotative:

John tiptoed	John revealed
John sneaked	John squealed

So can adjectives:

He was confident	He was proud
He was pushy	He was arrogant

So can adverbs:

He moved quietly	He moved decisively
He moved stealthily	He moved ruthlessly

So can whole phrases or sentences:

He was persevering	He was firm
He was stubborn	He was pigheaded

The words of the poet, politician, advertiser, or anyone wishing to persuade are chosen for their **connotation.** Such words are used to appeal to characteristics like our pride, partriotism, charity, affection, and self-esteem. The words of the scientist, investigator, or objective observer are chosen for their **denotation.** Such words are used to present facts and observations without bias or slant, to represent things as they are without emotional overtones.

Remember that a word is the right word only if it has the right denotation and the right connotation. It is accurate only if it conveys to the reader the meaning that the writer intended.

Euphemisms

A **euphemism** is a word or phrase that is used in place of a more blunt term which might be offensive. Euphemisms are sometimes justified, but often they are misleading, vague, or phony. For example, in an effort to hide what some consider to be an unpleasant occupation, the friendly garbageman has been called a "sanitary engineer." Nothing is wrong with this, but the term "sanitary engineer" may confuse anyone who still thinks of an engineer as a highly skilled, technically oriented professional. Similarly, euphemisms may be deliberately used to cloud the truth—to make something appear more acceptable than it actually is. No one likes to endure a depression in this country, so government officials carefully refer to a depressed period as a "mild recession" or a "downward trend in the economy." Thus, the euphemism acts the same as the sugar coating on a bitter pill. Finally, euphemisms are used, in some instances, to deceive—to completely hide the truth. Recently, in modern warfare, the term "protective reaction strike" has been used to explain what actually might have been an unprovoked bombing raid to support illegal seizure of territory. In the same way, those who feel that our penal codes are too harsh prefer to think of the habitual criminal as "a socially maladjusted person" or "a victim of his environment" who should not be denied personal freedom even though he threatens the safety of every other member of society.

There are many euphemisms that we do not recognize as such because they have become an accepted part of our daily language. Many have resulted from the efforts of advertisers to create markets for their products. Now, you no longer have to settle for an ordinary used car; you can buy a "previously owned" or "reconditioned automobile." Also, some of us who like to eat no longer need to worry about being fat or overweight; now we simply have a "problem figure" or "weight problem." The local "practitioner of funeral arts," who buries people when they die, prefers to "lay the loved ones to rest after they have passed away."

How many of the following euphemisms can you supply a standard definition for?

expecting
stretch the truth
halitosis
exceptional child
culturally disadvantaged
slow learner
reasoning together
distortion of the facts
meaningful relationship
liquidate
surreptitious entry
your services are no longer required
revenue enhancement

EXERCISE IXd

For each word listed, give a word of similar meaning (the same denotation) that expresses your approval, and one that expresses your disapproval (the connotative meanings).

EXAMPLE

Neutral term	Approval	Disapproval
horse	steed	nag

1. father _____ _____
2. car _____ _____
3. inexperienced _____ _____
4. inexpensive _____ _____
5. boss _____ _____
6. teacher _____ _____
7. woman _____ _____
8. businessperson _____ _____
9. police officer _____ _____
10. old _____ _____

EXERCISE IXe

In each of the following sentences, there is a word or phrase with a wrong connotation. Decide which word is wrong and substitute a better word for it.

1. Hitler declared that if he repeated a fib often enough, he could make anyone believe it.

_____

2. Last night on television, we saw a wonderful performance of *Romeo and Juliet* with Janice Gray, the champion of Juliets.

_____

3. Before he was elected president, Nixon was a highly regarded shyster.

_____

4. Mrs. Jones was sent to a psychiatrist because she was nuts.

_____

5. The notorious statesman from England addressed the Senate.

_____

6. Al Capone, the famous crook, was caught for income tax evasion.

_____

7. The delicate stench of the roses filled the room.

   _____

8. The sawbones was suggested for a Nobel Prize.

   _____

9. The banquet featured steak and lobster, and the booze flowed freely.

   _____

10. Our cur is adorable.

    _____

CHAPTER X

from paragraph to essay

To go from writing a single paragraph to writing a short essay involves applying the principles you have already learned in *Writing Clear Paragraphs*. It is an expansion of the basic pattern of introduction – body – conclusion.

Introduction and Thesis Statement

An essay, just like a paragraph, requires one clear controlling idea. In the paragraph, we call the statement of the controlling idea the topic sentence. In the essay, we call it a **thesis statement.** The thesis statement, then, is a statement of the controlling idea for the whole essay, whether it be three, four, or a dozen paragraphs in length.

No matter what the length or purpose of your essay, you must make a clear statement of your central idea almost immediately. In the single paragraph, the topic sentence **is** the introduction. In the essay, the thesis statement is a **part** of the introduction. Throughout this text we have urged you to put the topic sentence for your paragraph first. One of the best places to put your thesis statement for the essay is at the end of the introduction.

You might begin your introduction with a brief quotation, a bit of factual information, an incident from personal experience, or the news of the day. Often your introduction suggests to the reader why you have chosen this subject to write about. Placing your thesis statement at the end of the introduction points up the controlling idea of the essay. It puts the controlling idea in the right place to focus your reader's attention. Thus strategically placed, the thesis statement lets your reader know early the main point of your essay and leads directly into the supporting body.

Body

The body of the essay may be just one well-developed paragraph, or it may be several paragraphs in length. When there are several paragraphs of development, each will have its own topic sentence, related to the thesis statement in the same way that subtopic sentences are related to the topic sentence in the single paragraph. The topic sentence of each paragraph in the body of the essay, then, introduces some aspect of the controlling idea expressed in your thesis statement. Thus, the essay simply expands the structure of the single paragraph.

Conclusion

Just as the first paragraph of your essay is the **introduction,** the last paragraph is the **conclusion.** If the introductory paragraph serves as an opening wedge to your discussion, the concluding paragraph serves as a pedestal on which your discussion comes to rest. Thus, the concluding paragraph of the essay serves the same purpose as the concluding sentence in the single paragraph.

Basic Structure

Look again at the basic structure:

I.	INTRODUCTION:	One paragraph including the thesis statement
II.	BODY:	One or more paragraphs, each with its own topic sentence clearly related to the thesis statement
III.	CONCLUSION:	One paragraph reasserting the idea of the thesis statement

The following three-paragraph essay illustrates this basic pattern.

A sailor returning from sea duty to the broad prairies of the Dakotas was heard to say, as he looked out across the snow-swept plains, "Just like bein' at sea." Despite the long miles that separate ocean and prairie, the sailor, by his experience of both, was able to see the common element. *The essence of living on the prairie or on the sea is a natural loneliness.* (thesis statement)

Beneath the stars on a long sea voyage or under the vast blue vault of the prairie skies, one is alone with nature. Its immensity stretches away from the individual and dwarfs him to his true smallness, his insignificance in the universe. Yet, at the same time, he is intensely aware of his own being as an individual. It is his own muscle and bone on which he must rely. It is his own energy and intelligence on which he must depend for survival. There is no shield or buffer to wall him off from nature or to shut out the reality of his existence. He is nature's creature, and he knows it. Once having faced up to the towering power of North Altantic storms and the white fury of prairie blizzards, he comes to terms with nature in all its harshness and tenderness. What is more, he comes to terms with himself. "Maybe," he might say, "I am a little insignificant guy—but I am."

Thus the vast expanse of nature, experienced most truly on the prairie and the sea, builds within the individual a lonely ruggedness. But the loneliness is not the loneliness of alienation, for it is shared with everything that lives. Every blade of grass and every spear of wheat, every flying fish that darts through the waves has its individual life, separate and discrete. When one comes to terms with nature, his loneliness is natural.

Outlining

An outline is the blueprint for your paragraph or essay. At first, it may seem to be additional work, but it saves you time and prevents you from putting in irrelevant ideas or omitting ideas necessary for clear and adequate development.

The same three-part organization that you have used in writing all your paragraphs will serve you well in developing your essay. In fact, the three-part organization can be expanded to suit almost any essay you will be called upon to write.

In the Sentence section of Chapter IV you were given a simple formula for developing the paragraph about father's "keen sense of humor" That formula could easily be applied to develop an essay on the same subject: the pattern is simply expanded. The sentence "My father has a keen sense of humor." would then become your thesis statement, and each of the three subtopic sentences would become topic sentences for three paragraphs of development.

I. He loves to tease my mother.
II. He constantly jokes with our next-door neighbor.
III. He can even joke about his own misfortunes.

(Each Roman numeral indicates the topic sentence for a paragraph in the body of the essay.)

Thus each of the basic parts of the single paragraph are expanded in developing a complete essay. The topic sentence becomes the thesis statement (statement of the controlling idea for the whole essay), which is the focal point of the introductory paragraph. The subtopics of the single paragraph become topic sentences for paragraphs of development (each, of course, requiring detailed support). The concluding sentence becomes a concluding paragraph to tie together the various parts of the essay and reinforce its controlling idea.

For the longer, more formal essay, you need a more detailed outline; the pattern needs to be further expanded. Regardless of the length or purpose of your essay, however, you must first decide on your subject and your attitude— your thesis statement. That is the first thing you write down for your outline.

After writing your thesis statement, write down the most important points you intend to cover in your essay. Make sure that each of these main points supports the controlling idea expressed in your thesis statement. Working from main headings to subordinate ones, proceed to develop your outline with supporting details until you have a complete skeleton for your essay.

The relationship among the supporting details is made clear with an accepted form of numbering:

Thesis statement: _____

_____

I. First major support for thesis statement
   A. First major support for I
      1. First detail supporting A
      2. Second detail supporting A
   B. Second major support for I
      1. First detail supporting B
      2. Second detail supporting B

II. Second major support for thesis statement
   A. First major support for II
      1. First detail supporting A
      2. Second detail supporting A
   B. Second major support for II
      1. First detail supporting B
      2. Second detail supporting B

Conclusion: If it is included in the outline at all, it is not numbered or subdivided. A brief statement of the purpose of your conclusion, however, may be of help to you.

Note that since outlining consists of dividing the whole writing into its parts, each element in your outline has to have at least two parts. (After all, you can't divide anything into less than two.)

After reading the following excerpt from "Letter from Birmingham Jail" by Martin Luther King, Jr., (1) pick out the thesis statement, and (2) find the major supports for the thesis statement.

You express a great deal of anxiety over our willingness to break laws. This is certainly a legitimate concern. Since we so diligently urge people to obey the Supreme Court's decision of 1954 outlawing segregation in the public schools, at first glance it might seem rather paradoxical for us consciously to break laws. One may well ask: "How can you advocate breaking some laws and obeying others?" The answer lies in the fact that there are two types of laws: just and unjust. I would be the first to advocate obeying just laws. One has not only a legal but a moral responsibility to obey just laws. Conversely, one has a moral responsibility to disobey unjust laws. I would agree with St. Augustine that "an unjust law is no law at all."

Now, what is the difference between the two? How does one determine whether a law is just or unjust? A just law is a man-made code that squares with the moral law or the law of God. An unjust law is a code that is out of harmony with the moral law. To put it in the terms of St. Thomas Aquinas: An unjust law is a human law that is not rooted to eternal law and natural law. Any law that uplifts human personality is just. Any law that degrades human personality is unjust. All segregation statutes are unjust because segregation distorts the soul and damages the personality. It gives the segregator a false sense of superiority and the segregated a false sense of inferiority. Segregation, to use the terminology of the Jewish philosopher Martin

Buber, substitutes an "I—it" relationship for an "I—thou" relationship and ends up relegating persons to the status of things. Hence segregation is not only politically, economically, and sociologically unsound, it is morally wrong and sinful. Paul Tillich has said that sin is separation. Is not segregation an existential expression of man's tragic separation, his awful estrangement, his terrible sinfulness? Thus it is that I can urge men to obey the 1954 decision of the Supreme Court, for it is morally right; and I can urge them to disobey segregation ordinances, for they are morally wrong.

Let us consider a more concrete example of just and unjust laws. An unjust law is a code that a numerical or power majority group compels a minority group to obey but does not make binding on itself. This is *difference* made legal. By the same token, a just law is a code that a majority compels a minority to follow and that it is willing to follow itself. This is *sameness* made legal.

Let me give another example. A law is unjust if it is inflicted on a minority that, as a result of being denied the right to vote, had no part in enacting or devising the law. Who can say that the legislature of Alabama which set up the state's segregation laws was democratically elected? Throughout Alabama all sorts of devious methods are used to prevent Negroes from becoming registered voters, and there are some counties in which, even though Negroes constitute a majority of the population, not a single Negro is registered. Can any law enacted under such circumstances be considered democratically structured?

Sometimes a law is just on its face and unjust in its application. For instance, I have been arrested on a charge of parading without a permit. Now, there is nothing wrong in having an ordinance which requires a permit for a parade. But such an ordinance becomes unjust when it is used to maintain segregation and to deny citizens the First Amendment privilege of peaceful assembly and protest.

I hope you are able to see the distinction I am trying to point out. In no sense do I advocate evading or defying the law, as would the rabid segregationist. That would lead to anarchy. One who breaks an unjust law must do so openly, lovingly, and with a willingness to accept the penalty. I submit that an individual who breaks a law that conscience tells him is unjust, and who willingly accepts the penalty of imprisonment in order to arouse the conscience of the community over its injustice, is in reality expressing the highest respect for law.

How to Write an Essay Examination

Once you understand how to expand the paragraph into an essay, you can apply this skill to any type of essay writing, including the essay examination. Everyone is happy to see his or her examination booklet come back from the instructor sporting a large A. But how do you manage to do this? Do you have to be born with a big brain or, perhaps, an oversized will-power to stick to the books? Well, these things help, naturally, but taking exams is a skill that can be learned.

First, of course, you must know enough about the subject to have the raw materials for an answer, but facts—and opinions based on facts—are just that: the raw material, which by itself is only good enough for a C or a C+. With raw material only, you can't get that A. If you are aiming for a good grade, then you must know **how** to present your material.

Read the whole examination carefully

Make sure you understand the directions before you start answering any questions. You might see five essay questions on a test, but that doesn't mean you should automatically answer all five questions. If you read the directions first, you might find that you are supposed to choose only two of those questions.

Budget your time

Decide on how much time you can spend on each question, and **don't panic.** It only wastes time. If you have a half hour to spend on each question, you can't spend ten of those minutes worrying about how you are going to answer the question. One way to help ease test anxiety is to answer the first question successfully, so begin with the question you know the most about.

Read the question: What does it ask you to do? Look closely at the verb. Notice some of the types of activities required in the verbs below:

explain	give the reasons for something
evaluate	decide on the value or significance of something
analyze	break something down into its parts
illustrate	give examples of some generalization
define	state the precise meaning of a term
compare	point out similarities
contrast	point out differences
discuss	tell all you know about a subject

Think before you write

Jot down any details that you can think of that might help you answer the question. Listing major points in a rough outline will help you get a general answer in mind before you begin to develop it. Think about your topic sentence (subject plus attitude). Think about what the topic sentence commits you to. If you can't come up with a good topic sentence of your own, you can frequently make an acceptable topic sentence by turning the question around, as in the following example.

Identify and discuss the monarchs of England who did most to strengthen the monarchy during the 11th and 12th centuries.

Your topic sentence begins:

During the 11th and 12th centuries, the monarchs of England who did most to strengthen the monarchy were . . .

Then you might devote a paragraph to each of the monarchs you identified.

Develop your topic sentence

Once you have decided upon a topic sentence, develop it as completely as time allows. If you have approximately 25 minutes to answer an essay question, you can be sure that your professor is expecting more than a one-paragraph answer. The key to writing a good answer on an essay test is learning how to select the most important information and how to present it in a limited amount of time. Therefore, try to avoid long, rambling introductions. Get to the point.

259

Don't pad your answer

Remember that complete development does not mean padding an answer. Padding consists of wordiness, repetition, and irrelevant detail. The following answer from an American History essay test, for example, would never get an A, because half of the answer consists of irrelevant details. See if you can find them.

What were the North's major advantages in its battle with the South during the Civil War?

The North had more money and more manpower than the South. While the South had about five billion dollars worth of capital, the North had over twice as much—approximately eleven billion dollars. Thus, the Union was in a better position to purchase food, clothing, and equipment. With approximately 23 million people in 22 states, the North also had the security of outnumbering the South, whose population consisted of about eight million people in eleven states. The North's greater industrial capacity also gave her a distinct advantage over the basically agricultural South; with almost three times as many railroad lines as the South, the North could feed, equip, and transport an army more efficiently than her opponent. The North, however, was at a serious disadvantage in military leadership. The Confederate generals were more competent than most of the Union commanders. Lincoln had to fire a number of generals before he found one who could match the South's Robert E. Lee. The fact that the South was fighting a defensive war also put the North at a disadvantage. The South just wanted to be left alone; all she had to do to win was keep the North out of her territory, but the North had to fight an offensive war. In order for the North to win, she had to conquer the South; she had to invade and hold Southern territory.

As you have probably discovered, the last part of the answer deals with the North's disadvantages. Although this material is correct, it has nothing to do with the question. The time spent recording this irrelevant matter about the Union's disadvantages could have been used to discuss more of her strong points, such as her political leadership and her naval supremacy.

By applying the principles of composition illustrated throughout this book, you can do the writing necessary for success in college. Furthermore, the same principles of organization used in writing the paragraph and short essay can serve you in writing on any subject at any length. The simple three-part organization of introduction, body, and conclusion can be adapted and expanded to suit various types of expository writing, including on-the-job writing of business and technical reports. Your ability to write clearly will determine, to a greater extent than you may imagine, your chance for success in whatever career you choose. With the principles of organization and development firmly in mind, you can proceed confidently toward further developing your skill as a writer—a skill that can go a long way in determining your future.

index

Boldface page numbers refer to definitions of indexed terms, and italic page numbers refer to exercises.